NILES PUBLIC LIBRARY

Niles, Illinois

FINE SCHEDULE

Adult Materials . . . . 10 per day
Juvenile Materials . . . . . . 04 per day
Video Tapes . . . . . . $1.50 per day

WAR WITHOUT WINDOWS

WAR WITHOUT WINDOWS

A TRUE ACCOUNT
OF A YOUNG ARMY OFFICER
TRAPPED IN AN INTELLIGENCE COVER-UP
IN VIETNAM

BY

Bruce E. Jones

THE VANGUARD PRESS
NEW YORK

Library of Congress Cataloging-in-Publication Data

Jones, Bruce E., 1942-
War without windows.

Bibliography: p.
Includes index.
1. Vietnamese Conflict, 1961–1975—Military intelligence—United
States. 2. Vietnamese Conflict, 1961–1975—Personal narratives,
American. 3. Jones, Bruce, E., 1942– . I. Title.
DS559.8.M44J66 1987 959.704′38 [B] 87-21029
ISBN 0-8149-0934-5

Designed by Tom Bevans

Frontispiece map of Vietnam: Reprinted from *Vietnam:
Order of Battle* by Shelby Stanton, copyright © 1981 by
U.S. News and World Report, Inc.
Updated and reprinted by Kraus Reprint and Periodicals,
Route 100, Millwood, New York 10546, in April, 1986.

To the memory of Colonel Gains B. Hawkins
and
to Colonel Maggie

ACKNOWLEDGMENTS

I extend my deepest appreciation and respect to Samuel A. Adams, once of the CIA, who was singularly responsible for exposing the truth about the intelligence cover-up in Saigon. The information he uncovered made it possible for this book to be written. Equally important were the advice and support he provided during its preparation. We didn't have many heroes in the military and intelligence bureaucracies; Sam Adams is truly one.

Also vital was the assistance of Major General Joseph A. McChristian and Colonel Gains B. Hawkins, fine officers who created an outstanding intelligence system and then saw it destroyed by their successors and superiors. I have been honored to know these good Americans and soldiers.

My appreciation is also extended to Robert Baron of Cravath, Swaine, and Moore, counsel to CBS in *Westmoreland* v. *CBS*, 1982–85. The firm's generosity in making available copies of statements made by Army personnel, CIA officials, and others in the course of the proceeding aided immeasurably in the preparation of this book, to say nothing of helping me to unravel the events of 1967–68 that surrounded me in Saigon.

My gratitude to Eric P. Swenson, Gail Mabbutt, Mary Morgan, Melodye Condos, Lydia and Joan Wilen, and Robert Swandby; to Navy men Michael Leaveck and Thomas C. Hall; and to John Middlesworth, Robert Mueller, Glen Halsey, and Jack Peffley, Marines. Thanks also to Robert Guis, another Marine, and his Copy Mat gang; the folks at the Torch Club ("known from Maine to Spain"); and so many more.

My patient editors, Bernice Woll and Nancy Brooks, deserve medals for their long tour of duty in bringing the manuscript up to fighting trim. My deepest thanks for their diligent and thorough support.

Finally, I salute the Columbia Broadcasting System for producing and defending their 1982 broadcast "The Uncounted Enemy."

—B.E.J.

CONTENTS

FOREWORD

In the months before and during the Viet Cong Tet offensive of 1968, U.S. intelligence doctored its books to make the enemy forces in South Vietnam seem smaller than they really were. The motive was political: to convince the American people, Congress, and the press that things were going well in Vietnam, and that perhaps with a bit more time and effort, we might soon win the war. The cuts were huge. Hundreds of thousands of VC cadre and soldiers, including large numbers of their best troops, either disappeared from, or failed to enter, the official U.S. lists.

The result was catastrophic. The unexpected size and number of the Tet attacks—many carried out by soldiers who were not supposed to exist—were the biggest shock to America since Pearl Harbor. The offensive is now generally acknowledged to be the watershed of the Vietnam war.

Yet the story of the intelligence fakery is making its way only slowly into the history books. One reason is that any falsification of our own intelligence would be so self-defeating and destructive that it seems inherently improbable and unbelievable. Another reason is that the story appears so complex. Some still call the controversy only a technical debate about statistics and such arcane matters as whether this category or that belongs in our official estimate of enemy strength, that is, the order of battle or OB. History will ultimately recognize the truly disastrous consequences of the intelligence cover-up in Vietnam; a major reason will be this book by Bruce Jones.

I first talked to Bruce Jones in mid-1983. I was then a defendant in what may be America's most famous libel case, *Westmoreland* v. *CBS*. The lawsuit concerned a documentary by CBS that told the story of the fakery. The network had hired me as its consultant because of my two qualifications: first, I had been the CIA's chief analyst on VC manpower in 1967 and 1968; and second, during the 1970s I had gathered most of the information that the documentary reported.

I had always been confident about winning the case. But after my initial half-hour conversation with Jones, I didn't see how we could lose. In fact, the documents he brought back from Saigon came to be called "Jones's smoking guns" as our defense progressed. I believe that one of the reasons that General Westmoreland abandoned his legal action was these documents, which were the only direct evidence that came from within the MACV headquarters demonstrating that an arbitrary ceiling had been placed on reports of the enemy strength.

War Without Windows is the first book by an eyewitness to what went on within the MACV headquarters in the months surrounding Tet. Jones was in a perfect position to see what occurred. His job was to keep track of enemy units in I Corps, where most of the heaviest fighting took place. In his book Jones cuts through the complexity and the smokescreens. He not only demonstrates that there were larger numbers of enemy troops out there, but he also reveals how intelligence analysts were ordered to tamper with their own data. Further, he shows that it was not an "academic debate" about statistics, but a life-and-death struggle for truth about actual enemy units and soldiers who engaged, fought, and killed our men.

Most of all, Jones's book tells the human story of the deception, the emotional cost to those soldiers who were ordered to implement the OB manipulations. The dissension within the headquarters, the dismay of the young analysts, many just out of college, the cynicism and disgust of intelligence professionals—all this is part of the tragic consequences of the cover-up.

I am grateful to Bruce Jones not just for the help he gave me in the Westmoreland case, but, more important, because of the courage he has demonstrated in coming forward to tell his story at considerable cost to himself. *War Without Windows* offers an important explanation of why we lost the war in Vietnam and how we abandoned the goal and ideal of intelligence: to tell the truth, no matter where it leads.

—Samuel A. Adams

PROLOGUE

This is not the way you ought to do it. You don't start at an
end figure and work back. But we did.

> Colonel George Hamscher
> Defense Intelligence Agency

We were caught. We were caught up into this wheel. You
couldn't get out of it. . . . Truth was not allowed to get into
this system. It couldn't exist.

> Colonel Russell Cooley
> OB Studies, CICV

In 1967–68, I served as an intelligence officer in the United States
Army. I was assigned to the headquarters of the Military Assistance
Command, Vietnam (MACV) in Saigon as an analyst of the enemy's
order of battle, or OB—that is, the strength and disposition of his
forces. Some fifteen years later, on 23 January 1982, CBS aired a
ninety-minute "special report" called "The Uncounted Enemy: A Vietnam Deception." Its premise was that our intelligence reports on the
enemy had been deliberately held below a ceiling established by MACV
under General William C. Westmoreland. The program evoked a libel
action brought by General Westmoreland against CBS. My affidavit in
that trial produced the only direct physical evidence from within the
headquarters (in the form of internal operational documents) of the manipulation of intelligence figures.

One man had long believed that the size of the enemy army was
much greater than MACV was reporting. Samuel A. Adams worked for
the CIA on enemy-strength figures in Vietnam and Cambodia from late
1965 to 1973, reading thousands of captured documents and prisoner-
of-war reports.[1] As he read in 1965, he noted a pattern that was consistent with U.S. operational reports: units of the Viet Cong and the North
Vietnamese Army were taking heavy casualties and had high desertion
rates. The latter especially interested him. Using enemy unit rosters, he

developed an average monthly desertion rate for all similar units that he multiplied out to obtain a nationwide average.

The desertion rate came out to at least 50,000 a year. Military intelligence was then recording the enemy strength at 270,000, and simple arithmetic showed that continued pressure would soon lead to a collapse of the VC/NVA effort. But in the face of such high body counts and desertions, how could an army of just over a quarter million continue to be as active as it was? Adams started looking for new indicators. He found one on 19 August 1966, when he received the translation of a captured document from Binh Dinh province that put the number of guerrilla-militia (also known as "irregulars") in that area at more than 50,000. Our OB records showed only 4,668. Adams looked for further discrepancies in enemy documents, and he found them.

At this time, MACV was working hard to update its own intelligence through the increasingly effective system established by General Joseph A. McChristian, a West Pointer known for his attention to detail. His organization, J-2, was struggling to codify the complex enemy structure and, using tons of newly seized enemy documents from the first major Allied operations in 1966, his staff was beginning to get a clearer picture of the enemy's field command and combat units. The less understood VC irregulars—that is, the guerrillas and self-defense forces (the latter also called "home guards" or "militia," and labeled "secret" if they worked out of our "controlled" villages)—were being studied by a team of specialists in the RITZ program. In addition, the VC political infrastructure (the Communist leaders of the underground movement) was being analyzed through the CORRAL program.

But these studies could not be fully pursued until MACV had recruited and trained special teams to work in the field. McChristian was a cautious and pragmatic man who believed in process, and he would not offer mere estimates until his field reports were completed.

At the CIA, Adams was, in this area, ahead of the MACV research because he had been working solely on the VC irregulars. From his process of extrapolation, he thought he had made the biggest intelligence find of a war that was being managed by statistical analysis: there were twice or even three times as many guerrilla-militia as recorded by MACV. "Force ratios"—the number of our men needed to prevail in a guerrilla war—ranged from 10:1 to 3:1. Even the most optimistic ratio indicated that a whole new look at the war was in order.

Adams pressed on with his research. By December 1966, he had concluded that the strength of the entire enemy army was more like 600,000 than the 270,000 MACV carried. Only an army of at least that size could have absorbed the number of known casualties, deserters, and defectors.

In February 1967, General Earle C. Wheeler, chairman of the Joint Chiefs of Staff, called a conference in Honolulu of all the key intelligence agencies. Early in the session, a colonel from MACV stood up and announced, "There's a lot more of those little bastards out there than we thought there were!" The speaker was Colonel Gains Hawkins, chief of J-2's Order of Battle branch.

But the shadow of a cover-up loomed. In February, MACV sent a report to the Joint Chiefs showing "during 1966 a steady, and in January 1967 a sharp, increase in enemy large-scale attacks." In response, on 9 March 1967, General Wheeler cabled Westmoreland with this order:

1. I have just been made aware of the figures you now report for battalion and large size enemy-initiated actions. . . .
2. If these figures should reach the public domain, they would literally blow the lid off of Washington.
3. Please do whatever is necessary to insure these figures are not repeat not released to News Media or otherwise exposed to public knowledge.

Two days later, Wheeler sent another cable that put his concerns into even clearer language:

The implications are major and serious. Large-scale enemy initiatives have been used as a major element in assessing the status of the war for the President, Secretary of Defense, in Washington. These figures have been used to illustrate the success of our current strategy as well as over-all progress in Vietnam. . . . Your new figures change the picture drastically. . . . I can only interpret the new figures to mean that, despite the force buildup, despite our many successful spoiling attacks and base area searches, and despite the heavy interdiction campaigns in North Vietnam and Laos, VC/NVA combat capability and offensive activity throughout 1966 and now in 1967 has been increasing steadily. . . .

I cannot go to the President and tell him that, contrary to

my reports and those of the other Chiefs as to progress of the war . . . the situation is such that we are not sure who has the initiative in South Vietnam. Moreover, the effect of surfacing this major and significant discrepancy would be dynamite. . . . [U]rgent action is required. . . .

General Wheeler had put his finger on the pulse of the war: the enemy *did* have the will and ability to take the initiative, regardless of our massive build-up. Sadly, the result of that perception was only that a team went to Saigon to write a new standard for measuring enemy-initiated attacks, shifting the criterion from size to a judgment of "significance." Soon the number of VC/NVA initiatives would decrease in MACV reports.

The policy was clear. The military was not going to give bad war news to the civilians. Westmoreland had to understand the rules of the game.

At about this time, Hawkins began work on the estimate of Viet Cong irregulars. He described the approach as a "slow and methodical study by MACV analysts at the village level where the irregulars operated—an approach which promised greater validity than figures produced by analysts in Saigon and Washington."[2] Hawkins was suggesting that the MACV process was more detailed than Adams's one-man overview could be; still, he always found both sets of conclusions to be compatible.[3]

Later in the spring of 1967, the J-2 staff was finally ready to release its troublesome findings. McChristian first presented the new analysis to Westmoreland sometime between 10 May and 15 May 1967; he has described the meeting:

> Although I usually sent my intelligence reports directly to CINCPAC and DoD, in this instance I took the cable to General Westmoreland before sending it because I thought he would be interested in knowing that we were finally able to support and defend strength figures in these categories and could discard for the first time the . . . figures we had received from the South Vietnamese before I became J-2. I expected General Westmoreland to be pleased with our effort. . . . I was surprised by his reaction. After reading the cable [he] said: "If

we send this to Washington, it will create a political bomb-shell." I offered to take the cable personally to Washington and explain its contents in greater detail to the appropriate personnel. General Westmoreland did not accept the offer. He said "Leave it with me. I want to go over it." . . . This was the first time that General Westmoreland had ever held up one of my intelligence reports. I was disturbed by General West-moreland's expressed concern over political considerations. At no point during our meeting did he ever question the methodology or the evidence on which these estimates were based.[4]

The cable embodying the new analysis contained updated estimates for the irregular (198,000) and political (88,000) categories, raising the overall enemy numbers to some 429,000 from the previous 270,000. McChristian further stated that each group of VC and NVA "posed a threat to the lives and safety of our forces and our military and civilian allies and was capable of adversely affecting the accomplishment of our mission."

Westmoreland wanted a full briefing on the new intelligence, which was delivered on 28 May by Colonel Hawkins. Afterward West-moreland again expressed concern about the possible public reaction that we had not made progress in the war. According to Hawkins:

General Westmoreland would not accept the revised esti-mate. . . . [He] instructed me to take another look at the fig-ures. In the context of his concern about the political impact . . . there was no mistaking the message in his instructions: I was to reduce the estimate. . . . I then arbitrarily reduced the enemy strength figures and returned to General Westmoreland to brief him on my second, lower estimate. [He] also rejected this. . . .[5]

This second presentation was given on 14 June. His lowered estimate also rejected by Westmoreland, Hawkins *further* reduced the enemy-strength figures, contrary to the best evidence then in hand. Meanwhile, the CIA had finally approved the use of a total figure of 500,000, and that was the figure they had taken in June to the Board of National Intelligence Estimates (an annual meeting of all the intelligence agencies). This higher estimate of the enemy force was so controversial that the meeting—usually a week long—dragged on until September, when the debate moved from Washington to Saigon at Westmoreland's request.

Compromise was finally achieved in the week of 9–14 September. In essence the resolution, heavily in favor of the MACV position, was this: all categories of enemy strength were reduced and the self-defense militia and the political cadre would be dropped from the order of battle. The NIE presented a range of 224,000 to 249,000 for the enemy army. It was a resolution based on politics and personalities, not intelligence evidence, and it seriously compromised battlefield truths.

But I knew nothing of any of this when I flew out of Travis Air Force Base near San Francisco, my point of departure for Vietnam, on 11 August 1967.

PART ONE

Saigon Warrior

AUGUST 1967

Ode to a Saigon Warrior
(sung to the tune of "Sweet Betsy from Pike")

Saigon, oh Saigon, a wonderful place
But the organization is a damn disgrace
There's Captains and Majors and light Colonels too
With their hands in their pockets with nothing to do.
Chorus:
Dinky dau, Dinky dau, Dinky Do.
With their hands in their pockets and nothing to do.

They sit at their desks and they scream and they shout
They talk of a war they know nothing about
Against the VC they are not doing well
But if paper were cordite we'd be blown to hell.
(Chorus)

A Saigon commando is an unusual sight
He wears his fatigues tho he's not in the fight
A knife and a pistol, his daily motif
But you'll find him for lunch at the Cercle Sportif.
(Chorus)

The Saigon Warriors all draw combat pay
And in Saigon for years they will stay
They won't leave the compound, just sit at the bar
Draw the same pay but don't fight the war.
(Chorus)

1

Most Saigon Warriors all wear a Bronze Star
They got them for writing reports on the war
They've never been shot at, or seen a VC
But they know they deserve it, they work for MACV.
(Chorus)

When this war is over we'll all go home
We'll meet Saigon Warriors wherever we roam
We'll know them by sight; They're not in our class
For they don't have diarrhea, just a big chairborne ass.
(Chorus)

Author unknown

1

Bien Hoa and Camp LBJ

WELCOME TO SUNNY SAIGON

Pan Am Billboard

As our Pan Am 707 entered Vietnamese air space, I hungrily studied the incredible countryside below. It was an emerald land—shade upon shade of green, streaked with blue waterways, checkered with rice fields. But it seemed strangely passive and docile, to my eyes unmarked by the shellholes I had assumed would be everywhere.

Once I was sure I saw an explosion below, a little puff of smoke, perhaps a flash, out in the middle of nowhere. Maybe I imagined it; perhaps it was just a cloud below me. Or else it was smoke and mirrors of my own making.

Smoke to cloud the mind, mirrors to dazzle the eye. In Vietnam, as we'd been told by the vets at Fort Benning, you were never sure what was real, what was camouflage. You knew that a lot of your fears about Vietnam were created by your own imagination and confusion. And it was all complicated by the military's own "public information," propaganda meant as much for the troops as for the press and public back home.

I was an Army brat, so the service was not new to me. I went in knowing that a lot of the Army in general and Vietnam in particular would be bullshit in the uniform of the day. Still, I had volunteered for Vietnam and was considering following my father's steps as a professional officer. He had retired as a lieutenant colonel after twenty-five years of service, during which I had grown up on military bases in Japan, Germany, and the States. I hoped my background might give me an edge in Nam.

At Fort Benning, the oldtimers, the Nam vets, had enjoyed warning us that the passenger jet we flew in on would have to dive into its landing to avoid groundfire from the edges of the jungle. As the plane began its descent, I realized I had the armrest in a death grip. Quickly I tried to feign composure—the young first lieutenant could not appear to be without that school-taught "command presence."

The jet did not dive and, strangely, I felt cheated of my legendary welcome to Vietnam. The 707 skimmed the palms until the lush green flashed into raw red stripped earth and the comforting gray of solid American concrete at Bien Hoa air base. The hundred or so GIs actually cheered as the wheels touched down. That stateside training had accomplished its job: it had turned a bunch of clean, green American boys into gung-ho grunts eager for combat. Didn't they know that our strategy would send them crawling into ambushes so we could find the VC and bring down our artillery and airborne heat?

It had been a long trip, an exhausting twenty hours of some 13,000 miles with brief stops at Hawaii, Wake Island, and Guam. The Pam Am crew had to hate this flight not only because of its length; they knew some of their passengers would soon be dead.

As the jet taxied toward the buildings, many of the men began to move around, contrary to the orders of the cute but intense stewardesses. I had joked with one about it not being a luxury flight if we didn't have an in-flight movie. But she was as stiff as her lacquered bouffant. Surely I couldn't expect a luxury flight to Vietnam, she'd snapped.

A skinny young PFC, Infantry, was talking excitedly, a light southern accent in his voice. Suddenly his attention was on me. His eyes had a wild bright glare, almost as though he were on drugs. Nam was his drug.

"Hey, Lieutenant, we're here! Finally, we're here! You take care of yourself, Lieutenant! You hear, you keep your butt down, sir!"

I thought, I'll keep my butt down all right, in some nice air-conditioned headquarters chair doing paperwork, but you, you poor son of a bitch, you're headed for the boonies.

The PFC pressed his hand into mine and told me again to take care of myself. His eyes were brimming, and I had to look away. I wished him luck, told him to be careful, waved to his buddies, who were watching closely, and escaped quickly to the front of the plane where the officers would disembark.

Many of my classmates from Fort Benning, Georgia, and Fort

Holabird, Baltimore, were on the plane. We'd been moved as a packet, or group, through the nine weeks of infantry platoon leaders' training at Benning and the four weeks' intelligence indoctrination at the Bird. Waiting for the door to be opened, I said, "Well, it's all downhill now!" and one of the guys snarled, "Can it, for chrissakes!" Back during the training days, whenever we had reached some milestone marking progress through the tedium, someone could be counted on to yell out, "It's all downhill now!" to our cheers. But it wasn't funny anymore.

As the door was cranked open, I braced for that fabled and cursed heat and humidity—every day, 75 to 90 percentage points of wetness. Hot and blinding bright it was, with a heavy succulence to the air, but not any worse, at first flush, than the hottest summer day in my home state of California. Until we started walking with our overnight bags. Then the humidity soon turned our khaki uniforms into dark, wet, clinging sweat suits. Why we were ordered to travel in these easily wrinkled cotton khakis was beyond me, but my orders, dated 26 May 1967, had read:

> INDIV WILL ARR IN VIETNAM WEARING KHAKI TROUSERS AND SHORT SLEEVE SHIRT, AND WILL HAVE IN POSS BASIC RQR KHAKI UNIF FATIGUES AND CBT BOOTS. ARMY TAN AND GREEN UNIF OPT FOR OFFICERS ONLY. DRESS UNIF NOT RQR. SUMMER CIV CLOS DESIRABLE FOR OFF-DUTY WEAR.

The orders also directed that "THE INTRODUCTION, PUR AND POSS OF PRIVATELY OWNED WPN IS PROHIBITED IN RVN." (RVN was the Republic of Vietnam; SVN was South Vietnam. Same thing. And GVN was the government.) We'd already heard that support troops in Saigon, where I expected to be assigned, weren't issued weapons, primarily because support troops tend to shoot each other when they've been drinking, and support troops were known to drink a lot. But I'd heard too much about all the terrorists not to want at least a handgun, even an old clunky .45.

We were herded onto a snappy new bus, all bright chrome and soft seats, with individual air-conditioning vents for each passenger. Made in Japan. The modern American war of high technology could spare no costs for the comfort of our GIs. But the wire mesh screens on the windows—grenade-proofing—made the flashy bus look like a prison vehicle.

I asked where we were being taken and the enlisted man driving replied, "Long Binh. The 90th Repro Depot is there." Army talk. Repro is reprocessing. On arrival we did our basic inprocessing. And for the remnants, a year later, there was outprocessing.

There was no armed guard on the bus, and that made me nervous. Everything made me nervous. Knowing I would sound like the typical newcomer—hell, that's what I was—I had to ask the driver about security on the road.

He laughed. Greenies were always good for a laugh. "Don't worry. The 90th isn't far, and it's a fast, paved road." He glanced over his shoulder with a bit of a grin. "Wouldn't advise driving it at night, though."

I nodded and settled back, a little more relaxed, for my first on-the-ground survey of Vietnam. I enjoyed seeing the farmers wearing the traditional straw conical hats in the rice fields with their great black water buffalo. I hadn't seen those two-thousand-pound beasts doing the work of a tractor in the paddies since my family's year in Japan.

My first overwhelming impression of Vietnam was one of movement and traffic. Little people everywhere, maybe half the men in fatigues. Small Japanese trucks and cars, motorcycles, bicycles, all loaded with wares and fruits and vegetables. A bounteous land. The women were bounteous, too, graceful and often beautiful. I was amazed by the plentiful bosoms on such slender creatures.

"I think I'm going to like it here!" I said to my seatmate. But in time I discovered that one of the legacies of the French occupation was padded bras.

The depot was named Camp LBJ, also known as Long Binh Junction. In another sense the whole damn country was Camp LBJ. I didn't like LBJ. This was his war, he had created it with his Gulf of Tonkin Resolution, he was running it from the White House, and it didn't seem he was doing a very good job of generaling. ("LBJ" also stood for Long Binh Jail, the primary stockade in Nam. That seemed a more appropriate use of the initials.)

We were taken to a newly built half-tent, half-wood structure, shadowly lit by uncovered hanging bulbs. Red, raw mud-earth and new buildings were everywhere. Nothing seemed finished, even the red dirt, torn up and churned by the daily monsoon storms. War was a growth industry, and Camp LBJ was new and expanding. I grabbed a lower bunk next to the door and the wood slats that let some air flow into the billets. We were told by a Transportation Officer that we'd have a day or so to rest before going through formal briefing and relocation. In spite of our fatigue, we wanted to check out the base and wound up at the officers' club, a nondescript hut that served only Lone Star beer. LBJ's war, LBJ's beer.

For the first time, we used our MPC, Military Payment Certificates, instead of American green. They had taken our real money away and given us play paper, even down to five-cent certificates. The idea was to keep the dollar off the black market and to allow the military to make surprise design changes of the currency, trapping speculators with worthless paper. This era of MPC had the image of a beautiful round-eyed woman, perfectly coiffed, with a proper Mona Lisa smile, subtly reminding us of the home front.

Sitting in the O-club in our sweaty, wrinkled khakis made us feel self-conscious even though the jungle-fatigued officers who came and went paid no attention to us. New troops were the business of this place, material to be processed. We headed back to our billets as the clouds began to bunch up for one of those monsoon storms we'd heard so much about, rain you could drown in.

While the others crashed, I headed for the latrine complex. In the long hall of showers were only two guys, who, you could tell from their echoing conversation, were drafted enlisted men. As I soaked in the wonderful hot water, I listened to them.

". . . wasn't fucking bad, that fucking place. All I did at Hood for six fucking months was fucking peel potatoes. Just peel fucking potatoes, you know? Not bad, fucking easy. Then at night we'd go out and get fucking stoned and next day I'd peel more potatoes. Not too bad to peel potatoes with a fucking hangover, right? Better than fucking marching. Damn fucking easy. I hope I peel some fucking potatoes over here!"

Something about the military made everyone say "fuck" a lot. At Benning even the Army's favorite "outstanding!" had become the ultimate superlative, "outfuckingstanding!"

I was asleep the moment I hit the bunk. My next sensation was of roaring sound and wetness. A wall of water poured outside the hut and the rain was driving through the door and the vents, soaking my sheets. I felt too weak to do anything but stare dumbly at the incredible downpour that was turning the accumulated red dirt on the concrete floor into a swirling dark liquid. You couldn't help but think of pooling blood.

Some flares burst into the night, slowly drifting down on their parachutes. A siren started churning out its wail, and I thought I heard the *chrump-chrump* of mortars, a sound you hear during training and never forget. Not an attack, not on the first night, not on this big secure base! They hadn't even told us where the bunkers were. I looked down the line of beds. No one had moved. No one had heard the siren. Outside, a man, totally naked, ran through the rain and mud. I sat on my bunk trying to shake off my grogginess, confused, unsure if I was dreaming or if I should wake everyone to find some shelter. Flares continued to drift down, but the siren stopped and the night was silent again.

I crawled under the wet sheets and was sucked back into drug-like stupor. Day one, 12 August 1967, was over.

"GOOOOOOOD MORNING, VIETNAM!"

I shot straight up in my bunk, jamming my head into the wire supporting the mattress above me. The Beatles' "Sgt. Pepper's Lonely Hearts Club Band" blared from a clock radio. A hand crept out of a pile of sheets to turn it off, and an unfamiliar face poked out to grin at me.

"Favorite disk jockey," he said. "Time to get up if you want chow." The red-haired, freckled face fell back and was lost under a dirty sheet. He was not one of us, the Holabird class of 14 July 1967. I swung my feet over the side of the bed, saw the swamp of mud, and pulled back. A sheet dangled from the bed above me and I pulled on it. There seemed to be someone up there, but he didn't wake. I let the sheet fall into the muck so I could stand on it while I pulled on my shoes. The cloth sucked up the red water and disappeared into it. Maybe that'll happen to me if I get up; I won't get up, I thought.

I looked down the line of bunks and could see hazy faces peering out of their sheets, some trying to sit up, then falling back, a slow-motion ripple of bodies rising, then collapsing, as I did. I didn't wake up again until twilight. Most of the Holabird guys were still there, some just sitting on the edge of their bunks in a daze.

"This fucking heat just sucks you up. I wonder if I'll ever get used to it," said an indistinct voice down the hall.

Then from the door came another voice. "Well, you survived. Better hurry or you'll miss dinner too." I recognized the freckled face from the next-door bunk. He sat on his bed and watched me.

"You want a beer?"

"Love a cold beer, but I don't think I have the energy to walk to the O-club."

He moved a pile of dirty clothes at the head of his bed and there appeared a small box-sized refrigerator. He removed two bottles from an ample stock.

"You got a refrigerator here?" I asked in amazement.

"Yeah, I've been here two weeks, thought I might as well get comfortable."

"You mean to tell me they might keep us hanging around this dump for two weeks until they figure where to ship us?"

He grinned. "Only if you're lucky. The Army has, I believe, lost my records, and I think you can say I'm on TDY."

I laughed. Temporary duty indeed. Some of the other guys were drifting by now, to hear the story of this forgotten second lieutenant. He was supposed to be going to the 9th Infantry Division, he told us, but no transportation could be sent for him when he arrived, his outfit being under attack at the time.

"O.K. by me!" He laughed, then asked where we were going to be assigned. We explained we were in the Army Intelligence and Security branch, recently renamed Military Intelligence. Some of us would go to the field, the rest to Saigon.

"Better to go to the field," he offered. "The idea of terrorists in Saigon scares me to death, never know where they're coming from, who they are. Can be a kid or an old lady with a grenade. Say"—he brightened—"did you ever hear the story about this guy, a major, who walked every day at 0730 hours to the same BOQ mess, a few blocks away from his billet? This VC guy stalked him for a month before one morning he comes up on the major, waiting for a light to change, and places a .45 almost up to the back of his head, blows him away like an execution. I'll bet that really stopped the traffic!"

One of the guys said, "Yeah, we've heard stories like that, dozens of 'em!" We all knew the sixty-five-dollars-a-month combat pay was well earned, even in the rear areas. Many grunts would not even come into Saigon, its uncertainty too much for them.

I added, "The vets at Benning and the Bird spent half their time giving us this stuff. They thrived on it, sort of like saying, 'Well, Jack, I went through all this shit and I survived, and now you're on your way, maybe *you* won't.' Remember when that colonel at Benning told us to look to our left and right, one of us wouldn't be coming back? Classic stuff."

9

One of our lieutenants approached us. "Listen, while you gold-bricks were Z-ing, a captain from Transportation said we got to be at a briefing on Vietnam culture tonight at 1900 hours and to gather up tomorrow at 0700. We'll be moving out then."

I said to the TDY lieutenant, "Well, it looks like we'll be parting company. No lost orders for us."

He waved as we headed out for chow. "Yeah, well, maybe I'll see you all here a year from now. Should have the billets looking pretty good by then!"

At 1900 we showed up at a small conference room where a tall and handsome black lieutenant was waiting before a map of Vietnam. An enlisted man gave each of us a copy of *Stars and Stripes* and "A Pocket Guide to Viet-Nam," DoD PG–21, DA Pam 20–198, NAVPERS 93135, AFP 190–4–3, NAVMC 2593, published by Armed Forces Information and Education, Department of Defense. I scanned the table of contents of the slick little 130-page book, and saw chapters for history, the home life of the Vietnamese, their religion and culture, the mountain tribes, and a reading guide. The first chapter promised "Opportunity Unlimited":

If you are bound for Viet-Nam, it is for the deeply serious business of helping a brave nation repel Communist invasion. This is your official job and it is a vital one. The dangers of ambush and raid will make sight-seeing impossible in some areas; but, when security restrictions permit, be sure to see something of the lovely country you are visiting and get ac-quainted with the charming—and tough and courageous—people who call Viet-Nam home. . . . Wherever you go, remember that Viet-Nam is a land of dignity and reserve. Your good manners, thoughtfulness and restrained behavior will be appreciated by the Vietnamese. You will benefit, as will the country you represent, in terms of friendship built on a solid foundation of mutual respect and admiration. . . . By helping the people of this proud new nation repulse the ag-gression of the Communist Viet Cong, you will strike a telling blow for democracy. By doing it in a spirit of friendship you will be adding greatly to the strength of the bonds that unite freedom-loving people throughout the world. . . .

The *Stars and Stripes*, the military's worldwide newspaper, was even better. I hadn't seen one of those since we had left Germany after my graduation from Frankfurt American High School in 1960. Dated Summer–Fall 1967, this issue was labeled "MACV Orientation Edition." MACV, for Military Assistance Command, Vietnam. Pronounced Mac-Vee. The overall command, Westmoreland's empire.

Under the banner with the two draped American flags in living color, the fine print read, "An Authorized Publication of the U.S. Armed Forces in the Far East." You wouldn't find too much war criticism in the old *Stars and Stripes*. And indeed, the two lead articles were classics.

The first was VIETNAM TOUR—YOUR YEAR OF CHALLENGE, which explained to us that we were in Vietnam to fight Communist aggression organized and directed by North Vietnam and "backed by Communist China." It further declared that the security of the Free World depended on the outcome, since the Communists regarded the conflict here as a test case for their "so-called 'wars of national liberation.'" The article maintained that the whole world was judging "the value of an American commitment" and "the value of America's word." President Johnson was quoted throughout the piece, urging us on, finishing with this stirring pledge:

> "We will not be defeated. We will not grow tired. We will not withdraw, either openly or under the cloak of a meaningless agreement. . . . We will stand in Vietnam."

At the bottom of the page was an article accompanied by a somber picture of General William C. Westmoreland, Commander, U.S. Military Assistance Command, Vietnam—COMUSMACV. The four stars on each of his collar points shone out, their silver color-coordinated with the elegant gray of his neatly trimmed hair. Our first military hero since . . . who? MacArthur?

The headline read, MACV COMMANDER WELCOMES YOU. Westmoreland held that we were winning the war and overcoming the enemy:

> We have consistently beaten him in the field and in the 17 month period since 1 January 1966, a total of about 35,900 former insurgents came over to the government side—partly

because they were out-fought, partly because they saw a new way of life on the free side.

Additionally, we had a "great opportunity" to serve our country and "all mankind." Each of us could be important in nation building, as a "soldier-diplomat":

> Every member of our Free World forces in Vietnam is en-gaged one way or another in what is called "Revolutionary Development" by the Vietnamese, "Civic Action" within your units. By either name it is a vital task and your image should be that of an ambassador of good will as well as a fighting man. Your appearance, your manners, and your understanding of the people of Vietnam can make or break this image.

Westmoreland was impressive indeed and had effectively taken the war to the VC. I was glad to hear we were "outfighting" the enemy, but it was quite a challenge to be an "ambassador of good will as well as a fighting man."

The briefing officer was into another routine about the war and Viet culture. We already had heard it three or four times and had learned little from the efforts. He kept looking at me. When he finished he came up, checked my nameplate, and said, "I thought I recognized you." We had been in the same platoon during boot camp in 1963 at Fort Riley in Kansas. We shook hands and he apologized about the briefing.

"I know it's boring, but it's from a script I have to use. I'm trapped here, giving this damn thing to everyone who comes through the 90th."

"You mean that's all you do?"

He told me he had other occasional assignments, but this one was part of his regular work. "I can't believe I came to Nam just to do this. It isn't going to do my career a bit of good."

Ah, a career man, I thought. Good luck. Like me, he'd come out of the Reserve Officers Training Corps, and ROTC officers could spend a life in the service but they hardly ever went beyond colonel.[1] But then, a lot of people were happy for the regular paycheck and the travel. The wars were only occasional.

I said good-by to my boot-camp colleague and we wished each

other luck. It was clear his worst enemy was terminal boredom, and maybe a stagnant career. My father still wanted me to make the Army a career. The future ahead for our briefing officer showed me the risks, but I wasn't ready to reject the idea.

We were still tired and hit the bunks early. Tomorrow we would be moving on to our assignments. For us the war would begin on or about 14 August 1967. It was about time. We'd been waiting for it forever. And perhaps I had been waiting even longer than the others.

I had heard my first solid rumor of wars-to-come as early as 1962 during my ROTC training at the University of Wisconsin, Madison. In one of my classes, a young captain fairly leered at us, declaring, "You guys are going to get *your* war!"

The cadets looked at one another with anxiety, and the instructor held back his explanation for effect. Finally he announced, "Vietnam! Bet you never even heard of it, but Kennedy has sent helicopters and some troops! He'll get to you too!"

It was a sobering thought. On that day began my quest, ultimately passion, to understand the mysteries of Asia and its wars. I checked out references to Southeast Asia in our ROTC manual, *The History of War,* dated July 1959. There I read:

> The most difficult problem of all was in Southeast Asia. The end of the war in Korea enabled the Chinese Reds to step up their aid to the Communist rebels in Indo-China. Despite extensive American material aid, the French and loyal native forces in the area were unable to hold. . . . In the end a settlement was reached in a conference at Geneva in 1954 providing for partition of Viet Nam much as Korea had been partitioned and for the withdrawal of the French from the area. The settlement left the whole of Southeast Asia dangerously exposed to further Chinese Communist aggression.
>
> To bolster defenses in the area, the United States . . . entered into the Southeast Asia Collective Defense Treaty . . . signed on 8 September 1954 by the United States, France, Britain, New Zealand, the Philippine Republic, Thailand, and Pakistan. The contracting parties recognized that aggression in Southeast Asia should be regarded as a common danger. . . .

Chinese Communist aggression. It always came down to that. Korea would never end, even if the conflict had to be played out again elsewhere in Southeast Asia.[2] During my father's tour in Korea in 1951–52, he had worked in the field, advising the Republic of Korea Central Procurement Agency on their war industries and supply system. Hard living conditions and the harsh winter almost killed him with pneumonia, a threat worse than the occasional artillery, snipers, and MIG strafings that he experienced.

After my father's Korea tour, our family was stationed in Kobe during our year in Japan. There I became a war freak at the tender age of ten, reading *Stars and Stripes* for news about Korea, saving pages for my scrapbook. Years later, before going on my own active duty, while making my will and cleaning up personal files at home, I found those souvenirs from 1952 and 1953. As a boy fascinated by my father's war, I'm sure I never noticed the articles about Indochina on the same pages as the hot Korea stories. In the spring of 1967, I could not yet know how close they were to prophecy.

One article, dated 26 June 1952, declared, U.S. TO SEND MORE ARMS TO INDOCHINA:

> The promise of bigger and faster American arms shipments also came a few hours after Secretary of State Dean Acheson said communist aggression in Indochina has been checked and "the tide is now moving in our favor." He said that once again the policy of meeting aggression with force is paying off.

Another article, on 7 March 1953, stated: BIG VIETNAM VICTORY IN TWO YEARS SEEN. General Raoul Salan, Supreme Commander of French Union forces in Indochina, predicted a clearing of the Red River Delta by 1955 and a move northward into the Communist rear territory. The war was then six years old, and the general saw "considerable improvement in the military picture" in most of Indochina, though fighting in Tonkin was still "grim." It was noted that the enemy's casualties "were being replaced at a steady rate," but that the Allies had fifty-four new battalions "composed entirely of Vietnamese who in time are expected to assume military responsibility which at the moment is in the hands of the French forces."

Thus the French were trying to "Vietnamize" their war the year before it was ended for them at Dien Bien Phu. Optimism prevailed even at their eleventh hour in spite of awareness that the enemy kept replacing his losses. America would replay that scenario almost to the last detail only a dozen years later.

But in 1962, eight years after the French surrender and just as my ROTC instructor was warning us about Vietnam, the United States was beginning to Americanize a war then dominated by the Viet Cong. I wasn't too worried about it. I planned to go to law school, and a subsequent delay for the bar exam could keep me from active duty until 1969. Hell, Korea lasted only three years, and I had a six-year cushion for this war to run its course. Still, in my senior year, when it was time to list my three branch preferences, I agonized over including Infantry.

"Join the Infantry," insisted my old man. "It's the only *real* Army!" He'd put in a lot of rifle-company time before a knee injury shifted him into Quartermaster, but Infantry was not for me. Years ago I had rejected his urgings for West Point; I'd have to let him down again.

A new branch had just been formed, Army Intelligence and Security, or AIS. Stay away from the Security half, I was warned. That's all boring radio and electronic stuff. Perhaps because it was the time of the first James Bond movies, Intelligence had, if not a romantic feel, at least a sense of mystery and elitism. Without the impact of Infantry bullets.

So AIS was my first choice. But all the other Army branches were so mundane—Signal, Transportation, Quartermaster, even Armor. Finally, I put Infantry (known as the "Queen of Battle") as my second choice and Artillery (the "King") as my third. To my shock, I later heard that if you put Infantry for *any* of your choices, you were assured of getting it!

That's when I really started thinking seriously about Vietnam. Maybe I wouldn't be accepted into law school, or maybe I'd flunk out in time for the war. I had to be sure I got Intelligence.

I frantically started pulling the few strings available to me. As a student senator at Wisconsin, I'd become friendly with the dean of men, who was known to have been high in the national intelligence hierarchy during World War II. He had always liked me, and he promised he'd do what he could to get me into AIS. I wrote letters seeking "career information" in intelligence from the CIA, the Department of the Army, and even the FBI, and I sent copies to the ROTC commandant and the dean.

For whatever reasons, the AIS assignment came through. The insignia was a little brass button that some called an "earring," with a design of a sword laid over a sunburst. It was a strange symbol, maybe a little mysterious.[3] But I was *in,* and the day I got my commission—8 June 1964—in an auditorium at the University, the dean rose from his chair just to shake hands with me and offer congratulations and good luck. I think he did get me AIS, and it is possible he saved my life. Infantry platoon leaders in Nam had a terrible casualty rate.

In 1964 I felt good about my commission and branch assignment. Maybe it would be a career opportunity after all, and certainly a chance to upgrade my résumé. I could get something out of the Army, instead of its taking a piece out of me. Maybe "Army intelligence" *wouldn't* be a contradiction in terms!

I started law school, but massive boredom and unclear expectations led to a second-year flunk-out. So the Army came sooner rather than later, and in June 1967 I found myself undergoing platoon leaders' training at Fort Benning. Browsing on a Saturday in the base bookstore, I found a volume entitled *Combat Intelligence in Modern Warfare* by Lieutenant Colonel Irving Heymont, who wrote:

> The decisive factor in warfare has often been combat intelligence. It has been of major influence in every battle, campaign and war in history, affecting the outcome of struggles between squads and armies. Yet, no other single factor has been so consistently ignored and neglected by unsuccessful commanders. Nothing else has been so universally used and emphasized by successful commanders.

I underlined that. When I was assigned to J-2 (the intelligence section in a joint command)[4] at Westmoreland's headquarters in late August 1967, I still believed passionately that intelligence was of vital importance, that it was an objective research process, and that it could make the difference in Vietnam.

I had a lot to learn.

But first, I was to spend a week as a company executive officer in an obscure little outpost on the edge of Saigon. That, too, would be an education.

Everything about Vietnam was an education. And we all learned the hard way and never in time.

CHAPTER
2

The 519th MI Battalion

You will be transferred to a distant branch office with in-creased pay.

> Chinese fortune cookie,
> opened before departure,
> July 1967

About half of us would be going to Saigon. One or two of the men had already been pulled away for field assignments, but the majority of our class was still unsure what jobs we would get. We had an idea, though, from our MOS—Military Occupational Specialty. Each of us was a 9300, for "Military Intelligence Officer." Then we were each given another MOS for our "specialty"; these differed, even though we'd all had the same training and none of us had any real expertise. Some arbitrarily got the number for documents exploitation, others were assigned 9306 for prisoner-of-war interrogation, still others—including me—had a 9318 for order of battle. Most of this group were to find themselves at MACV headquarters, or so I hoped.

Whatever the number, we were all called "spooks." That was the classic name for spy types, though it was a romantic misnomer: most of intelligence duty was paperwork. A lot of us were heading into sector assignments as advisors to province-level units of the Army of the Republic of Vietnam (abbreviated ARVN, pronounced Arvin) at some desolate—and vulnerable—base. Even worse than a sector job was the possibility, so often made clear to us at Fort Benning, that if there was need for a replacement of a zapped platoon leader or company executive officer, we could be called to combat duty. Intelligence work was not *always* paper-shuffling.

As the morning heat built up and our skin drooled sweat, we watched a series of vehicles whittle down our class as the various units came to pick up their new men. On the back of a deuce and a half (a two-and-a-half-ton truck) from the 9th Infantry Division was old Swans, looking desolate and lost as they hauled him away. Second Lieutenant Bob Swandby—I had nicknamed him "Standby" or "Swans" but most called him "Swamprat"—was one of the two officers I had roomed with at the Bird. With him I had developed the closest friendship of the class. A slim, quiet fellow who never complained, he was comfortable to have around. I wished he were coming with me to Saigon. We pledged to write and trade experiences—I wanted to know about the field and how my classmates were coping with the real world.

His MOS put him in the prisoner-of-war business. It would mean trips into the boonies, and you had to wonder if the Intelligence types ever got full protection from our Infantry. At Benning they had looked down on us; spooks wouldn't be their top priority. During training, the grunt lieutenants had ribbed us with a marching chant:

A-I-S, A-I-S,
In the Army
More or less!

We had countered with a self-mocking variation of the Airborne Rangers' refrain:

Chairborne,
Chairborne,
All the way!

As Swans's truck pulled away, I threw him a salute. He returned a small, sad wave. I wondered if I'd ever see him again.

"You the guys for the 519th MI Battalion?" called an enlisted man standing by an open truck. About a dozen of us jumped into the back, facing each other nervously on hard wood benches. And we were off, pulling onto the four-lane superhighway, wonder of American technology, headed for the 519th on the outskirts of Saigon.

On its edges, the "Paris of the Orient" was not what you'd call beautiful. A lot of huts, many made from cardboard and corrugated metal sheets—anything that could be scrounged. The more substantial buildings were white concrete and tile blocks with fancy air holes, swirls, and vents carved in them. Stores and even some houses were fronted by ugly sliding metal grates that were closed for security at night. Behind their accordion fences some building fronts were left open, ventilation being the key point of the design. But the huts that came with the huge refugee population had to be hellholes in the heat. That's why, I guessed, so many of the displaced slept out in the open on straw mats, their possessions clutched around them. Saigon was a city of up to four million—officially. There was no way to count the homeless crammed into every unused space.

"Damn, this place has worse smog and traffic than Los Angeles!" I yelled over the numbing sound of hundreds of motorbikes and tiny Japanese cars and trucks. Honda was king in Saigon. Some of the bikes carried loads of four or more people, plus all their worldly possessions. The density was almost as overpowering as the heat. Furthering the discomfort was the sooty vehicle exhaust that billowed in tandem with the dust, combining to coat the skin and nose and ear passages with a vile greasy sheen. The traffic was thickened by pedestrians who lurched into the flow without a care. Bicycles and Hondas skipped around the slower pedicabs—rickshaw carts on two wheels for passengers behind or in front of a one-wheeled bike frame. Countless produce-laden carts pulled by manpower or buffalo rumbled with determination through the confusion.

The people seemed stonefaced and cold. I didn't remember that degree of "Oriental inscrutability" from my family's tour in Japan.

The scene was so fascinating that I forgot my fears about terrorists, at least until a Honda would pull alongside our open truck. It would be so simple for a VC to toss a grenade in our laps and be gone in the flurry of traffic.

We made a stop at a small outpost (the 525th MI Group), then headed deeper into Gia Dinh, the province that surrounds Saigon. The driver seemed bent on mayhem, and the density of the traffic was claustrophobic. I was sweat-nervous again by the time we came roaring into a small compound through a white-painted arch that declared the post to be the Parker Motor Pool.

After an enlisted man raised the candy-striped pole, the truck stopped in a graveled lot surrounding a handsome villa with broad steps that led up to its veranda. The French influence was obvious and no doubt the place had been an imposing residence in colonial days. Now it was hemmed in by a series of pre-fab huts, painted white against the sun.

"Why have we stopped in a motor pool?" I asked the driver.

"This is the 519th MI Battalion. That sign is supposed to be some kind of camouflage. Don't fool no one." He gestured to a hut. "That's the company headquarters. You check in there."

No sirs or salutes, and there was no one to meet us as we unloaded. We followed the EM's directions. I supposed I'd have to get used to Nam informality.

Inside, the sole occupant was a specialist four typing on an ancient Remington. As the dozen lieutenants crowded into the tight space, he glanced over his shoulder at us, then went back to his typing.

One of the lieutenants cleared his throat and said, "Ah, we were told to report here for processing. We're new in-country."

As if the khakis didn't make it clear.

"Just a minute," said the enlisted man. I was getting annoyed. The informality was being pushed a little.

The EM stopped his typing, pulled out a drawer of his gun-metal-gray desk, poked around in it, and said, "We're out of the forms. I'll have to order some. Come back in an hour or so."

Groans from the group. More Army hurry-up-and-wait. We walked outside and looked around, hunting out meager shade along the side of the villa. But it was almost noon and there was precious little. Our already funky khakis, dust-covered, had turned muddy with sweat.

Worse than the heat was not having anything to do. Here we were in the big Nam and we wanted to get on with it. I fiddled with my wallet to occupy my mind, going through the duty cards the Army had been issuing us since Fort Benning. These were reminders that we were supposed to carry with us so that at opportune times we could refresh our memories about duty, honor, and country.

The most important one was the "Code of Conduct for Members of the Armed Forces of the United States," GTA 21–50, dated June 1958; it was a military offense not to have this card on your person. It declared:

1. I am an American fighting man. I serve in the forces which guard my country and our way of life. I am prepared to give my life in their defense.

2. I will never surrender of my own free will. If in command I will never surrender my men while they still have the means to resist.

3. If I am captured I will continue to resist by all means available. I will make every effort to escape and aid others to escape. I will accept neither parole nor special favors from the enemy.

4. If I become a prisoner of war, I will keep faith with my fellow prisoners. I will give no information or take part in any action which might be harmful to my comrades. If I am senior, I will take command. If not, I will obey the lawful orders of those appointed over me and will back them up in every way.

5. When questioned, should I become a prisoner of war, I am bound to give only my name, rank, service number, and date of birth. I will evade answering further questions to the utmost of my ability. I will make no oral or written statements disloyal to my country and its allies or harmful to their cause.

6. I will never forget that I am an American fighting man, responsible for my actions, and dedicated to the principles which made my country free. I will trust in my God and in the United States of America.

You couldn't help noticing that four of the six points had to do with being captured. The Armed Forces code of conduct was really a warning not to surrender and if you got caught to keep your damned mouth closed. It was a legacy of Korea, where many POWs did poorly under intense brainwashing.

We also had a MACV card called "The Enemy in Your Hands," the other side of the coin. This outlined what we were supposed to do with captured VC, and Westmoreland, it was said, personally demanded that the troops carry it and respect its rules. The front of the card offered this:

AS A MEMBER OF THE US MILITARY FORCES, YOU WILL COMPLY WITH THE GENEVA PRISONER OF WAR CONVENTIONS OF 1949 TO WHICH YOUR COUNTRY ADHERES. UNDER THESE CONVENTIONS:

YOU CAN AND WILL
DISARM YOUR PRISONER
IMMEDIATELY SEARCH HIM THOROUGHLY
REQUIRE HIM TO BE SILENT
SEGREGATE HIM FROM OTHER PRISONERS
GUARD HIM CAREFULLY
TAKE HIM TO THE PLACE DESIGNATED BY YOUR COMMANDER

YOU CANNOT AND MUST NOT
MISTREAT YOUR PRISONER
HUMILIATE OR DEGRADE HIM
TAKE ANY OF HIS PERSONAL EFFECTS WHICH DO NOT HAVE
SIGNIFICANT MILITARY VALUE
REFUSE HIM MEDICAL TREATMENT IF REQUIRED AND AVAIL-
ABLE

The tag line was: *"ALWAYS TREAT YOUR PRISONER HUMANELY."*
The inside of the card folded out to advise us to:

1. *HANDLE HIM FIRMLY, PROMPTLY, BUT HUMANELY.*
The captive in your hands must be *disarmed, searched,* secured, and watched. But he must also be treated at all times as
a human being. He must not be tortured, killed, mutilated, or
degraded, even if he refuses to talk. If the captive is a
woman, treat her with all respect due her sex.

2. *TAKE THE CAPTIVE QUICKLY TO SECURITY.*
As soon as possible evacuate the captive to a place of safety
and interrogation designated by your commander. Military
documents taken from the captive are also sent to the interro-
gators, but the captive will keep his personal equipment except weapons.

3. *MISTREATMENT OF ANY CAPTIVE IS A CRIMINAL
OFFENSE. EVERY SOLDIER IS PERSONALLY RESPONSI-
BLE FOR THE ENEMY IN HIS HANDS.*
It is both dishonorable and foolish to mistreat a captive. It is
also a punishable offense. Not even a beaten enemy will sur-
render if he knows his captors will torture or kill him. He will

resist and make his capture more costly. Fair treatment of captives encourages the enemy to surrender.

4. *TREAT THE SICK AND WOUNDED CAPTIVE AS BEST YOU CAN.*
The captive saved may be an intelligence source. In any case, he is a human being and must be treated like one. The soldier who ignores the sick and wounded degrades his uniform.

5. *ALL PERSONS IN YOUR HANDS, WHETHER SUS-PECTS, CIVILIANS, OR COMBAT CAPTIVES, MUST BE PROTECTED AGAINST VIOLENCE, INSULTS, CURIOSITY, AND REPRISALS OF ANY KIND.*
Leave punishment to the courts and judges. The soldier shows his strength by his fairness, firmness, and humanity to the persons in his hands.

Another of the duty cards was quite popular with the troops, especially the grunts. "Standing Orders, Rogers' Rangers" was written in 1759 by Major Robert Rogers, who led a company of frontier rangers in the last of the French and Indian Wars. He fought in classic guerrilla style, and his unit was the prototype of the Army's elite Rangers. His nineteen rules of combat began with, "Don't forget nothing." His third rule made a lot of sense in combat: "When you're on the march, act the way you would if you was sneaking up on a deer. See the enemy first." His fifth made a lot of sense anywhere, anytime: "Don't never take a chance you don't have to." Rogers had even anticipated a chronic mistake made in Vietnam that caused many casualties: "Don't ever march home the same way. Take a different route so you won't be ambushed." But for me, a 9300, the most impressive order was, "Tell the truth about what you see and do. There is an Army depending on us for correct information."

We also had the "Intelligence Officer's Check List" from Fort Holabird and the "M-16 Rifle Tips" from Fort Benning. I'd fired an M-16 only once at Benning, and it had jammed on me. I doubted I'd ever even touch another one, I was so sure I'd be chairborne, but I kept the card buried in my wallet.

Then there were the "Nine Rules for Personnel of U.S. Military Assistance Command, Vietnam," nine rules for getting along with the Vietnamese people:

1. Remember we are guests here: We make no demands and seek no special treatment.

2. Join with the people! Understand their life, use phrases from their language, and honor their customs and laws.

3. Treat women with politeness and respect.

4. Make personal friends among the soldiers and common people.

5. Always give the Vietnamese the right of way.

6. Be alert to security and ready to react with your military skill.

7. Don't attract attention by loud, rude, or unusual behavior.

8. Avoid separating yourself from the people by a display of wealth or privilege.

9. Above all else you are members of the U.S. Military Forces on a difficult mission, responsible for all your official and personal actions. Reflect honor upon yourself and the United States of America.

It was a bad sign, I thought, that no one took this card seriously. At least as an Army brat I was used to living overseas with the "natives" and educated in the importance of public relations.

Rule 9 impressed me: "Reflect honor upon yourself and the United States of America." Yes, that was it, the thing to get me through Vietnam. I didn't want to kill anyone, I didn't want to be zapped. Give me my job at a nice desk, let me work my butt off, give me the chance to figure out what's going on over here, and let me get out of here *honorably.*

A jeep roared out from the back of the compound. When the driver saw us, he jammed to a halt, spraying gravel in all directions. He was a tall, lean captain in dusty jungle fatigues, a camouflaged Australian campaign hat tilted up on one side of his head. In TV coverage of the war, I'd seen men wearing these wide-brimmed cowboy-like hats, one edge of the brim tacked up on the side. It had a snappy look. This guy also had a bright red railroad handkerchief tied around his neck and at his waist was a hand-tooled black leather pistol belt for his .45, the squat bullets in loops around the sides and back.

"Well, there's your answer about dress requirements over here!" laughed one of our men.

The lieutenants immediately gravitated toward this imposing figure who swung an M-16 over his shoulder to complete the image. They saluted and he nodded regally in return. He eyed the greenies and started holding forth, wiping his face with the handkerchief. I watched him suspiciously. His close-cropped hair was graying and his face was craggy with wrinkles.

"Christ, he has to be at least forty-five years old," I muttered. "A middle-aged captain. What does that tell you?"

"Dunno," answered the guy next to me. "A late joiner?"

"Hell, he's stuck in grade. He's a deadbeat. A showboat, too."

Already the lieutenants were mesmerized as the captain held court. The scene looked like a field training session back at Fort Benning. I stayed at the back, curious about his stories though skeptical of the source.

". . . always drive fast coming into this shitcamp. Did they tell you about the ambushes?" There was a chorus of nos from the lieutenants and you could hear the anxiety in their voices.

"That's Grenade Alley out there! The only road between here and downtown Saigon. The plainclothes VC hang out in the market crowds, especially in the rainy season, and when a lone vehicle comes along, slowing down at intersections, they just lay a grenade on ya. Gentlemen, you gotta drive fast, jam through these intersections, reduce your target."

When he mentioned Grenade Alley, we turned as one to look at the busy road outside, full of innocuous-looking Vietnamese peasants, many carrying baskets. How many grenades can you get in a basket? Suddenly all the bustling activity seemed more menacing.

". . . you'll get the clap, of course. No big thing, like a cold, easy to cure, comes with the duty. But those damn crabs are a bitch. Stay away from the street whores. They're the dirtiest. Buddy of mine got that new strain of syphilis they can't cure. He's with the others in Okinawa and they can't go home till there's a cure."

There was a low whistle from the group. They were ready just then to give up sex for a year.

"You see the Saigon River right behind the post? At night, and even in the day, you'll hear a lot of shooting from that direction. The ARVNs guarding that bridge there, one of the main ones out of town to VC-land, are checking it out for floating mines. The VC like to float mines or satchel charges down the river to see what they can blow up around here. So the little ARVNs shoot at anything they see that comes passing by. Floating turds have been known to be machine-gunned into diarrhea!"

The captain laughed at his joke, and so did his audience. I gave it up and walked toward the lone guard at the front gate. His job was, apparently, to raise the pole. He didn't even have an M-16, just an old M-14 rifle. As I approached, his slouch against the wall was upgraded to a lean and he delivered a reasonably accurate salute, kind of the Air Force variety, high and mighty, taking off like a B-52 with droopy wings. Hardly your crisp, extended-fingertips-to-eyebrow, snap-it-down-to-your-side textbook variety. Well, at least it was a salute. He had an acne-scarred face with an ample brown mustache, and curly hair too long for stateside duty. I figured him for twenty-one or twenty-two. I noticed a kind of glint in his eyes, as if life constantly amused him.

I asked him if he knew anything about the captain.

"Yes, sir, he comes in every couple months from Phu Bai to get stuff and do whatever he does."

"Do you know what that is?"

"Yeah, sir, he's in the Phoenix program."

"What's that?"

The EM grinned. "You *are* new, aren't ya, sir? That's the real fun program for you officers in MI who get to go live with an ARVN unit in the boonies and hunt down the VC infrastructure and kill 'em. Or vice versa."

"What's 'infrastructure' mean?"

Another grin. "That's the VC shadow government, the political officers who give the orders."

"I see. Sounds great."

"Yes, sir, but at least you don't have to hang around the MACV or CICV headquarters." He pronounced it "sic-vee."

"What's CICV?"

"Most of us work there, bunk here. It's the Combined Intelligence Center, Vietnam, near the MACV headquarters. It's part of the HQ but it includes Vietnamese Army types so it has to be a separate building."

"Why's that?"

The EM laughed. "Because some of them have to be VC spies and they don't want them in the main headquarters building."

"Oh," I said, a bit startled. "Is this what you do, security here at the compound?"

He laughed again. I was glad I could keep him amused during boring duty. "No, sir, I work in I Corps Order of Battle at CICV." (He pronounced it "eye-corps.") "We have to pull duty here all the time in addition to our jobs there. It's a bitch. CICV and the compound are always fighting over us, and the compound here has red tape and harassment you wouldn't believe."

"Like what?"

"O.K. Once the crew that works at night at CICV was woken up at noon to fill sandbags for three hours, then sent right to work without sleep. Another time they had us fill up sandbags for a detail, then they threw them away."

I looked around. The outer perimeter could have used them.

"Then there was the time we tried to get a jeep lubed, because they wouldn't update the trip ticket till the vehicle had the maintenance. But we couldn't get the jeep lubed without an updated trip ticket. Catch-22, ya know?"

"O.K., I get the point. Well, thanks, you've been most helpful."

I gave him a salute, he more or less matched it, and I turned to leave.

"Lieutenant, excuse me. Haven't they told you *anything?*" he asked.

I turned back to him and threw up my hands. "Sure doesn't seem like it, does it? We can't even get processed, the damn clerk ran out of forms."

This really amused the EM. "You're being rat-fucked, sir! That clerk, Wadsworth, we call him the Wad, he hates everyone he has to do paperwork on. He rat-fucks every MI type he can, especially the new guys who don't know any better. Ah, excuse me, sir."

"You mean he's got us out here getting sunstroke so he can get his kicks?"

"Yeah, something like that."

I gritted my teeth and swore, pointed my finger at him like a gun, and said, "Thanks!" Then I headed for the company hut.

As I stepped out, the EM called to me once more. He was grinning again.

"Lieutenant?"

"Yeah?"

"Welcome to Vietnam!"

I hit the swinging door hard and it popped open. The clerk was reading *Stars and Stripes*.

"So, Specialist Wadsworth, how goes it with the forms?"

He barely glanced up. "We're working on it."

"But not too hard, it seems."

He finally looked at me and I saw distaste in his eyes. "I called MACV for them."

"But MACVs not that close, is it, and there must be some processing we could be doing instead of standing out in the sun." My voice was getting louder.

"Not till I get the forms," he insisted.

"Not till you get the forms, *sir!*"

The clerk stared at me sullenly.

"O.K., Wadsworth, get me the company commander."

"He's not here."

"Sir, damn it!"

"Yes, sir," he mumbled indistinctly.

I heard the door open behind me. Some of my classmates were gathering at the door.

"Hey, Jones, we can hear you way across the compound. Come on, lighten up, it's gonna be a long war!"

I spun around. "You're damn right it's going to be a long war and I'm not going to start it being jerked around by a goddamn clerk. *You* lighten up!"

The second lieutenant who had spoken actually appeared embarrassed and, to my surprise, said, "Yes, sir." Up until then no one had ever acknowledged that my being a first lieutenant actually meant anything. We'd all gone through the same training, but the handful of us who had been in graduate school were automatically kicked up a grade when we left Benning, simply because by then it had been three years since receiving our commissions.

I turned back to the clerk. "O.K., where's the executive officer?"

"We don't have one. Sir," he added reluctantly.

"How about a first sergeant? Does one of those come with this unit?"

"Yes, sir, he's in his hooch."

"Get him!"

The lieutenants formed a path for the EM as he hustled off, trying not to look like he was in a hurry. In minutes a smiling five-striper sergeant appeared. Young, with blond hair slicked back country-style that looked too long for regs.

"Excuse me, gentlemen, do we have a problem? Please come in out of the sun. Now, who is the good lieutenant who's concerned about the processing?"

"I'm not concerned about it, Sergeant. I just want to do it."

"Yes, sir, no problem! Let me see . . ." He went to a file cabinet, pulled out some forms, and said, "O.K., these will do it."

I turned to the clerk, who looked like a trapped animal, but before I could unload on him, he said quickly, "Sarge, those are out of date."

"They'll do, Wadsworth. We can update later. Now, gentlemen"—he turned to us with a big smile—"let me show you the recreation hall, where you can fill these out and have a cold beer, and I'll arrange transportation for you into your Saigon billets."

I figured the sergeant for a lifer. He probably had a high school education, maybe less, and had found a home in the ranks of the non-commissioned officers where a slick and smooth operator could live long and well.

I was still annoyed and tried one more shot. "Does anyone around here ever spend any time in his office?"

The sergeant laughed. "We get it done, sir! Now, please follow me and I'll get you over to the recreation hall."

We were being greased, and by this time it felt O.K. The "recreation hall" was a porch on the second floor of one of the nearby buildings overlooking the Saigon River. It was edged by palms and enclosed by screens that let in enough breeze, pushed by large fans around the room, to make it comfortable. A couple of NCOs were playing pool and paid no notice to our group. We got beers all around, more Lone Star.

"I wonder if all the facilities are integrated here," I said. My classmates stared at me strangely and I added, "I mean, mixing NCOs and officers. I thought that was against military traditions."

One of the guys said, "Yeah, well, a lot of the stateside traditions don't seem to apply over here."

"That's a roger," said another.

"But the worst of it," said Kernsky, who had been one of my squadmates at Fort Benning in the J–K platoon (we had been organized by last-name initials), "is no weapons in Saigon. Can you believe we don't get no goddamn gun?"

Kernsky was crazy about weapons, a passion from his street-gang days. For a moment I felt like teasing him with the old Army routine for making trainees learn nomenclature. If you slipped and said "gun," the instructor would make you hold your rifle at present arms, chanting, "This is my *rifle*," then you'd have to clutch your crotch, saying, "This is my *gun*. This is for *fighting*," again the rifle held forward, then a hand back to the crotch, "This is for *fun*." Doing that just once before your laughing platoon made you remember your fucking nomenclature.

But I didn't remind him. The joking of the training days was over, and anyway Kernsky, a tough city kid, didn't take kindly to joking or perceived slights.

The sergeant returned to collect the paperwork and said he'd be back when the truck was ready. Tomorrow we would get our uniforms and be interviewed by the commanding officer of the battalion before our final assignments were confirmed. It seemed this would be the last time together for the dwindling Holabird class of July '67. As we got further into our beers we talked about the war, what it meant, what we hoped for.

One of the guys offered, "Like John Steinbeck said, 'I'm not a hawk, I'm not a dove, but I'm not a pigeon either!'"

"Right on!" said another, raising the two-finger peace sign. "Peace . . ." he said, then lifted a third finger to make a W and continued, "but otherwise, look out!"

". . . Vietnam, love it or leave it!"

". . . I don't want to have to rely on a bunch of ARVNs for my life. *Fuck* a bunch of ARVNs . . ."

". . . you've got to expect losses in Southeast Asia . . ."

". . . whatta they gonna do, send me to Vietnam?"

". . . fuck 'em if they can't take a joke . . ."

It went around and around, the beer kept flowing, and so many memories, recent but already so far away, flooded back. I remembered how at Fort Benning we had played games with the traditional military order "As you were" when the officer-in-charge reduced our standing at attention to a state of ease. Each time a new smart-ass wisecrack would come from the troops. Toward the end of training, one of the lieutenants, acting as student platoon leader, barked it off: "As you were, troops!"

From the ranks came back, "As you *should* be!" Then, "As you *might* have been!" Another voice added, "As you *yet could* be!" Finally the topper: "Right, and as you will be when you get out of this fucking Army, and that's if you're still in one piece, but you'll still be screwed up!" We had all let out a whoop after that, and never went through the routine again. There wasn't anything more to say.

Probably because of the beer, I decided to volunteer what was on my mind. "What I want," I said intently, "is to get through all this without having to kill anyone, and to serve *honorably—*"

Gregory started laughing. He was a tall, arrogant first lieutenant who had been promoted when I was, and I'd never liked him. I'd always felt he was looking down on me. He had height, I was "average," he came from East Coast money, I was an Army brat from California, he'd finished law school well, I hadn't finished at all. Old Gregory no doubt saw me as substandard issue.

"Honor? You got to be kidding, Jones! What the hell does that mean, some ancient romantic concept of chivalry?"

I felt like a jerk for setting myself up and just stared at him, sweating more than the heat required. He sneered at me down that long nose and said, "Anyway, your 'honor' equates to nothing more than the absence of dishonor, especially in this idiotic war!"

I didn't care to argue the point. It was still my goal to do the best job I could, regardless of any idiocy. At the end of the Benning training I had said to a bunch of Infantry officers that I, for one, would work night and day to get the info to them that could save their lives. I had an overwhelming respect, an awe, for these combat platoon leaders. It seemed beyond comprehension to me, going into soggy jungles to be ambushed and boobytrapped. My sense of "honor" was to give it my all, to do everything I could to make it a little easier for the grunts. Gregory could shove it. Too many guys like him would just try to skate, to coast through their tour.

I was saved by the arrival of the sergeant. Our truck was ready. As we were about to board, we started talking about Grenade Alley again. We all began worrying, each man's fears fueling the next's. I suggested that the most senior of us should ride in the front with the driver, per regs, and I volunteered myself, mostly to ensure that someone up front would be watching the road closely.

Gregory cut me off, implying his date of rank had me by a few days. "I'll ride in front if you don't mind, Lieutenant Jones!" The troops enjoyed that, but I insisted he watch the road *close,* an unarmed truck of Intelligence officers was a damn good target. The laughter stopped and, for the whole ride, no one was in a joking mood. We were in a canvas-covered truck this time and could see nothing but the dust out the back while the driver drove like a maniac into Saigon, making Indy-like screeching skids through the traffic.

The truck finally jerked to a halt across from a high-rise hotel in downtown Saigon, and the enlisted man yelled back through the cab window, "Here's your billets, gentlemen." We flooded out of the truck, eager to get into a secure building. I noticed a pile of garbage, the height of a man, on the corner. It was to remain there and grow over the coming year.

Behind me I heard a yell of pain and a thud to the ground. I spun around and saw a lieutenant rolling on the concrete sidewalk, bent over and moaning loudly. In his eagerness to get off the truck, a feeling we all shared, he had caught his foot and ripped the cartilage in his knee. He was soon medevaced out of Vietnam, never to be returned to the war zone. He was our first WIA—"wounded in action." The VC were everywhere. Especially in our heads.

I hardly took notice of the hotel, the Meyerkord, a transients' facility where we were to stay for a few days until spread out to permanent billets. We did hear that it was also the home of the USO and Red Cross personnel, as well as visiting show-biz types, but at that point we didn't care. We were too uptight, tired, and dirty, and more important, the place had hot showers.

I was given a room on the eighth floor, above the constant roar of the hotel's generator, where breezes flowed and mosquitoes didn't. I liked it fine, until the middle of the night when my roommate came crashing in, a huge Australian wearing his flap-up hat. He punched me awake to wish his "mate" a good morning and proceeded to hold forth on the nature of the war for half the night while swigging from a bottle of booze.

I grunted occasionally, thinking in amazement that Aussies really do talk that way. Finally I pleaded with him for sleep, and he laughed about "pussy Americans" before finally leaving me alone. When I awoke in the morning he and his gear were gone. It was as if he'd never been there. But I don't think I could have dreamed such a presence.

The truck was coming at 0700 and it was assignment day.

3

Life in the French Foreign Legion

Rear-echelon pogues and their silly-assed paranoia.
Dale A. Dye
Run Between the Raindrops

"What's the colonel doing?" I asked.

I was standing with one of the Parker compound oldtimers by the door of the company headquarters hut. We were watching the lieutenant colonel in charge of the 519th MI Battalion.

"Inspecting his jeep."

It was my first day as executive officer of the company that had processed us two days earlier. I was deeply depressed. The clerk avoided talking to me, the first sergeant worked around me, and I still had not met the company commander.

"What's he inspecting his jeep for?"

"Bombs. Does it every day."

"Bombs?"

"Right."

"But the jeep's been sitting in the compound all day."

"Yes, sir, but there's Vietnamese coming and going in the compound all day."

"The workers?"

"Yeah."

"But the guards search them when they come in mornings and leave at night. The jeep's been sitting ten yards from the fucking front gate and the guard!"

"Yeah."

"So what's the old man worried about?"

"Bombs."

I sighed. Parker was proving to be a little backwater insane asylum, and the madness had begun the day of the interviews with the CO.

We had been sitting in the chow hall in the basement of the villa head-quarters, sucking on coffee, writing letters home. I had a little notebook in which I planned diligently to record all the significant bullshit. My insightful entry for the day was intended to be philosophical:

> O.K., here we are in Vietnam, where to now. Do I do brain-work or pain work. Count VC or kill them. Operate figures or figure operations. I hope I kill every VC I meet. I hope I don't meet any VC. Kill a Commie for Christ. They say kill an Imperialist for Ho. Comes out the same.

"Hey, Lieutenant Jones," yelled the first sergeant through the door. "The colonel's ready to see you first!"

I groaned. One of the lieutenants called, "Hey, Jones, that'll teach you to raise hell with the clerks. They always get you back!"

I told the lieutenant to screw off and expressed the wish that he find himself stationed with the poor man's John Wayne up in Phu Bai. "And I hope you get his crabs!"

My classmate laughed. "See you in the bar later. Good luck!"

This was it. The field or an office, dust and mud or concrete and air conditioning. It was now in the hands of the good Lieutenant Colonel "Flakjacket."

The story behind his nickname wasn't inspiring. It was said that on the day he took over the battalion, some ambitious VC shot a rifle grenade into the Plum Farm, one of the 519th's other compounds. It fell short and dug a little hole in the parking lot. Many of the men slept right through it. The new commanding officer took the radio report and declined to come out for an inspection. Days later he called in advance to determine if the area was "secure" and maintained full radio contact with his destination on the way, constantly inquiring if there was any change in condition. His convoy arrived at the Plum Farm in style with a cluster of well-armed men, himself resplendent in flakjacket, helmet, and web gear with grenades slung all around him. He continued to wear the flakjacket around the Parker compound, and his trips to the Plum Farm, or anywhere, were rare.

At the top of the steps to the villa was an engraved wooden plaque ordering "Knock," which I did, while removing my brand-new olive-drab baseball cap.

"Come in!" A booming voice bounded through the breeze inlets around the door. I breathed deeply, then pushed on. After the bright sun I was blinded in the cool darkness, and I had only vague impressions of a sizable room with a ceiling fan and perhaps even some potted palms. I could have expected to see Claude Rains seated at the large desk, with Humphrey Bogart lounging in the corner.

Instead, it was the first sergeant, whom I'd named "Slick," standing with a notebook behind LTC Flakjacket, in whose direction I saluted.

"Sit down, Jones, relax, relax. I'll be brief, I know how tiring inprocesssing can be. Now, we do have a subsector spot open in II Corps, but it'll be easy to fill. You're a first lieutenant and you come from a military family so I'd like to make you executive officer of one of our companies, some three hundred and fifty men. How does that grab you?"

Not well. "Executive officer of one of the companies?" I repeated lamely.

"Right. Actually, it's our only company here. The others are scattered across the country. One is a small admin contingent in Phu Bai but it's just a clearinghouse for scattered order-of-battle types in I and II Corps. The other one is only a company in concept, handling the paperwork for the covert types across Nam. You know, the cloak and dagger types." I presumed he was referring to the Phoenix program.

Flakjacket continued. "I'm in Armor myself. Why they gave me a spook battalion, I'll never know. But there's not that much real Armor work over here, so we have to take what we can. So, you think you can handle the admin side of a company? Remember, these men aren't here that much, working long shifts, so it's mostly paperwork, not playing chaplain to a bunch of homesick GIs. The first sergeant will handle that anyway."

I figured that First Sergeant Slick, smiling confidently in the background, handled most everything.

"Well, sir, I would like to say that my MOS is order of battle and I was hoping to do that at headquarters."

"Headquarters, shit!" he snapped. "The HQ is the world's worst place. Total bureaucracy, constant state of panic, spit and polish! I'm doing you a favor, believe me. Lots of free time, your own jeep, a good mess. It's good duty, Jones!"

"Yes, sir, I'll do my best at whatever I'm assigned to." I felt weak at the thought of being stuck in limbo in a backwater administrative post halfway between the field and headquarters.

"I believe you will! We'll get the captain in here to break you in. Meanwhile, get with the sergeant here tomorrow and he'll show you around."

I thanked him, saluted, and broke out into the heat. I avoided my classmates and went straight to the recreation hall. I needed a drink. Already the Army was messing with my morale.

The orders for my assignment as executive officer, dated 16 August 1967, read: "Dy asg: Executive Officer, Pkt 519E1-A (OB) 519th MI Bn (FldA) APO 96307." However, the military nomenclature on the sign outside the building was "Headquarters and Headquarters Company." And I'd seen a reference to a 45th MI Company. I didn't know what the hell I was executive officer of, and cared a notch less.

Paragraph three of the orders announced "Fol indiv APPOINTED" and, funny thing, each of the sixteen additional duty items had printed after it, "JONES, Bruce E 05533920 1Lt MI." I had received "add dy" as: Soldier Voting Officer, Unit Fire Marshal, Unit Savings Officer, Unit Information Officer, Unit Material Readiness Officer, Unit Records Management Officer, Unit Safety Officer, Unit Supply Officer, Unit R&R Officer, Unit Historian, Unit Security Control Officer, Unit Motor Officer, Unit Arms Officer, Unit CBR Officer, Unit Commo Officer, and Unit Crime Prevention Officer.

First Sergeant Slick told me not to worry about it, that he and Wadsworth would keep things flowing to me for signature. It bothered me no small amount that I was now at the questionable mercy of the punk clerk. Whenever I came into the office, he was busy at the files; somehow he always knew when I was coming. Not seeing me meant not having to respond in a military fashion, but I wasn't about to call him on it. I needed him too much. My first letter home said, "I'm moving slow in this job. Have no choice, since I don't know what I'm doing!"

That was one hell of an understatement. But one thing I did know about was security, and as the newly appointed Unit Security Control Officer I inspected the compound. I got scared again. Never, even on small stateside Army bases, had I seen such miserable security. Along Grenade Alley there was a wire fence of wide mesh without any barbed wire along the top. A single stacked row of sandbags, about thigh-high, leaned against the villa's original concrete fence, a low, openwork structure with perpendicular and crisscrossed columns. The entrance at the candy-striped pole was closed up at night with a swinging gate that a pedicab could have broken through. On one side of the compound was a huge old barn-like building, almost windowless, where the enlisted men slept in sweltering heat. Its long outer wall was also the outer edge of the compound. An alley, open to any pedestrian, ran along the wall. A single VC could have placed charges along the building and blown away the majority of the enlisted men in Intelligence at MACV headquarters. I reported my concern but it didn't get past the first sergeant. The true chain of command was becoming clear to me.

On the side of the compound facing the Saigon River even the wide mesh fence had holes in it, and there was no sandbagging. A guard tower did overlook the river, but it was rarely manned. At the corner of the compound, close to the EM's barn (which, after one guided tour, I was told by Sergeant Slick to avoid henceforth, it being enlisted-man sanctuary), was a fairly well constructed pillbox. Its viewing holes were screened by wire mesh to keep out the occasional tossed grenade. Fortunately, it had never been field-tested by the VC. However, one corner of the mesh, at a blind spot facing down Grenade Alley, had been bent upward. I was told later by enlisted men that the opening had been made to allow the guard to dump out his beer or soda if any duty officer came diddy-bopping by. A grenade could have been dumped right back into the bunker just as easily.

I was insistent about having that mesh fixed, but the sergeant said he had no personnel for that kind of work. I offered to do it myself if he'd get the tools, but he said an officer couldn't be seen doing manual labor. Right. I went back to my little office and sat at my olive-drab wooden field desk. I wrote a letter home and went to the mess for coffee, then left for the Meyerkord.

The next day the sarge came in beaming. "Lieutenant, got that bunker screen fixed! Did it myself!"

I was indebted. I thanked him profusely. Damn, one of my orders had been fucking executed! That mesh repair was my most important accomplishment—in fact, my only accomplishment—as executive officer at the Packet 519 E1-A of the 519th MI Battalion.

The colonel finished his inspection for bombs and was off, driven by his personal aide. The jeep passed under the archway, on which was inscribed, "Remember YOU are the guest here. Drive carefully." A sign next to the gate elaborated the point: "Whenever you leave this post, you represent our unit. Stay alert. Be courteous. Represent your country well."

On Grenade Alley the drivers were alert, all right, but there was little sign of careful driving. On the day of our interviews, the EM driver had yelled through the back window to warn us that we had reached Grenade Alley and that this was where "we get it all the time." The checkered flag was down again as he drove the deuce-and-a-half like a race car, and this time we could see the Vietnamese jump and scurry, screaming their curses at us.

I subsequently learned from a post veteran that danger on Grenade Alley had become history during the last dry season, when the Army Engineers straightened, smoothed, and blacktopped the road. No more ruts, no more mudholes, no more bogged-down U.S. vehicles. And no more incidents of terrorism as soon as the normalized traffic was no longer offering an easy target.

We were being rat-fucked again. The next time a driver pulled the Grenade Alley routine on us, I locked his heels, stood him up against the wall, and quickly brought about a more civilized style of driving.

We had gotten our issue of jungle fatigues and jungle boots, those half-leather and half-web creatures that let sweat and paddy water evaporate out. The jackets, which hung comfortably outside the trousers for ventilation, had oversized pockets everywhere; the trousers had extra pockets on the thighs. We were allowed to roll up the sleeves as high as they'd go and the outfit actually looked pretty sexy—after we had it tailored, of course, to smooth out the baggy fit. The Army told us it was against regulations to wear tapered jungle fatigues. Mine were done skin tight, with the blouse tucked in nicely. Later, a lieutenant colonel at CICV commented on the snug fit. I smiled and blamed supply for giving me too small a size. He replied with the traditional Nam acknowledgment of the unavoidable and unresolvable: "Right," drawled Colonel Mac with the prerequisite half-smile. I think that was the start of our friendship.

On the left shoulder we wore the patch for the U.S. Army in Vietnam, an upright sword in a three-striped field of yellow, blue, and red in vertical columns. On our jungle fatigues, all patches were in camouflage colors, black and jungle green. Early generations of troops had gone through the boonies with their colors and ranks shining, letting the VC have nice bright aiming points. Officer ranks of silver and gold were always high-priority targets. I much preferred the muted approach, even in the Saigon boonies.

The day we had gotten our uniforms, we also received our first antimalaria pill, which, at least for those in Saigon, had to be taken only once a week. My first pill planted me on the throne for thirty minutes of excruciating runs. The supply sergeant had told us when he gave them out: "When the pills were first used in Vietnam, someone said that they'd make you turn yellow. So everyone took them and turned yellow. Then someone said you'd get the runs for days. So everyone took them and got the runs for days. Then someone said they'd make you impotent. So everyone stopped taking them!"

One of the less sophisticated guys later asked in great concern, "Do you really think they'll make you impotent?" and a more tuned-in lieutenant replied in all seriousness, "Sure! You remember how they put saltpeter in our food at Benning, don't you?"

Amazing how some legends persist through the military generations, and there is always some round-faced, wide-eyed innocent to buy them.

The company commander came in the next day, just to meet me. He too was an aging captain, though not as far along as the poor man's John Wayne of Phu Bai. He was friendly and easy to talk to. I was encouraged—until he said, "You'll be running the company, Jones. You and the first sergeant. I don't come in too often."

"Come in? From where?"

"I have a villa downtown, with my mama-san. It's behind my bar."

"You have a bar?"

"Yeah, on Tu Do Street." He gave me a small advertising card. "But we don't talk about it, do we?" he continued with a grin and a wink.

"Oh. Right. Sure, we don't talk about it. Yes, sir!"

"But come on down. I've got some outstanding girls there. They'll take good care of you!" He was gone after that and in my week at Parker, I never saw him again in the compound.

I learned later that he was into at least his third extension in Nam, seeing his stateside family only on leaves to Hawaii. It could be profitable to serve your nation in Vietnam.

4

Saigon Curfew

In the rear with the beer.

GI slang

On or about my twenty-fifth birthday—August 19, 1967 (I was not prepared to think of my birthdate in that reversed military sequence)— we received a memo dated 18 August 1967 from Robert L. Ashworth, Brigadier General, USA, Subzone Commander, at the U.S. Army Headquarters Area Command. Not a great birthday present. Entitled "Rising Terrorist Incidents," it included this:

> 2. Terrorist initiated activities and threats in the Saigon/Cholon area have sharply increased this week. Personnel walking alone after dark have been accosted and threatened by armed individuals on foot or in slowly moving vehicles. Rifle fire has been directed against US billets, guard posts and installations. One grenade attack on a US vehicle resulted in several injuries. There have also been a number of attacks on Vietnamese polling sites and personnel. The VC have openly and clearly declared their intent to continue, on an increasing tempo, this type of activity up to and during the coming Vietnamese elections.
>
> 3. There is no cause for undue alarm. However, you are advised to limit your movements during the hours of darkness, as much as possible, to move in pairs, avoid large crowds, and poorly lighted streets and alleys.

The day before the memo was issued I had written to my father at his office so that my mother would not get the letter first. She was a heart patient, and I didn't want to scare her. My letter said:

I've decided I need a gun pretty badly and there's no guarantee they'll issue me one. The main reason is the elections. It'll be the roughest terrorism Saigon has ever seen—has already begun. The last 2 nights there has been firing around the hotel. Each day trucks are grenaded. They've been running 10 of us Lts. in open trucks with *no* weapons and it's unnerving me. I know a .45 is no equalizer, but it'll help my peace of mind a great deal. (Don't worry about *overconfidence*.) An officer may wear a weapon—however, they're just not handing them out. Perhaps a shortage. Whatever the reason, it's hairy enough around here that I'd feel a lot better if I had one.

Just before leaving for Benning, my father and I had gone up into the dry yellow hills of Santa Barbara, our home town, to practice with his .45. He wanted me to stand up formally as at a firing range, but I insisted that in Vietnam I wouldn't have much time for that. Quick-firing from my hip at a log some twenty feet away, I blew up a lot of dirt with the two-and-a-half-pound mini-cannon but never hit the target. Not an accurate weapon, the .45—it had a maximum range of fifteen hundred meters but was effective only under fifty. Or maybe five feet. It had gone into service around 1911, after Americans learned that lesser handguns wouldn't stop the frenzied attacks of Filipino insurgents. The monster .45 slug had such power and impact, it could knock your enemy over even if it hit him in the hand. Probably blow off the hand, too. But you had to be close to your target to hit anything. At Benning I had qualified expert on every weapon, but I never learned to like the .45, especially because it was so slow to activate. You had to hand-crank the bullet into the chamber before it could be fired. But it was all the Army issued.

In my letter home I promised I would be staying off the streets "at least" until the elections were over—the president and vice president would be chosen on 3 September and the National Assembly elected later in the month. The elections were supposed to be a major test of the nation's democratic potential. At first the flamboyant Nguyen Cao Ky, head of the Viet Air Force and the past premier, was going to oppose

Nguyen Van Thieu for the presidency. It was said that the Americans had convinced Ky to settle for the vice presidency to avoid a serious clash between the two men and their factions. There were also ten civilian candidates, including a peace candidate, Truong Dinh Dzu, who may have had Viet Minh and Viet Cong affiliations. Some 4.8 million people voted and Dzu actually came in second, although distantly.[1]

I wasn't going anywhere, although the Meyerkord wasn't a bastion of safety. The first day I noticed the neat crisscrossed taping across the windows in an attractive lattice pattern. I learned that tape reduced the shower of splintered glass from the concussion of a bombing. The hotel had been bombed twice since the American occupation with devices smuggled in by the Vietnamese maids. The maids tidied your room, cleaned and pressed your fatigues, and shined your boots for a monthly fee of around twenty dollars in piasters. Some of them could also blow away your lunch. I always gave my maid a bonus.

My father's .45 would not have got to me in time; even with it, I had no intention of going out on the streets after dark. The 2300 curfew seemed highly cavalier to me, especially after reading General Ashworth's memo. I had talked to a captain down the hall at the Meyerkord, a married man also new in-country, and we both agreed that a guy could stay in the hotel, read books, go to bed early, and work hard at his job. We could make it a "sabbatical," a year of work, contemplation, and education. He said he was going to "save it all for his wife."

Two nights later I ran into him on Tu Do Street as he and some friends came out of a rock 'n' roll bar next to a steambath with a sign that promised a "scientific massage." An aging Viet woman stood out front, yelling at us, "Hey, Joe, sucky-fucky?" The captain and I shared embarrassed grins and shrugged. So much for sabbaticals.

The Meyerkord's charms were wearing thin on me already, even though we had heard that Miss America was staying there and that we had at least four USO and/or Special Services women. "Donut Dollies," they were called, but never to their faces. I never figured out exactly what it was they did, except escort show-biz V.I.P.s on their tours and hand out donuts and coffee to the troops.

I had my share of the traditional male military attitude about civilians in general and civilian women in particular in war zones. Stories about them abounded, fueled by incidents such as one that occurred not long before I arrived. Some of the Donut Dollies had gotten a little too drunk one evening and hung a captured VC flag from their balcony. Possibly it could have been seen from Independence Palace, where President Thieu lived and worked, two blocks away. Certainly the Korean embassy on the next block had a full view of it. In minutes the hotel was converged upon by the Vietnamese police (Americans derisively called them "White Mice" for their white uniforms), our MPs, and Korean MPs. The White Mice wanted to arrest our terrified Donut Dollies, but some fast-talking Americans eased them out of it. Stern lectures would follow.

I kept my distance from our "roundeyes." Except for one; Sheila, a slender, sexy redhead in her early twenties. She was just starting as a general's secretary at MACV headquarters and we dated for about a month, well into the time that I was transferred to CICV. Before we'd go to dinner, I'd shower and change clothes at her fine two-story villa with maid service, where she lived with another secretary.

Sheila had demanding tastes. At even the modestly priced Viet restaurants and the officers' clubs, she could make dinner into an expensive proposition. Finally one night, in an attempt to alter our costly routine, I gathered a basket of picnic goodies from the PX, including a bottle of champagne, for a romantic feast on her veranda in the tree-lined backyard. Sheila was furious. She didn't want PX, she wanted French restaurant. We ate at a nearby club in silence. She didn't invite me back to her villa and I never called her again. I swore off roundeyes for the duration.

I saw Sheila again, months later. She was at the Meyerkord for a night. I'd heard rumors she'd lost her villa and was living in a hot, dusty tent at U.S. Army Headquarters, Camp LBJ, after her general had been transferred. She'd be eating PX now. And I heard she was making good money there, doing hundred-dollar short-time tricks for soldiers. At the Meyerkord our conversation was brief. "So you're out in Long Binh now—no more villas, I guess."

"Yes, but I actually like it," she said.

"So I've heard," I said. She averted her eyes and walked away. I never saw Sheila again.

The Meyerkord was designed like a square donut around a large open-air core that allowed breezes to circulate. You could stand on the inside walkways and watch rain pour through the hotel to land on the green corrugated plastic roof over the snack bar on the ground floor.

Weather permitting, most of us met almost nightly on the roof of the hotel for movies. We'd all bring our drinks up—it was interesting how many had converted to the Graham Greene gin and tonic—and watch distant flares drifting down around the edges of Saigon, dripping magnesium light as they floated on their parachutes. It was said that they cost fifty dollars a shot and they kept coming, one after the other, all night long, out where the jungle met the urban limits or the base perimeters.

And, in awe, we watched the B-52 strikes that were regularly flown close to Saigon. "Arc Light" was the name for the program with the big 500-pound bombs. Many of them went into the "Iron Triangle," a VC stronghold among the rubber plantations and jungle only some twenty kilometers northwest of Saigon. The concussion of those monster explosives was impressive even from a distance. It was said that if the dug-in enemy avoided the fire and shrapnel, a string of B-52 bombs would still blow out the membranes of the ear and sometimes create a vacuum that could suffocate an unlucky VC.

One evening I watched *In the Heat of the Night* up on the roof as flares, bombs, and monsoon lightning popped and flashed around our humid horizon. But even spectacular light shows and free movies soon became mundane and I was itching from cabin fever.

I took my first pedicab trip, enjoying the hell out of it, to my captain's bar on Tu Do Street. The place was nothing fancy, but it did have a number of young ladies sitting at the tables. I asked the Vietnamese bartender for the proprietor and in a moment the captain came in, smiling expansively, and shook my hand. He asked if I was settled in at the compound, then introduced me to his mama-san, an attractive middle-aged woman. Over a drink he explained that he'd established ownership of the bar in her name so she'd have something after he left Vietnam.

"It seems the only fair thing to do," he said earnestly.

It occurred to me that this arrangement would also make it harder to trace his profiteering. If the Army cared to check out these things.

I stayed and drank with one of his bar girls, a woman close to thirty who was pleasant and spoke English well enough to hold a conversation. A little embarrassed, I asked the captain whether it would be all right if I went home with his employee. Money changed hands with her before we left the bar. I presumed my commanding officer would get a piece of it.

We arrived at her house by taxi just before the 2300 curfew. Hers was one of the typical concrete-block buildings honeycombed with air vents. Not much furniture, but family portraits were abundant. A number of small gecko lizards—for good luck and mosquito control—prowled the walls and ceiling. I asked the woman naive questions about VC terrorists in the neighborhood.

Of course, there never were any. Here was safe, Saigon was safe, she insisted.

I met her mother, an ancient, shriveled, smiling dot of a woman with the typically betel-nut-stained teeth of the older generation. (These nuts were chewed for their mild euphoric effect.) She bobbed and bowed, chattering in Vietnamese. The woman and I settled into bed, her mother in the next room. There was no door between the rooms, and the old lady's snoring was almost in my ear. I asked the woman if her mother minded about men being there.

No. It was necessary.

I slept hardly at all. Every mosquito in Saigon found my location and even with a fan aimed at me, I was buzzed and bitten all night. They didn't bother her. I said something about "VC mosquitoes" and she laughed. At dawn, I hurriedly pulled on my civvies and taxied back to the Meyerkord to get ready for work, dragging through the day after vowing to find a better outlet for future extracurricular activities.

At the compound I was issued my own .45 about the time my father replied to my earlier request for a weapon. In Korea, he wrote, he had suffered similar fears of "occasional shots and grenades":

> The chief of staff ruled that sidearms made priority targets out of us and were worthless. Concealed sidearms were easily spotted and seemed to invite the knife in the back. Of course —the feel of the sidearm at one's side was comforting—but one might as well suck one's thumb.

Still, he said he'd be happy to send his .45 if I needed it:

> I wouldn't care if it came back—so long as you do! If something happened to you without it—I'll always have to wonder if it would have made a difference. If something happens with

you having it, I'll always have to wonder if you might have been spared if you were un-armed!...If one or two pistols return fire after an attack, it is pretty certain that another grenade will eliminate everyone promptly.

Then he added a postscript. By chance he had run into a man who had just left Vietnam as General Westmoreland's courier. He reported that the private pistol had gotten top command attention and was *"out."* The courier, who had lived in Saigon, told my father this:

"We wanted to come home alive—so we sat in quarters night after night. No *night prowling* of the city—and damned careful in the day!! Many is the night we stayed and slept on our desks when things were bad in town."

Good advice, indeed. But by then I'd already hit the streets, the rock 'n' roll bars (where you bought expensive nonalcoholic shots of "Saigon tea" for a "hostess" while she played with you under the table), the "scientific" steambath-and-massage parlors. My hotel was about a twenty-piaster taxi ride from Tu Do Street and the alternative to boredom was just too tempting. Being out and around somewhat reduced my anxiety about terrorists; the incidents were just not as frequent as one would expect. Still, the occasional report was chilling. Like this one:

A captured member of a VC assassination unit disclosed that the unit had the mission of killing 3 American military or civilian personnel per month. The assassinations would take place as opportunities arose. When a lone American was spotted, he would be followed until he entered an isolated area. If the area contained several streets or alleys that would facilitate the assassins' escape, the American would then be shot. This modus operandi was employed in the majority of the 10 incidents involving Americans in the Saigon/Cholon area since May 1967. Six of the Americans were killed, while 4 were wounded.

But there were some places I'd never go. Cholon was the Chinese suburb of Saigon, a city unto itself, and I avoided it except for quick runs to the main PX there. VC terrorism seemed to concentrate on that area, perhaps for racial reasons. (Just before the elections the VC had even conducted propaganda lectures there in broad daylight.) I would never be able to go to the My Canh restaurant, located on a boat moored in the Saigon River. On 25 June 1965 a bomb went off inside the restaurant, creating panic as American and Viet diners tried to get back to shore over the narrow gangway. Then the VC set off two Claymore mines that took out the ramp and everyone on it.

A Claymore is a shallow curved box set up on little legs. It is detonated by a long wire that keeps its owner at a comfortable distance from the site, and its charge blows a six-foot-high blast of pellets into a wide killing zone of some fifty yards. It is sort of a wide-gauge shotgun with a very short barrel.

Forty-four people died, eighty-one were wounded that day at the My Canh restaurant.

On 21 August I wrote home:

> I feel a lot better about the terrorists now. I know how they work and how to watch them—stare at the Viets' hands as we travel and the occasional bad guy won't make a move. He wants to terrorize and get away—not get shot. He's also short on grenades, so he doesn't waste them. The percentages are *well* on my side that I'll never see a Charlie. They have been sneaking in town with mortars to hit the airport, but they've been getting wiped out. Which is a *real* deterrent!!

Years later, rereading my letters, I saw that constant, irresistible pattern of putting a good face on everything I sent home to try to relieve my parents' concern. Each of my mailings from APO 96307, San Francisco, was its own little exercise of smoke and mirrors. I think I even came to believe my own letters as time went by.

I should have understood then that MACV would be no different in its public proclamations. But they would affect a lot more than just home-front morale. In time the incessant, insane optimism would lose the war.

A letter from Swandby—"Swamprat"—reached me, to my great pleasure. He was at Bear Cat, a base camp forty kilometers east of Saigon, working with brigade IPW (Interrogations Prisoners of War) teams. He said the 9th Division was spread out "all over hell" with the 3d Brigade's base camp at Dong Tam in the Mekong Delta and a battalion camp at Tan Am, also in the delta just south of Saigon. Other elements were scattered and he would be traveling to them. He was living in a tent with five other officers, but they had electricity and a small refrigerator. Monsoon rain could and did take over their living space on occasion, flooding them out.

Later he told me how when he got to Tan Am he discovered, to his dismay, a total absence of bunkers. On the day of his arrival their sister unit at Dong Tam was mortared and everyone in the headquarters wounded. Swans made his first project the construction of a bunker for his team. They used up all the standard gray sandbags they had, then used the green variety the next shipment brought. When the bunker was finished, the brigade CO, in his spitshined jungle boots, came by for a look—and ordered it torn down and rebuilt in "all one color." That same colonel was subsequently responsible for losing most of a company in an ambush by a VC battalion.

Fortunately for Swans, not everyone there was an idiot. He wrote that he was being shown the ropes by a lieutenant who spoke Vietnamese, a rarity for Americans, and who did some of the VC interrogations himself. Swans had a lot of time on his hands, since "business fluctuates a good deal depending on whether there are operations, etc." But all in all he was pretty happy with his assignment.

I wasn't. Late one afternoon I started writing another letter home, laying out my unhappy status in the French Foreign Legion. I told my folks about everything, from the snotty little clerk Wadsworth to First Sergeant Slick who belonged to the company commander and "kisses his posterior frequently." I explained the captain's living arrangements (skipping, of course, the part about going home with one of his girls), and said even the field looked good to me now. And I laid out how Lieutenant Colonel Flakjacket had got his name.

I was about halfway through when it was announced that a jeep was available to take me back to the Meyerkord. Another day had gone by with nothing but coffee, a few signatures, and letter-writing. Life in the war zone. I put a paperweight on the letter and took off.

That night I felt a sudden intense itch in my penis. I looked into my shorts and saw a vile yellow stain.

"Oh, shit, I've caught the clap!"

A case of V.D. from my commanding officer's whore.

In the morning I called the compound to tell them I'd be late. At a nearby U.S. hospital, they took a smear, confirmed gonorrhea, and gave me a shot and a bottle of antibiotics. Eight pills a day for five days.

No big deal, just like a cold, comes with the duty, I tried to tell myself.

Arriving at the compound late in the morning, I discovered that my letter home was not on my desk. How stupid that I hadn't put it away from inquiring eyes. Maybe my morale problem was now being discussed throughout the company . . . some damn intelligence officer, I thought.

That day or the next, into my in-basket came a memo giving me one more "additional duty": I had been named Unit V.D. Officer. I was to prepare a briefing on the types of venereal disease in Nam, their symptoms, consequences, and the greater glory of abstinence. It was my first good laugh since arriving in Saigon. It was true what they'd told us at Benning: in Vietnam everything got twisted around, up, and over. I took two of my penicillin pills and looked at the bottle. At least I'd already prepared my graphic aids.

I rewrote my letter home and made sure the replacement was properly sealed and posted. Later in the afternoon, in came the first sergeant, full of energy and purpose.

"Lieutenant Jones, change one!" (Army talk for a first set of corrections.) "You've got new orders! You're moving out to CICV! Gonna have a shot at order of battle after all!"

My mouth fell open. I was torn between jubilation and anxiety. What did I do wrong, I wondered. Except leave a compromising letter sitting out.

"When do I go?"

"Now. We've got a jeep waiting. Grab your personals and they'll brief you at CICV."

I had to find out what was behind this. "You don't know if I, ah, did anything wrong, do you?"

The sergeant laughed. "Lieutenant, you haven't been here long enough! There's a first lieutenant coming in off a stateside X-O assignment, so it makes sense to put him here. Also, the CICV people asked why you weren't passed through to them. They have a vacancy in I Corps OB."

"I Corps?" I repeated.

"Yes, sir, the northernmost sector. The hot one! You'll have your work cut out for you."

As I carried a box of my effects out past the clerk, I observed him poring over a file and wearing the slightest of smiles. Sure there were reasons for me to be going to CICV, but I couldn't help feeling that the S.O.B. had finally gotten his revenge.

And sweet revenge it was for me too. I was escaping the backwater and plunging into the fast current of the war, where the decisions were being made. I was surely going to have to paddle like hell.

CHAPTER

5

Combined Intelligence Center, Vietnam

> CICV became the most sophisticated and capable [intelligence] production facility I have ever known in direct support of wartime operations and planning.
>
> Major General Joseph A. McChristian
> J-2 MACV, 1966–68

On my insistence, the enlisted man was driving at a moderate speed down Grenade Alley. Despite the demise of the street's killer status, I was glad I wouldn't be traveling it anymore.

The driver was carefully eyeing the women we passed, but I didn't think he was looking for VC. They wore the traditional *ao dai,* and they were beautiful and graceful. The dress with its long sleeves was closed at the neck, and at the waist became two flaps of cloth down the front and back. Either black or white silk pants were worn underneath.

"Enjoying the scenery?" I asked.

"Yeah. VPL!"

"What's that mean?"

"That's 'Verify the Panty Line.' The girls with the white silk pants, you can see through them pretty good. Kind of sexy!"

I did a quick VPL and confirmed the field intelligence.

The jeep driver asked me what I'd be doing at CICV.

"Order of battle, apparently."

"You were trained for that, Lieutenant?"

Good question. In four weeks at Fort Holabird, they skimmed over a lot of things in record time. In a day-long field exercise we performed as an "OB shop" and wrote up the eight OB factors—composition, disposition, strength, tactics, training, logistics, combat efficiency, miscellaneous—for make-believe enemy units. As one of the few first lieutenants, I had run a shop and was more or less successful.

"Sure, they taught us the eight OB factors. And I missed three of them on the exam," I said with a grin.

The EM didn't know if I was joking. "Oh, well," he said, "gotta expect losses in Southeast Asia."

"So I've heard," I replied.

But it wasn't a joke to me. The challenge was awesome. Coming directly into a war without any stateside military experience seemed the worst possible way of doing things. Training didn't have the persuasion of actual duty time. At the schools we constantly fought the Great God Zonk: to us, "stacking arms" meant giving it up and zonking out over arms cushioned on the desktop. You take dehydrated lectures, powder-dry manuals, mix in raw greenies, dilute with maximum quantities of coffee, and cook for four weeks. Presto! Instant intelligence officer. Serve immediately in Vietnam.

And we had only a year to do our job. The Westmoreland formula for one-year tours was meant to give the GI and his family a not impossibly distant target date for returning home. Of course, you could extend for half-year segments if you so desired. My father had shaken his head in disbelief over the one-year policy. His wars had been "for the duration." It'll take you two, three months just to learn your job well, he told me. Then a half-year later, you'll start counting the days until rotation. He was sure they'd get only a decent half-year's work from each man.

True. For the combat grunts who, too soon, burned out in the jungles, one year seemed O.K. But the officers and support troops should have been assigned for two years, or at least the greater part of their legal commitment (ROTC graduates were then required to serve only two years, including training time).

"That's Tan Son Nhut air base over there," the driver said, pointing at a fenced perimeter and an MP guardpost beyond an intersection of several roads. "MACV headquarters is down about a mile on that road beside the airfield."

He jerked the jeep to the right onto an almost unnoticeable dirt and gravel road across from the 3d Field Hospital. "And this goes to CICV." On our left was a weed-infested stadium. Sitting high on the bleachers under a primitive tin roof were several long-haired goats who watched us complacently. Beneath the stands were the artifacts of a homestead. I later learned that refugee families had made use of the comparatively superior shelter, and some of the CICV Americans occasionally gave them PX goods and money. I figured it would be a great place for a VC agent to keep tabs on the workers and visitors at CICV. I doubt if this small community was ever checked out by any counterintelligence teams.

After some hundred yards on the road, we pulled into a parking lot outside several one-story windowless white square buildings with flat red-tiled roofs. I had a quick picture of my aunt and uncle's house in Santa Barbara, a Spanish casa built on the foundations of the fort that preceded the city. But their adobe didn't have a guard outside, a Vietnamese soldier strolling the grounds with a carbine slung casually over his shoulder. The Combined Intelligence Center, without windows and designed for security, was said to be both mortar-proof and the largest fully air-conditioned single-story structure in Southeast Asia. It had opened on 17 January 1967, replacing a crowded, makeshift warehouse at Tan Son Nhut whose original function had been the targeting of B-52s.

Inside the front door was a counter and a small office where a Vietnamese woman was checking arrivals. I was given a visitor's badge while a call was made announcing me.

Suddenly two men rounded the corner, a first lieutenant whom I'd never seen before and my Benning and Bird classmate, old Second Lieutenant Kernsky.

The first lieutenant was very glad to see me—I was his replacement. Kernsky also shook hands, but he looked even stormier than usual. I didn't understand why he was meeting me.

"Because I'm working at I Corps, and now I'm supposed to help get you settled in." He looked at me grimly, his dark eyes flashing. "I hope we'll be able to work together." He didn't sound as if he expected we would. Nor was I sure. I had alternately liked and disliked Kernsky. He could go from hang-loose to hard-ass with only minor provocation. We'd had good moments at Benning, but also some confrontations, and now I would have to be giving him orders. It would not be easy.

The two escorted me down a long hallway busy with American and Viet personnel. Doors were marked with overhanging brown wood signs in English and Vietnamese, such as "CHIEF, ORDER OF BATTLE" and, above it, "TRƯỞNG-BAN TRẬN-LIỆT."

Then we reached the door for I Corps Tactical Zone (CTZ). Inside was a most amazing room. Plastic-sheeted maps at 1:100,000 scale, full of unit symbols, covered almost all the available wall space. Desks and bodies were clustered in a density that seemed to make work impossible. (I learned there was also a night crew.) Almost every desk had a reel-to-reel Japanese-make tape recorder and an amplifier-tuner with an enlisted man embedded in earphones and his private world of music and work. Akai and Sansui seemed to be the PX brands of the highest favor.

I was surprised by the abundance of electronic gear. It didn't seem "Army" to me, more like a college dormitory. I soon learned that in these close working quarters, the earphones cut out distractions and reduced conversation. You had to adapt in Southeast Asia.

I was introduced around and was pleased to find the EM who had tuned me into reality that first day at the compound. We had a Hispanic sergeant, but all the OB analysts were white (the blacks were all out on point in combat patrols). Except for one or two, they all had college educations.

Every work area had its assortment of mementos, some taped on adjacent wall space or on the side of a file cabinet: *Playboy* nudes, photos of the girl back home, Vietnam souvenirs, cartoons, and occasionally some OB lists. Every desk had its large desk pad, and under its plastic cover was more of the same, plus the inevitable short-timers' calendar for crossing off each day toward going home.

In charge of the section was a captain, a young man only a little older than I was. He was in extremely good spirits, just a couple of weeks from going home, and he was busy wrapping up his last project.

There was another first lieutenant, nicknamed Thorny, who had just extended for six months and was expecting to become the officer-in-charge when the captain left. Thorny was about to go on the one-month leave that came with an extension, and it was announced that I'd be the acting OIC in his absence. After maybe two weeks of office time, I would be in charge of the OB shop for the most active war zone in the country! I tried to hide my shock and maintain some of that vital command presence.

I met our ARVNs, three of them, called "counterparts." They were all very formal, barely smiling and untalkative, but polite. Their senior officer was a second lieutenant. There was also an "aspirant," a training rank for second lieutenant, and an enlisted man. Lieutenant Tri had a hard, cold look to him, and he would not look at me. Immediately that made me nervous. (Had I read my "Pocket Guide to Vietnam" more closely I would have understood his behavior: ". . . a Vietnamese might

55

avoid looking a superior in the eye when talking to him. This does not mean the man cannot be trusted. It means he is being polite by not 'staring' at a person of greater standing.") Of the group, Tri was the most formidable in appearance, taller and tough-looking. The other men, like most youthful Vietnamese of both sexes, had a fragile, soft look.

I soon learned that the Vietnamese generally remained aloof until you smiled at them. Then the returned grin and animation were sincere. Too many Americans never got beyond that initial Asian restraint and carried forever a dislike of those aloof "slopes," our current term of derision.

I was introduced to the OB Book,[1] which was the most important document produced by CICV. Formally, it was the MACV Monthly Order of Battle Summary; informally, some called it the Green Hornet, for the color of its cover. It was our bible, setting out the key information on the enemy army then confirmed and accepted by MACV.

That army, a complex structure which had been evolving since 1946, had many levels, essentially reflecting the maneuverability of the forces. The OB Book of August 1967 gave these definitions:

> *North Vietnamese Army (NVA) Unit:* A unit formed, trained, and designated by North Vietnam as an NVA unit, and composed completely or primarily of North Vietnamese. At times, either VC or NVA units and individual replacements appear in units that are predominantly NVA or VC at the command level.

> *Viet Cong (VC) Main Force (MF):* Those military units which are directly subordinate to Central Office South Vietnam (COSVN), a Viet Cong Military Region, or Sub-Region.

> *Viet Cong (VC) Local Force (LF):* Those military units which are directly subordinate to a provincial or district party committee and normally operate only within a specified VC province or district.

> *Irregulars:* Organized forces composed of guerrilla, self-defense, and secret self-defense elements subordinate to village and hamlet level VC organizations. These forces perform a wide variety of missions in the support of VC activities and,

in fact, provide a training and mobilization base for the VC maneuver and combat support forces.

These "irregulars" were further described as follows:

Guerrillas: Full-time forces organized into squads and platoons which do not always stay in their home village or hamlet. Typical missions for guerrillas are collection of taxes, propaganda, protection of village party committees, and terrorist and sabotage activities.

Self-Defense Force: A VC para-military structure responsible for the defense of hamlet and village areas controlled by the VC. These forces do not leave their home area, and they perform their duties on a part-time basis. Duties consist of conducting propaganda, constructing fortifications, and defending home areas.

Secret Self-Defense Force: A clandestine VC organization which performs the same general function in GVN controlled villages and hamlets as do the self-defense forces in VC controlled areas. Their operations involve intelligence collection as well as sabotage and propaganda activities.

Finally there was the "Viet Cong infrastructure," the shadow government, the most important VC organization of them all. This was defined as

the political and administrative organization through which the Viet Cong control or seek to control the South Vietnamese people. It embodies the party (People's Revolutionary Party) control structure, which includes apparatus (Central Office South Vietnam) at the national level, and the leadership and administration of a parallel front organization (National Front for the Liberation of South Vietnam), both of which extend from the national through the hamlet level.

These designations were largely of American construction, and most of them did not follow Hanoi's own nomenclature. There was only one Communist army and that was the People's Army of Vietnam

(PAVN), a term that came into use in the late 1940s after several previous names were abandoned. Contrary to what we'd stated in our OB Book, Hanoi did not specifically designate units as "NVA." However, much was made of the Viet Cong or allegedly southern origin of all units and soldiers fighting the Americans and GVN. This was to present an image of conformance with the 1954 Geneva accords, which prohibited northern soldiers in the South, and to further Hanoi's claims that the war was a true "people's revolution" from within. It never was. The North ran the war and there were northerners in almost all VC units, even by mid-1967.

In the OB shops for the Corps Tactical Zones, our concern was solely the enemy's combat units; the irregulars and the political cadre were handled by smaller sections elsewhere in CICV. Our analysts had their hands full keeping current on the sixty-seven VC/NVA combat battalions in our sector as of August 1967; MACV had identified two hundred battalions for the entire war zone. For each unit the OB Book required our best efforts to provide a strength estimate; the location and date of last contact; and the current probable location and the date of that information. (Later editions of the book added columns for the date of arrival in the South for North Vietnamese units or, for a VC unit, the date the unit became operational.)

The book also reflected the status of identified units as "confirmed" (based on evidence of two sources, a PW/returnee and/or a captured document), "probable" (one source), and "possible" ("repeated reports from different sources," although lacking a PW/returnee or captured document for verification).

Other portions of the OB Book addressed the irregulars and the political cadre, as well as infiltration statistics. The first half of the document contained dozens of sometimes confusing charts with "recapitulations" of retroactive strength figures for the enemy. These were intended to be corrections of past published figures based on the subsequent receipt of more accurate data.[2]

The first edition of the MACV Monthly Order of Battle Summary, only sixteen pages long, was published in December 1966. By the end of 1968 it was about seventy-five pages. In mid-1967 some four hundred copies of the OB Book were being sent to seventy-five users in and out of Vietnam. By mid-1968 there were more than two hundred recipients.

Much of the OB Book's information was dated; time was our constant enemy. The time lag was inevitable because the documents found in the field, which already might be old, then had to be translated and the result moved up to our level. Even more frustrating would be having to wait, weeks sometimes, for the new OB Book to be published. (Each month the old one would be put in a burn bag, stapled up, and taken to the incinerator out back.) So you might have hot data in hand and not see it reflected in print for over a month. We would pencil in our newest information in the office copy of the OB Book, which was always heavily marked up before the new copy reached us. (All interim approved changes to the book were also cabled to the users, who presumably also updated their own copies.) In the field, where information had to be more timely, the OB Book, I learned, was less revered. Many or most unit G-2s (division intelligence chiefs) penciled in their own estimates of strengths and locations, sometimes even adding new units that were not yet—or ever—recognized in Saigon.

The OB Book was not intended to be the most current intelligence on the war. It was an academic baseline, a conservative record of what had been proved through review of the enemy's own records and interrogations of enemy personnel. That basic concept became lost as the pace of the war intensified, and the OB Book became a tool for the dissemination of current propaganda.

A standard-issue gray steel desk was waiting for me at the I Corps OB shop, and I settled in. The first thing I slipped under the plastic cover of my desk pad was my wallet card entitled "Intelligence Officer's Check List," which had been issued to us at Fort Holabird. All you needed to know on two little foldout pages. Or at least all they were able to teach us in four weeks. The eight OB factors were outlined:

COMPOSITION
  a. Unit identification
    (1) Number
    (2) Branch of service
    (3) Echelon of command
DISPOSITION
  a. Geographical location
  b. Tactical deployment

c. Movements

STRENGTH

a. Personnel

b. Equipment

c. Type of unit

TACTICS

a. Tactical doctrine

b. Special operations

TRAINING

a. Individual

b. Unit

c. Special

LOGISTICS

a. Systems

b. Current status

COMBAT EFFICIENCY

a. Combat experience

b. Morale

c. Other factors

MISCELLANEOUS

a. Personalities

b. Unit histories

c. Uniforms and insignia

Also listed on the card were the components of an Intelligence Estimate, a Periodic Intelligence Report (often called a PERINTREP), and an Intelligence Summary. The card proved to be the barest outline of the actual work load. I became Projects Officer, a position sometimes referred to as Dirty Little Projects Officer, responsible for all recurring reports as well as for meeting "right-now" data requests. And, in a couple of weeks, I would be acting OIC for a month. It would be a long hard autumn for me, covering the hottest war zone in Vietnam.

Throughout modern American military history, field commands have been divided into zones designated by roman numerals. In Vietnam there were four. I Corps covered the five northern provinces just below the Demilitarized Zone that had separated North and South Vietnam since the 1954 Geneva agreement. This was the smallest of the four zones, both in area and population; its terrain included low coastal plains that bore two rice crops a year, and rugged mountains, some over five thousand feet high. Then came II Corps, which included the Central Highlands. Next, III Corps, which was centered on Saigon itself. In the extreme south, IV Corps was in the Mekong Delta, the rice bowl of Southeast Asia with its amazing rivers and swamps.

The American forces in I Corps (there were also SVN and Korean[3] units) were largely the Marines who had come ashore at Da Nang on 8 March 1965, initiating our serious build-up. In time, they became the III Marine Amphibious Force (MAF), composed of the 1st and 3d Marine Divisions, and their original job was to protect the American airfield there from VC attack. The Marines, however, could never stay in static positions for long and soon began "search and destroy" sweeps out into the jungles and paddies (at least to the range of VC mortars). And so the war was begun in earnest.

There were also some Army components in Quang Ngai, the southernmost of the five provinces in I Corps. In April 1967 the Army's Task Force Oregon was reinforced and renamed the Americal Division, a reincarnation of a force that had fought in the Pacific in World War II and was afterward disbanded. MACV reported that the addition of this force allowed the Marines to concentrate on the DMZ and the northern provinces.

The Army and the Marines had never got along. (My father had always disliked the publicity given to the Marines' amphibious landings, while the Army had to do the dirty and unpublicized mop-up.) I wondered how relations were so far in this war. My suspicions were confirmed when I heard a full bird colonel from MACV J-2 declare, "Never met a Marine above the squad level who was worth a damn!"

On 25 August, my second day, I wrote my first letter home from CICV, reporting that I was already working on the history of an NVA unit that had newly infiltrated into I Corps. I noted that we worked with the Viets in our office only when one of "us" needed information that one of "them" might have. Hence, duplication of effort. But "that kind of duplication is O.K. since the Viets have to fight their own war as much as possible." However, it was "ticklish" working with people who might be VC spies since we had to be polite and share material with them.

So far I had figured out that our job was to "document the war and provide studies on past history with occasional predictions," even though Westmoreland apparently relied mostly on his own people for analysis. I had gathered the impression that CICV was not held in the highest regard by the MACV command.

I, however, was impressed by the center.[4] Its administrative branch had a teletype for immediate communication with all major U.S. commanders and senior advisors. Much emphasis was put on automatic data processing, and the ADP Section was apparently intended to be the primary clearinghouse of CICV's diverse data base (ultimately this would become a point of vulnerability). ADP could provide a narrative printout (bilingual if desired) and a graphic plot of intelligence for staff and field use.

For intelligence production, CICV had six branches: Area Analysis, Technical Intelligence, Imagery Interpretation, Research and Analysis, Targets, and Order of Battle. The Area Analysis branch supported combat operations through preparation of studies on enemy transportation, communication, and "military geography" (which addressed infiltration routes, avenues of approach, and general terrain analysis). This section's major products were "tactical scale studies." These were presented on 1:50,000 maps that described, in narrative and symbol, topography, entry zones, lines of communication, cultural features, telecommunications, cross-country movement, enemy installations, and potential avenues of approach. By mid-1967 about half of South Vietnam had been mapped, the balance scheduled for November.

Technical Intellegence analyzed the capabilities and vulnerabilities of the enemy's technical and support units: chemical, ordnance, engineer, quartermaster, medical, signal, and transportation. One of its major studies was on the enemy's use of mines and booby traps. Readouts from aerial photos, infrared photos, and side-looking airborne radar were produced by Imagery Interpretation. A specialty of this branch was photo study packets for specific areas designed for use by units in the field. The Research and Analysis branch developed studies on economic, political, sociological, and psychological aspects of the enemy's military and political forces in North and South Vietnam, Laos, and Cambodia. Strategic studies were produced on such topics as VC taxation practices, troop morale, the effect of B-52 strikes and herbicide operations, and characteristics of NVA soldiers. A typical study could be based on some six hundred sources. The Targets branch received input from all other branches to develop target recommendations, especially for B-52 strikes. Its main tool for attempting to locate the enemy was the pattern analysis, an analytical process that could use a data base of up to thirty-five factors on separate overlays. By combining these overlays into sets of up to five at a time and placing them over the base map, an enemy pattern might be discerned for targeting.

Finally, there was Order of Battle, considered by some the "heart of the center."[5] It had three components: Ground Order of Battle, Order of Battle Studies, and Political Order of Battle. The Studies group was responsible for countrywide analysis of enemy strength (especially of the VC irregulars), infiltration, effectiveness, and logistics. Political OB had teams organized to track each of the enemy's Military Regions. It developed analysis of the structure, strength, personalities, and activities of the Communist political organization, the "infrastructure" or shadow government.[6] Ground Order of Battle developed intelligence on the enemy maneuver units. It had five teams or shops, one for each Corps Tactical Zone and a Southeast Asia team concerned with North Vietnam, Laos, and Cambodia.

It was in Ground Order of Battle for I Corps that I was now trying to assimilate an incredible amount of information while facing work for which I had not been adequately trained. And just as I was getting started, I learned that the purpose and function of this intelligence system, so carefully constructed since 1965, had just come under attack from within and from its highest level.

Two or three days after my arrival the lieutenant I was replacing and the shop's senior sergeant took me out into the hallway, away from any eavesdroppers. After looking around to ensure privacy, they showed me a photocopy—a "burn"—of a memo that was nearly illegible but carried a clear message. It was dated 15 August 1967, the signature block was that of General Phillip B. Davidson, Jr., the new Assistant Chief of Staff, J-2, and it was addressed to his Deputy J-2, Production, with copies indicated for Colonel Charles Roberts and Colonel Charles Morris (see Appendix B).

The communication was not intended for further distribution. I was given the impression someone had smuggled it out of one of the senior staff offices for clandestine copying. The memo read, emphasis included:

1. Now that we are getting our revised format for our revised OB squared away I want to move boldly into a new procedure for determining OB on a *weekly basis*.

2. What we have got to do is to attrite main forces, local forces and particularly guerrillas. *We must cease immediately using the assumption that these units replace themselves.* We should go on the assumption that they do not replace themselves *unless we have firm evidence to the contrary.* The figure of combat strength and particularly of guerrillas must take a steady and significant downward trend as I am convinced this reflects true enemy status.

I was told that the memo represented "what was going on" in MACV, that this new J-2 was exerting pressures to drop unit strengths regardless of evidence. It was explained to me with great intensity that if we simply applied all the body counts to units known to operate in the area, in no time we would be carrying them at zero. Not only did the Allied units in the field often inflate their killed-in-action reports (they might count blood trails and parts of bodies each as a KIA, even if the several pieces and the blood could have come from one soldier), but these body counts also included irregulars and civilians. You just could not assume all the KIA came from the nearest unit of record, if only because our information on "current probable location" was rarely timely.

Of the highest importance, the lieutenant and the sergeant explained, was the continuing flow of plentiful replacements from North Vietnam coming down the Ho Chi Minh Trail, which quickly brought most enemy units up to strength after engagements. (I soon started reading the many documents that supported these findings.) I had to stand up to the pressure to drop unit strengths, they said, because the Davidson memo failed on its assumption that the units did not replace themselves. In fact, evidence consistently showed that the units did replace their losses in a timely fashion. When rare and valuable enemy unit rosters or especially knowledgeable PWs fell into our hands, we could modify or confirm overall numbers, and our findings almost always showed a unit in operational condition. The enemy might occasionally pull back into the jungle to rest and refit, or just to harvest crops, but they'd soon be back in action. The consistent experience of those who worked with the documents every day, I was told, simply overwhelmed Davidson's theory of nonreplacement, even though he was "convinced" it reflected the "true enemy status." He was flat out wrong, and the analysts believed he knew he was.

The men did not want me to make a copy of the memo, but I insisted. The lieutenant told me to put it in a safe place. "You don't know where you got it," he warned me.

These two old hands believed in the intelligence system set up by General Joseph A. McChristian, who had completed his J-2 tour just before my arrival. One of his chief deputies, Colonel Gains B. Hawkins, had been instrumental in putting together a superb Order of Battle section at CICV and was known as "Mr. OB," the ranking American expert on the VC/NVA forces. Hawkins had another couple of weeks before he would be going home, and the men who had worked for him spoke of him with respect and affection.

But the important thing was the process. McChristian's design for the MACV OB Book relied on two primary sources: captured documents and interrogations of PWs or "returnees," defectors from VC or NVA forces, called in Vietnamese *"hoi chanh"* (agent reports were also reviewed but could not be trusted—some paid informants were VC and all would tell you what you wanted to hear). McChristian had developed a mutually supporting system of "combined" centers (that is, staffed by both Vietnamese and American personnel) to process these documents and interrogations into finished intelligence. At the top of the system was CICV. In support was the Combined Documents Exploitation Center (CDEC, pronounced "C-deck"), located next to CICV, and the Combined Military Interrogation Center (CMIC, or "C-mick"), near the Pho Tho racetrack in Saigon.

An amazing number of documents were being located by our combat sweeps. During Operation Cedar Falls in III Corps, 8–26 January 1967, some 492,000 pages of VC documents were obtained; about 11 percent contained information important enough to warrant summary or full translation. By early 1967 the Allies were capturing a half million pages every month, about 10 percent of which contained useful information. Units were encouraged to send the material directly to CDEC,[7] where it was believed the organized teams of Vietnamese translators could more quickly identify the "Type Alpha" documents offering perishable, hot information of immediate value in the field. For these, "spot reports" would be issued in hours and returned to the Allied units that could then respond. "Type Bravo" documents offered strategic information, such as unit identifications or data on strength and disposition; these would be published in either summary or full translation format.

By early 1967 the center's daily production was some 1,400 pounds of reports. Its publications received a wide distribution both in and out of country, including the State Department, the Defense Intelligence Agency, the CIA, the Department of the Army, the U.S. embassy in Saigon, CINCPAC (Commander-in-Chief, Pacific Area Command), the Field Forces, III MAF (Marine Amphibious Force), and Free World Military Armed Forces (which included all the Allies, American, South Vietnamese, Korean, Australian, Thai, and Filipino). CDEC also had an automated document storage and retrieval capability that classified documents by subject and was supposed to provide the requesting agencies with photocopies of stored index material and, when necessary, copies of the original document. CDEC's data base had been put on 16mm microfilm, which was issued to users on a recurring basis.

The processing of prisoners of war was similar to that for documents. However, field interrogations ("tactical exploitation") were essential to obtaining any information of immediate value. This level of examination was usually performed within seven days at the division or separate brigade level, usually by combined U.S. and ARVN teams. Prisoners who were determined to have information of high or "strategic" interest were evacuated to the Combined Military Interrogation Center in Saigon. Here was produced and disseminated a "knowledgeability brief." The intelligence community then responded with specific questions for the source. The resulting CMIC Interrogation Report was published in both Vietnamese and English, the latter edition sent to ninety-two users in and out of country.

The MACV Intelligence Production Directorate (which included CICV) received all information and then analyzed, evaluated, and worked it up into production reports. These reports were "finished intelligence," that is, documents that could be used for planning in the field, at headquarters, and in Washington. (An example of finished intelligence was the OB Book.)

Out at Camp LBJ was another intelligence group, the Combined Matériel Exploitation Center (CMEC), which collected and analyzed the enemy's weapons and other supplies. At MACV headquarters a related effort produced the MACV Logistics Fact Book, updated annually and sent to some 180 agencies.

I was to learn that a Benning and Holabird classmate, a lieutenant called Klein, was over in the MACV puzzle palace, doing paperwork on matériel infiltration. He proudly told me, "I'm in charge of all this! Just me!" His Texan expansiveness, touched with some naivety, made him highly vulnerable to the pressure he too was soon getting. When he was later shifted out of his job after complaining about reductions of his estimates, he felt guilty, as if he'd failed his mission. The Davidson "downward trending" formula was, in time, to damage all of us.

On 28 August another letter to Santa Barbara attempted to explain again that yes, there was terrorism, but no, I wasn't in any danger. I noted that "Downtown is OK in regards to bombing since most everyone pays taxes to the VC." And traveling in the tiny Honda taxis was safe because it was hard to see into them and the drivers paid their taxes, too. So I had been told, and so I passed it on. But if you went even one kilometer out of Saigon, you'd be visiting the VC:

> Out on the far edges of the airport begins VC territory. Two weeks ago they hit a Korean compound there with an RR (recoilless rifle). I don't go out *there* either. . . .

I reported being able to keep my .45 after leaving the 519th. I was carrying it in my briefcase so it wasn't obvious, remembering my father's letter about his Korean experiences. The open-topped valise could be carried with my thumb outside and fingers inside, curled over the barrel of the .45, close, handy, and comforting.

I told my folks that my first briefing, to a colonel, was scheduled for the following week, and already I had three important research projects: what effect the B-52 raids had on enemy tactics in I Corps; what new offensives had been planned; and whether there was any enemy armor in the DMZ.

I discovered, to no one's surprise, that the VC didn't like the B-52s at all. The big bombs certainly were very hard on morale. But there were also statements in interrogation reports indicating that the enemy often knew when and where the big bombers were going to hit. As the B-52s left their bases on Guam or in Thailand, somehow that "primitive" jungle army found out; or, there were leaks in the in-Nam targeting process. Too many infiltrators said they just moved out of the way before the bombs fell.[8]

And there were, indeed, rumblings of armor in the DMZ. I wrote up the indicators, but no one took the possibility very seriously and my report did not prosper. Perhaps a better job of documentation could have changed the outcome at Lang Vei on 7 February 1968, a little over five months later. The poor bastards in the Special Forces camp at Lang Vei, near Khe Sanh, were surprised by thirteen North Vietnamese Russian-made light PT-76 tanks. The armor came right up to the camp's wire. The NVA drivers casually climbed out and smoked cigarettes on the turrets before buttoning up and driving over the defensive perimeter.

Ten American Special Forces KIA, eleven wounded; 316 CIDG (Civilian Irregular Defense Group, mostly Montagnards) dead or missing. Lang Vei was one of the few U.S. bases ever overrun in the war. The Special Forces had two 106mm recoilless rifles, which can take out a tank, and a number of M-72 LAAWs (Lightweight Anti-Armor Assault Weapons), previously used in Vietnam against bunkers and troop concentrations. Many of the LAAWs didn't work or bounced off the tanks, and one of the 106s was lost early in the attack. The Lang Vei defenders had simply not thought about the possibility of tanks. The intelligence process had failed them.

The what-ifs and the why-didn't-Is can drive you crazy.

Usually the four-cot room at the Meyerkord was all mine, but there were occasional transients. One night in early September I was joined by three doctors, two captains and a major, in from the 24th Evacuation Hospital on a brief Saigon R-and-R. They had their booze with them and wanted to talk about the war. They didn't think we were winning but wanted to believe we were, that we could. And they'd become more confused since arriving in Vietnam.

These men weren't pleased with their treatment by the Army. They were given tents to live in—at their base only the doctors and the prisoners of war lived in tents. They had to build their own hooches, and had bruised hands in surgery to show for it. Visits to the black market were necessary to get all the materials they needed, which they paid for with their own money. Still, my roommates were proud of the high level of treatment given to the wounded. They had to face as well an incredible array of diseases. Most medical men in Vietnam also on occasion treated Viet civilians. There were the intestinal parasites, especially those causing amebic dysentery. Tuberculosis. Liver cirrhosis from malnutrition. Malaria. Typhoid. Cholera. Polio. Plague. Meningitis. Smallpox. Hookworm. Round worms. The list went on and on.

My assignment fascinated them, and the doctors questioned me as if I had the answers to the war. I tried to let them believe it. One of the captains said, "So you speak of figures that show we're winning. But did you ever see a wounded GI all hacked up?" His voice was ragged. "A little while ago there was a kid—only nineteen years old—brought in. I went to take off his boot and his leg came off in my hands . . ."

We were silent for a moment. "The numbers are just paper figures to me—don't change them for me!" I pleaded. Then I added, "You're right. The blood is the ultimate argument."

We were getting deeper into the drinks and all of us had been tired even before the first one. "But we can't win!" said one of the doctors.

"We already *have* won!" I declared emphatically. The others stared at me. I smiled smugly and laid it all out for them. "As soon as we built Cam Ranh Bay, we won! I mean, our major installations on the coast and lowlands are secure. We can sit in them forever and the VC can have the damn jungles and we've still got all we need over here. The major population centers are in the government's hands, right?"

"Are you talking about the enclave theory? General Gavin pushed that, but he was blown out of the water, wasn't he?"

"I don't think it's a theory. You noticed the MP in the concrete post at the front of the hotel and all the fencing around us? *We're* an enclave. Every American installation is an enclave, and when we leave it we're out in a free-fire zone, whether it's the streets of Saigon or Highway One along the coast! So, all I'm saying, if we hold our enclaves, we've got all we need out of this war! Sooner or later there'll be a negotiated peace and some coalition government."

We talked about the "Big Picture," as the Army liked to call it, international politics, the Cold War, the spread of Communism. We agreed, there were balance-of-power considerations that couldn't be ignored. Finally I said, "And, anyway, we're here. So what do we do now?"

The mood had turned downward and they put their liquor away. "One thing we don't do is kill everybody and everything," one of the doctors said bitterly.

"Yeah," I mumbled. The debate was over, sleep was much needed. In the morning I left for CICV before they awoke, and they had gone by my return.

I had hoped my move to CICV had put behind me that "additional duty" as V.D. Officer. No such luck. I was scheduled to go back to the compound before the assembled troops and give them the word. I was still taking my penicillin pills several times a day. A tactical error in planning occurred when, as a reminder, I left the bottle on my desk, tucked into the edge of a three-ring binder. Enlisted men miss nothing.

So up comes PFC Shore, a twenty-one- or twenty-two-year-old with a long acne-blemished face, eyeglasses, and thinning blond hair.

CICV was loose in the relationships between the junior officers and the enlisted men. We worked too closely together, both physically and in our missions, to dwell heavily on traditional military formalities. Though the arrangement never slid away from the requisite "sirs" and "Lieutenant Joneses," some of the EM's kidding and wisecracks would have raised the spitshine off an oldtimer's boots.

Shore proved to be the ace of them all. He was also the best analyst in the shop. He came to be the spokesman for the rest of the men, and he was always the one with the joke, the zingers. Enough sometimes to drive a green lieutenant to distraction.

This time, he stood in front of my desk until I noticed him.

"Lieutenant Jones?"

"Yes, Shore, what is it?"

"Some of us couldn't help but notice, sir, and of course I don't want to be rude . . ." His delivery was dry and his deadpan masterful. In time you learned to know when he was setting you up, but even then there was no way you could do anything about it.

"Yes, notice what?"

"Why, Lieutenant Jones, the bottle of penicillin pills on your desk."

The room was very quiet. I could hear a suppressed giggle from the back.

Shore continued earnestly. "And we were just surprised, sir, to learn that officers have sex, too! Right, sir? I guess they *are* human sometimes?"

I was speechless. I snatched the pills off my desk and shoved them in my blouse pocket.

"These are just for a condition . . ." I said lamely.

Shore smiled brightly. "Yes, sir. But at least you'll be well prepared for your briefing on Saturday, right, Lieutenant Jones?"

The V.D. briefing. To the troops, at the compound. Saturday morning.

I covered my eyes with my hand and leaned heavily on my propped forearm. "Right, Shore. I'll be prepared."

"Yes, sir, we'll all be there, sitting in the front row, to learn about that VC V.D.!"

I nodded. "I'm glad to hear that, Shore. Carry on, now."

"Yes, sir," he said, doing a snappy about-face, and leaving me with a "You, too, sir!"

The room was alive with laughter, whispers, and side glances. I think even the Vietnamese got in on it. As quietly as possible, I took off for the snack bar for a Coke and a return of composure.

On Saturday, all the I CTZ enlisted men sat in a bloc along the front row. Shore was in the middle, his head resting on two fists, elbows on knees. With a big shit-eating grin on his face. I stumbled through all the varieties of gonorrhea and syphilis. I had learned, too late, that eight out of ten bar girls were carriers of V.D. I decided to omit the standard pitch about abstinence being the best protection—in the circumstances, I doubted it would be persuasive.

In the closing days of August or perhaps in early September, a cocktail party was held at a nearby club to bid farewell to the officers about to go home. Kernsky and I went over with the first lieutenant I was replacing. We talked about terrorists, whether the lieutenant had had any experience with them. He had. In a quiet part of Saigon he'd been on foot in civilian clothes when a couple of VC on a Honda shot off a weapon and dropped a grenade into a crowd of Viets, killing several.

"Wow! What did you do?"

"I dug in fast! Hit the ground and hugged it while they roared past me."

"You had no weapon, I presume?"

He shook his head.

"Bet you wish you did!"

"Hell, no, then I would have had a responsibility to shoot at them and I didn't want to be in no goddamned firefight!"

It was an interesting point.

He pointed out a cluster of officers talking in the middle of the room. "There's Colonel Hawkins, the man who put the OB system together. He's a hell of a good guy. You got to meet the Hawk before he goes home."

I had always avoided field-grade officers whenever possible and declined, but the lieutenant insisted and I was taken over to be introduced.

I shook hands with a short, rather squat man with a rich southern drawl and a down home, folksy speaking style. The white wisps of hair around his mostly bald head created the image of a grandfather rather than the "Genius of Order of Battle," the man who knew more about the enemy army than anyone but General Giap himself.

I felt uncomfortable standing mute in a group of majors and colonels as they engaged in small talk; at a pause, I thought that perhaps a toast would be appropriate. Raising my glass, I said something like, "May we, the incoming officers, do as good a job as you gentlemen!"

The officers appeared stricken and embarrassed. They mumbled a few words, then disappeared before my eyes. The lieutenant suggested, "It would probably have been better if you hadn't said that," adding something about their having troubles lately, resulting in friction between the analysts and the brass. He did not elaborate.

That day, or perhaps a day or two earlier, there had been another peculiar incident. Our captain, who was about to rotate home, had been at work on a last-minute project, and I had offered to help him, hoping to get some on-the-job training from a veteran. He had replied with a wry smile, saying he'd better do it alone, so that I could remain "pure" for a while longer. What the hell does that mean, I asked. And he said, "You'll find out soon enough."

My "purity" was indeed on the line. I would not remain without sin for long.

PART TWO

The Order of Battle

SEPTEMBER—NOVEMBER 1967

... the commander must know first of all what he is planning against. In developing every part of his command—from the first to the last—the commander must keep the enemy in mind.

*The Joint and Combined Staff
Officer's Manual, 1959*

Intelligence is for all commanders: leaders should take advantage of every available opportunity to learn about Viet Cong units, their strengths and weaknesses. In this war, intelligence governs our tactics no less than our plans and operations.

Training Operations—Lessons Learned
Department of the Army
Pamphlet No. 350–15–10
1 July 1968

If the Johnson Administration suffered from lack of credibility in its reporting of the war, the truth would reveal that much of the hocus-pocus stemmed from schemers in the military services, both at home and abroad.

General David M. Shoup
Past Commandant, U.S. Marine Corps
"The New American Militarism"
The Atlantic Monthly, April 1969

73

CHAPTER

6

On-the-Job Training

Once more, the enemy has been kind enough to give us the recipe of his victory. . . . No one can in all honesty blame General Vo Nguyen Giap for our own illiteracy in the field of Revolutionary Warfare or for our own doctrinaire blindness to military developments. . . .

Bernard B. Fall, *Street Without Joy*

At CICV we plodded along, reading captured documents and PW reports, trying to pull out enough hard data to update the OB Book and complete projects. Already life had become a blurring series of ten- to twelve-hour work days, often without time off (my first day off came three months into my tour), because it was our commitment to get the best possible information out to the men in the field.

Everyone, mostly, worked hard. The EM, the noncoms, the officers. We took it all very seriously.

There was so much to know and do. I was overwhelmed by the number of units and the detailed OB factors for each. You had to understand the geography, the general disposition of friendly forces, the terms, the military/political structure of the VC regions, the earlier reports on file, the overall history of the whole damn war itself. For all the stateside orientation lectures they had given us, a clear picture of the war had never evolved. Maybe that was a lesson in itself.

Vietnam was a nation of peculiarities which made the war into myriad mini-campaigns, and grasping the "Big Picture" wasn't easy. Military sources were surprisingly sketchy. The *Area Handbook for Southeast Asia* (April 1967, DA Pam. 550–55) described the insurgency into 1966 as follows:

The end of the Indochina War in 1954 left Communist North Vietnam with a highly developed composite politico-military organization, under the direction of Ho Chi Minh, capable of waging war both as a guerrilla underground force and as a conventional land army. This organization was then deployed throughout Vietnam, with about 90,000 military troops occupying portions of South Vietnam. With the signing of the Geneva Agreement in 1954, which partitioned the country, most of these troops were regrouped and evacuated to North Vietnam. Ho Chi Minh left many thousands of specially selected men (variously estimated from 5,000 to 10,000) and numerous caches of arms and equipment behind in hideouts in the remote jungles of the Mekong Delta and the mountainous region north of Saigon. When the government of the newly formed Republic of Vietnam refused to participate in the referendum, those men, known as the Viet Cong, served as the nucleus of military and subversive efforts to overthrow the government. . . .

Having received substantial increases in men and matériel in 1958, the Viet Cong embarked on a new campaign of terror and intimidation. Their strength mounted to about 12,000, and with relatively small units they increased the tempo of guerrilla harassment, sabotage and intimidation of additional areas of the country. . . . By 1960, the Viet Cong began attacking in company-sized units and, on occasion, in groups of up to several battalions in strength. Meanwhile, reinforcements infiltrated from the North in increasing numbers, and more local recruits were obtained.

By 1962 the Viet Cong numbered more than 75,000 and were divided into three main categories: full time guerrillas, part-time guerrillas and village activists. . . . These three groups have become known as main force units, local force units and guerrillas. . . .

By the end of 1963 total Viet Cong personnel in South Vietnam rose to about 30,000, exclusive of local irregulars and part-time guerrillas. Since that time, the figure has steadily mounted. Military infiltration from the North continued in growing numbers, and the flow of weapons from North Vietnam and Communist China increased, particularly those of larger caliber. The hard core Viet Cong force in early 1966 was estimated to be close to 90,000, reportedly including between 12 and 15 regiments of the regular People's Army of North Vietnam. The number of irregulars, including sympathizers and Communist party workers supporting the hard core troops, probably had reached 150,000 or more.

Of some help in my indoctrination was a MACOI (Military Assistance Command Office of Information) fact sheet, dated 19 June 1967, which presented the "Historical Background of the Vietnam Conflict" and included this:

The commitment of U.S. and other Free World forces... effectively halted what was clearly a military defeat in the making, and seized the initiative from the VC/NVA forces in the military arena.

It was generally acknowledged that in 1965 the VC had been on the verge of pulling down the Republic of Vietnam, and American intervention had stabilized the situation. But then the NVA build-up—and, in turn, the Americans'—had begun in earnest. The intensity of the war increased without any clear resolution, one stalemate after another.

I was able to fill in some of the gaps for 1965 and 1966 from the MACV annual summaries, unattractive mimeographed booklets with crudely drawn maps. The overall 1965 summary was only two pages and stated:

U.S. participation in the Vietnam war increased steadily through 1965. Total U.S. military strength grew from about 23,000 on January 1, 1965 to approximately 181,000 at year's end. Republic of Vietnam Armed Forces increased during the year from about 511,000 to approximately 565,000. Enemy military strength rose from about 103,000 to an estimated 230,000 by December 31.

As troop strength increased, the pace of the war quickened. More than 1,200 U.S. troops and some 11,000 ARVN forces were killed in action, while the enemy lost over 34,000 men killed and almost 6,000 captured.

The 1966 "Summary of USMACV News Events" was a much bigger deal, some ninety pages and more ringing in its rhetoric:

> Allied forces achieved notable successes against the enemy during 1966, inflicting heavy personnel and matériel losses on his forces... forcing him to remain on the move.... We have taken the initiative away from the enemy and dealt him some heavy blows. Heavier blows will follow. Any hope that the Viet Cong and North Vietnamese may have had of achieving a military victory is gone.
>
> During 1966, the enemy continued to build up his forces by recruiting in the South and by infiltrating from the North. During the year he placed increased reliance upon regular troops from North Vietnam. The infiltration from North Vietnam averaged more than 8,000 per month....
>
> His total strength in the Republic exceeds 280,000.... The enemy was hurt in many areas during 1966.... However, the enemy strength increased during 1966 (by some 42,000 men) indicating that he has been more than able to replace losses....

MACV had apparently recognized that the enemy had been more than able to replace losses by infiltration and conscription. This candid admission made an optimistic conclusion about the VC/NVA being kept on the "defensive" much less persuasive.

I was impressed by the amount of activity reported in I Corps as compared with the other three CTZs. That meant my shop received not only the most captured documents and PW interrogations but also the largest number of taskings for special projects. But you couldn't do many of the complex assignments without a good understanding of the history, and you couldn't study the history because of the crush of projects. Somehow I squeezed in the background files and available books, especially those by Bernard Fall, who had been writing about Indochina since his first visit in 1953 while researching a doctoral thesis. Many offices in MACV headquarters and most intelligence analysts had copies of Fall's books. They contained scholarly background and, more important, offered a sense of the war that could not be gotten elsewhere. He called the Indochina campaign *la guerre sans fronts,* the war without fronts. He also identified the Communist strategy as "the war of vast empty spaces" in a land of jungles and plains that gave easy refuge to a disappearing enemy. It was a "bottomless pit," he warned, because of the VC's political spirit and their access to "active sanctuaries" in Laos and Cambodia. His best known work was *Street Without Joy,* the title referring both to the sad path of war and a specific stretch of VC stronghold along Highway 1 between Hue and Quang Tri City in I Corps. In his last update of this book he reported that the West, this time America, was "still battling an ideology with technology" and the war would be long and uncertain. Fall was killed by a VC mine on 21 February 1967 while on a patrol with U.S. Marines north of Hue, very close to the Street Without Joy.

Ever since my arrival at CICV, I'd been hearing about how the troops in OB studies under Colonel Hawkins had completed the RITZ program for evaluating irregulars (the guerrillas and the self-defense forces) and the CORRAL program for the political infrastructure. These studies had provided MACV's first reliable data on those two components of the VC structure, and everyone was very proud of the work. Since the CTZ shops in Ground Order of Battle monitored only combat units, my predecessors hadn't been directly involved in those studies, but they had worked for months on the VC Military Regions that controlled I Corps. They had discovered that the northernmost Tri–Thien Region (sometimes called the Tri–Thien–Hue Region), which included the provinces of Quang Tri and Thua Thien, was directly subordinate to Hanoi, not to the VC headquarters in South Vietnam (the Truong Uong Cuc, or Central Office for South Vietnam, known to us as COSVN).[1] It had previously been believed that COSVN alone ran the show in the South, although certainly in conformance with Hanoi's directives. But now we knew that for the northern, DMZ portion of I Corps, Giap was in control as, we believed, he sought to annex the area to North Vietnam for the first step in his drive to victory. In time this belief became a compulsion that helped drive the events leading to the Tet offensive.

The flood of VC documents captured during our early operations in 1965 into 1967 had opened up a window on the Hanoi and COSVN structure. Finally, in early 1967, we were able to draw a picture of the enemy's chain of command from Hanoi down into the Military Regions of South Vietnam. It was a complex system, and figuring it out had been a major victory for CICV. My predecessor was getting a Bronze Star for his role in the work. I wondered if we, the new class, would be able to make any such breakthroughs, and whether we'd get our medals too.

The only way I could get my hero's badge was to study the documents closely, to learn from the enemy himself what he was going to do. Hanoi and COSVN made that a lot easier by the plentiful sources captured in the field that poured into J-2. One illuminating piece was an article entitled "New Developments in the Guerrilla War in South Vietnam" that appeared in the North Vietnamese Army daily newspaper and was also broadcast over "Liberation Radio" on 13 November 1966. Although it dealt with the guerrilla side of the war, it could be read as a guide for the large main force units as well: even when General Giap allowed massive, seemingly traditional large-unit engagements to occur, he was still using his divisions, regiments, and battalions in hit-and-run guerrilla tactics.

This treatise was by "Cuu Long," a name believed to be a pseudonym for a committee of key officials. They declared the guerrilla to be able to

> attack the enemy right in his cities and his political and economic centers through commandos' and special agents' activities, especially through . . . the people's forces, self-defense armed forces, and secret guerrilla cells in and outside cities, thus sowing dreadful fear among the enemy.

The authors stated that the guerrilla war alone was inflicting one-third to two-fifths of the U.S./GVN casualties.[2] They stressed that their guerrillas had tied down and scattered our troops because of their flexibility in attacking rear installations. I was impressed by a reference to the "movement to hold a hoe in one hand and a rifle in the other." Indeed, this was the core of the "people's war" and the strength of the VC in their villages. The paper also included the "guiding ideas and fighting mottos of guerrilla warfare": the "motto" of mobility, flexibility, surprise, and resourcefulness; the "motto" of "three-pronged attacks" by "three categories of troops" in "three areas"—the "liberated area, the disputed area, and the area under the enemy's temporary control"; and "Lenin's method of uprising: attack and only attack; for in this fierce struggle, to pause at the defensive is to invite the danger of being annihilated."

The North Vietnamese authors' next statement matched my own fear of how the war was going:

> ...the superiority of modern guerrilla science lies in the fact that guerrillas use a small force to fight against a greater enemy force, hit at the enemy accurately, face no difficulties concerning the supply of weapons... the enemy—no matter how numerous his troops are—will be bogged down increasingly deeply and unable to recapture or achieve any significant victory on the battlefield.

The official American interpretation of VC capabilities, as found in Army field manuals, did recognize the enemy's strengths. At CICV I again reviewed the *Handbook for U.S. Army Forces in Vietnam* (DoD GEN–25/DA Pam 360–521/NAVMC 2612), dated 10 June 1966, which described common enemy traits. Guerrilla forces, when hit hard, would "break into small groups" for escape and evasion. They made extensive use of concealed tunnels and bunkers and moved at night to fight under cover of darkness. Their most worrisome characteristic I had underlined in my text while at Benning: "normally he will not attack unless he has great strength." The handbook lauded the VC as an "elusive and determined foe," well organized, expert at camouflage, deception, and ambush, a "hardy and ruthless fighter, but not an invincible one." The conclusion was that the VC "can and will be defeated."

To inflict such a defeat, we had fully to understand the enemy's intentions, and perhaps our best effort was a paper published a couple of months before my arrival. In CICV Study 67–037, 29 June 1967, entitled *Strategy Since 1954,* was a description of the evolution of Mao Tse-tung's theories from China's revolution in 1949 through the Viet Minh war against the French to the Viet Cong insurgency:

> There is no "magic" in the formula proposed by Mao. Rather it is a pragmatic approach designed to meet the enemy's strengths only when unavoidable, while concentrating on his weakness in a protracted war of attrition. This approach is by no means unique; it is merely a logical outgrowth of a concept as old as the culture of the Orient: "... concealed

within strength there is weakness and within weakness, strength."

Thus, the Communists contend that the strength of the enemy becomes their own weakness; their superior equipment makes them roadbound, and destroys their strategic and tactical mobility. The weakness of the guerrilla becomes his strength; his wide dispersion keeps the enemy confused and off balance and erodes his morale.

The study showed how Mao's three phases of an escalating war had been adapted to the Vietnamese situation by General Vo Nguyen Giap, the legendary commander of the North Vietnamese Army and the conqueror of the French.[3] In his treatise "People's War, People's Army" (1959) he wrote of the "stage of contention, stage of equilibrium, and stage of counteroffensive." As before in the struggle against the French, presumably Hanoi would embark on the third phase against the Americans when it was felt they held superiority of forces over those of the enemy and that the local situation had evolved in their favor.

The CICV report also outlined Giap's strategy for a war of attrition:

attacking the enemy where he is most vulnerable, advancing deeply into the enemy rear and then withdrawing swiftly, and emphasizing dynamism, initiative, mobility and rapidity of decision in face of new situations.

This study also showed how an analysis of intelligence on the enemy had led to development of our own tactics:

The successes of the Allies during this period were based primarily upon the strategic exploitation of a basic weakness in Viet Cong doctrine. The concept of "one slow, four quick" —the notion that units must first plan and prepare slowly, then (1) assault quickly, (2) open fire quickly, (3) clear the battlefield quickly, and (4) withdraw quickly—was the key to US/GVN deployment. So-called "spoiling attacks" kept the enemy from gaining momentum or launching major attacks. Since the enemy's concentration around the DMZ and the buildup in War Zone C (around Tay Ninh) have been checked by Allied offensives, there is reason to believe that it will be necessary for the enemy to undertake a strategic reassessment.

This report demonstrated to me that proper use of intelligence could be translated into battlefield successes. (But not until many years later would the validity of CICV's prediction become apparent. This study was published in June 1967, stating its "reason to believe" the enemy would "undertake a strategic reassessment." In July the Hanoi leadership decided to conduct its unprecedented nationwide attacks during Tet of 1968.) I hoped that my shop with its new generation of analysts could produce finished intelligence as useful as *Strategy Since 1954* and offer the right data at the right time to help break the stalemate of the war. Already I had been awed by the significance of some of the taskings we received, and it seemed we were in a position to make a difference.

The work kept coming. Not the least time-consuming part of it was reading the multiple headquarters communiqués, Daily Intelligence Summaries (DISUMs), and interminable memos. Even keeping up with the Command Operations Center (COC) daily journal was a burden, since it was updated all day long, sometimes minute by minute as reports came in from around the nation.

There was a constant stream of "do-it-right-now" projects. By the middle of September, two were coming due almost every day. I had already completed reviews of the enemy armor potential and the impact of B-52 raids. We were often asked about artillery and antiaircraft capabilities, two areas that had only sketchy documentation. There were frequent taskings for an "Area Order of Battle Analysis," a description of all enemy units and their activities in a specific area within given map coordinates. The request for one of these products meant that an Allied operation would soon be going into that sector. The CICV desk jockeys took these studies very seriously, and "guesstimates" would not do.

The Monthly Order of Battle Summary (the OB Book) had to be constantly updated as the analysts confirmed the validity of new data from captured documents and PW interrogations. Then there were the recurring projects. The PERINTREP (Periodic Intelligence Report), which we had to produce by the third of each month, concentrated on the discovery of new weapons, equipment, and tactics. The ninth was the deadline for the MOP, Measurement of Progress, which described the activities of those enemy battalions identified and confirmed in contact that month. On the tenth came due the Monthly Wrap-Up, also known as the Composite Summary of Observations, a review of the past month's activities of the identified units carried in the OB Book. The MACV Intelligence Bulletin was due on the twentieth, but it became an optional, and therefore abandoned, report. A one-page quarterly review was due on the seventh of every third month; getting three months of I Corps OB activity onto one page was no easy chore. Later came a tasking for another quarterly evaluation, the QUARTEVAL, due on the twelfth of each third month. This one was more extensive and ultimately had three sections: a summary of major enemy activity; new enemy tactics, weapons, and equipment; and "Large Scale Significant Attacks, Large Scale Attacks, and Significant Attacks." (In March 1967 General Wheeler had expressed concern about the reaction in Washington to a MACV report showing an increase in enemy large-scale attacks in 1966 and 1967. As a result, this new standard of "significance" rather than size was adopted. By creating new classifications and definitions, conclusions and trends became more jumbled and difficult for us—and the press—to report.)

After gaining more experience and sophistication, I would use the first report due as the source for many of the others. Often essentially the same text would be recycled through the period under different titles. No one ever complained. Probably no one ever noticed.

Very quickly I learned how vital were the enlisted men who processed the huge inflow of documents. These men were generally college grads who had more intelligence training than the junior officers who commanded them. They were bright and hard-working. In fact, the enlisted men who were the order of battle analysts at CICV were the cornerstone of the MACV headquarters' intelligence system.

They read all the captured documents, agent reports, and prisoner-of-war interrogations that came into the shop. A Team Reader, usually an NCO, first scanned each source and channeled it to the proper analyst, who generally covered all enemy units in one of the five provinces (two EM were usually assigned to each of the more active provinces in the North; I CTZ OB, at its peak, had about seven enlisted analysts doing unit work).

The analyst wrote by hand into a Unit Notebook (he had one for each unit he followed) a summary of all the usable OB data that was contained in the source. He evaluated it for its veracity and entered any analysis he felt appropriate. If the document concerned several units, the analyst had to make entries in several Unit Notebooks. Then he had to make photocopies for filing in each Unit Source folder, a bulging compilation of all the key documents received concerning that unit. Ultimately the men would file the master document in just one folder and put an entry to that effect in each Unit Notebook. Our files were jammed with documents and finding room for all the raw intelligence received each day was becoming a problem.

After filling in his Unit Notebooks, which for a good source could take a major portion of a work day, the analyst often had at least two more data recording systems to deal with. The enemy did not label his units as conveniently as we would have liked. For every name that we relied on, such as the 38th VC Local Force Battalion, there might be several AKAs ("also known as") or cover designations. The 38th was also called Nghien Doan; Labor Union 38; 83d Battalion; Worksite 83; Thi Xa 38; 803d; 504th; Cong Ty 38; and the 48th Battalion. A source could refer to any one of these AKAs and our analyst had to decide if he was reading about a brand-new unit or one we already had listed. The enemy's intent, of course, was to confuse us and reduce the risks from capture of documents or soldiers. Sometimes he was successful.[4]

Our defense was an AKA file, with each designation alphabetically maintained on a three-by-five card and cross-referenced to the unit title used in the OB Book. For every name mentioned in a source, the analyst had to check through the file to see if it was already on record. If not, he was either learning about a new unit or simply running into a new AKA; his decision was made from his reading of the balance of the document. The OB Book included an appendix with many of the AKAs listed for each recognized unit, and the analyst had to keep that compilation up to date as well. The simple AKA card file was as vital to understanding the enemy as any sophisticated electronic system then in use by MACV J-2.

A card file was also maintained as an index to PW interrogation reports. Each report, filed under the PW's name, was described on a separate card. The card included a note as to where the report had been filed. As in any paper storage system, one of our biggest problems was prompt retrieval of key documents at a later date. The PW card file was one way to doublecheck what we had and where it could be found.

Other duties fell on these men like a constant mortar barrage. As Projects Officer, I often had to assign production functions, and the OIC would also have his own data projects. The analysts would sometimes get a "knowledgability brief" from the Combined Military Interrogation Center about a PW who had information on certain subjects. Our men then had to prepare questions to be put to the captive to satisfy our particular needs. (After going through this exercise a few times and not seeing our questions being asked, we didn't respond to many of these taskings.) Finally, these hard-pressed men had to type much of the finished intelligence. For only part of the year did we have a clerk-typist who could turn out decent copy. I was able to reduce one of their burdens by persuading Colonel Mac that our shops should not be responsible for ADP (automatic data processing) input. The men had been filling in the computer cards used in the data bank. It was time consuming and wasteful of their analytical skills. The function was shifted elsewhere in CICV.

All the officers were dependent on the material the enlisted men passed on as being significant. Even Kernsky, who oversaw the northern sector of I Corps and tried to read everything, had to rely on his enlisted men to identify trends. We were only secondary experts, our knowledge largely derived from the skills of the PFCs, corporals, and specialists. I think nowhere in the war effort could be found so few men who did so much that directly affected its conduct.

I wasn't the only newcomer trying to define his job. In September came a memo from Colonel Charles Morris, the new Director of Intelligence Production, the branch of J-2 that included CICV and CIIED (Current Intelligence, Indications, and Estimates Division). Morris wanted us to have "Some Random Comments" on how he would be running the show. The long memo was a bit of a pep talk, riddled with football analogies ("No football play ever goes off just as drawn out on the blackboard . . ."), but it showed his desire to maintain an effective, cooperative intelligence system. He had found upon starting his job that he had more than 800 men under his authority. He had quickly reorganized his area of responsibility to perform two functions: the maintenance of a data base by CICV and the production of current and estimated intelligence by CIIED (which was housed over in the MACV headquarters in a large windowless room known as the "Tank").

Morris had some sharp conclusions to offer, and I was impressed by his warning that "you are doing a job which, depending on how you do it, can mean the difference between life and death to some frontline soldier." And he really got to the heart of it with this: "Every time you hear of a unit that has been surprised, it is traceable to one of two causes: (a) failure of intelligence, or (b) failure of command to respond to intelligence. There can be no other answer."

To his memo he attached a statement of the J-2's (that is, Davidson's) "Intelligence Objectives," which included: "To provide COMUS-MACV that intelligence required for making sound and timely decisions." Then followed Morris's own set of objectives. His first priority was: "Maximum prior warning of impending military attack or reinforcement of enemy in an attack on the U.S./FW [Free World] forces in areas for which COMUSMACV has responsibility." Also in his list of areas to monitor was one that was reminiscent of Korea:

> USSR and Communist Chinese capabilities, posture, deployment and concepts for the employment of major forces in the area for which COMUSMACV has responsibility. . . .

Always that echo of the monolithic Red threat and the yellow hordes! Even so, the memo made me feel a little more comfortable after Davidson's "downward trending" directive of 15 August. Maybe this new colonel would be a good cushion between the analysts and the J-2. Time would tell.

And with time I was getting a handle on the battlefield data. In a letter home written on 16 September, I reported that in two briefings to senior officers, I'd been chewed out only moderately. The chewer was usually Colonel Mac, chief of Ground Order of Battle. We'd hit it off well, as early as the time he had noticed my tight jungle fatigues. But on occasion he could blast the roof off. His face would turn florid, the network of veins on his nose and cheeks prominent. His expression would become a grimace and his eyes flash during his explosions. But in minutes, as his blood pressure dropped, he would smile and usually offer some encouragement. I came to develop a true affection for him.

In my letter I had held forth on the greater glories of intelligence work and my role in it:

> Intell. is fascinating. There is nothing I could be doing in the Army that would be more worthwhile or fulfilling for me. . . .

> I work with a lot of field grade officers and have possibilities
> of even influencing the course of the war.

So I hoped, perhaps fantasized. And in fact, as the Tet offensive neared, I twice had vital information in hand that could have—*should have*—turned the VC attacks into a devastating Allied victory from the outset.

But Tet was still months away and indicators of an unusually aggressive "winter-spring campaign" by the VC had not yet begun to arrive at CICV. I was still plowing through the files to study past projects taskings and their products. Some were fascinating, others surreal. For example, on 24 June 1967, the officer-in-charge of Ground Order of Battle sent to the OIC of each corps this instruction on the subject of "Project 1878–67: Anticipated Intelligence Requirements":

> Each Wednesday, all CTZs will submit a list of proposed
> projects which each CTZ team OIC feels would anticipate
> intelligence requirements.

In essence, each section chief was being asked to make more work for himself. Stapled to this memo was the weekly series of routing slips that the I Corps chief had sent back to the originator of this idea. Each read, "No input." On 11 August, the chief of Ground Order of Battle sent one more memo in the series, tersely announcing, "Effective this date this project has been cancelled."

Only a few of the many file drawers contained general (and often superfluous) data and one-time projects. These included a CICV study on the VC use of rodents (even the rats were against us) and a poetic essay on the origin of beggar beads in Vietnamese history. The writing occasionally provided a laugh. One document reported, "The infiltration group was composed of ⅓ males, ⅓ females, and ⅓ party officials." Another analyst declared: "This unit had an estimated strength of about 2,000 men, of which 300 were women." Also I found, "Sex can be considered uniform throughout the ranks, although some females work for and with the enemy." Matters of gender apparently confused some MI types.

Now and then I came across a comedian ("VC agents reportedly have slipped slogan slips into the shopping sacks of Saigon shoppers"), or an analyst with a sense of the sardonic:

The need to abandon the critically ill or provide makeshift burial for the dead unquestionably leaves the survivor with a bleak outlook related to the possibility of health failing.

Such exercises did not always go unpunished. The files held a copy of a lesson some hapless EM had had to copy over and over:

Today I committed twenty seven (27) errors of a mechanical nature and four (4) errors of judgment. Each error and judgment was preceded by a period of profound thought and contemplation on the subject at hand. A decision was reached, thereby showing decisiveness if not intelligence or grasp of the English language.

These trivia-jammed drawers (much of the material wasn't even dated) had to be cleared to make room for my coming generation of files. I had obtained a wooden crate from supply and gathered up all the marginal files for review as time permitted. But other projects piled up and the box under my desk was neglected. Soon Kernsky became convinced I was "hoarding" data and responsible for every misplaced file in the shop. He aggressively addressed his complaints to me in front of the enlisted men and the Vietnamese. Unsure of myself, even though he had breached basic military protocol by his public criticisms, I waffled defensively and explained that I was reviewing only out-of-date material, not the vital Unit Sources folders. I appeared weak, lacking "command presence," and I knew my authority had been damaged.

The situation worsened later when I bent down under my desk to gather some files and found a surprise. Taped to the box was a copy of the familiar cartoon of an officer twisted so far over that his head was between his legs and stuck up his ass. I suspected Kernsky, but said nothing.

The next day I ordered an enlisted man to search all desks for the infamous missing files. They were soon located and, with righteous flair, I established a procedure whereby all removed files would be logged out by the user.

But more foolishness was to come. Kernsky and I were fated to have it out over his frequent loud criticisms. Finally I let him know privately that I considered him "insolent and egotistical" and that "while I'm OIC these qualities will not demonstrate themselves to the EM" at my expense. Then he sought a meeting in the snack bar and told me his life story: a poor urban immigrant family, a life on the streets, too many fights, a mother who grieved over his future. It seemed he needed a chaplain, not me. At last we got back to the problem between us. Kernsky earnestly declared, "It's a thin line between insubordination and speaking your mind."

I shot back, "Yeah, and I wish you'd learn where it is!" Surprisingly, he didn't explode, but merely nodded.

I opened up a little. "Listen, the real OIC will be back soon, and we'll be done with our problems. Meanwhile, let's talk more and we'll keep it positive and constructive. O.K.?"

We shook hands on it and, returning to CICV, I felt a burden lifting. I was beginning to learn personnel-management basics never taught in ROTC, but, as with everything else in the Army, it was the hard way.

I was stunned to discover that we had almost no "finished intelligence," that is, thorough, typed, up-to-date copies of background reports on each enemy unit that could be distributed as needed. These reports, the Unit OB Summaries, were compilations of all the available data on each OB factor for each unit in our area. Only one summary was available and it had been put on a mimeograph stencil, so it was difficult to update and modify as needed.

I wanted OB Summaries developed as quickly as possible. There was no standard operating procedure requiring that such documents be on hand, and I had never seen guidelines for their preparation, but their importance to us in understanding the enemy was clear. Only the barest data on locations and date of contacts got into the MACV OB Book. The analysts had a treasury of information in their often scribbled Unit Notebooks, but the data had to be organized and transcribed into a legible format for distribution to field units and headquarters.

But when I talked to the overworked analysts about the project, all that came back were complaints and concerns. Finally on 14 September I gave them a memo that set a three-month work period to produce these summaries for every independent enemy unit. I explained that these products would be distributed to units in the field and would "carry I CTZ's stamp of approval, even if they aren't CICV/MACV official documents." However, I made a mistake by beginning the memo, "Start preparing yourself for a major project."

Soon I learned no one was working on the summaries. I was more deflated than angry. Then PFC Shore cleared it all up for me.

"You see, Lieutenant Jones, you've only talked about the project. You've distributed the format but you've never *told* us to start producing them!"

I stammered something about being concerned about the men's work load.

"Yes, sir, there's always a heavy work load around here, but if something has to be done, we'll do it. But it has to be a clear order first."

Shore wasn't sharpshooting for a change. He was trying to help. The order was given and soon the OB Summaries started coming in, although it took months to finish the entire backlog of units in I Corps. These summaries proved vital in understanding the enemy's tactics. For example, a history of an important NVA division had appeared in CICV's *Strategy Since 1954*:

> ...the enemy took a bold stroke in the latter part of June 1966; a full division, the 324B, was moved across the Demilitarized Zone.... A successful US operation repelled the enemy's advances, however, and the NVA regiments were driven back to the sanctuary of the Demilitarized Zone....

We recorded movement data like this in our summaries because the information revealed the tactics and operations of the enemy. The authors of the CICV strategy report had offered an optimistic conclusion that "this major setback" had "probably marked a turning point in enemy strategic thinking." They hypothesized that the defeat may have halted Giap's progression into his "phase three" of conventional warfare as he sought to break out of the "equilibrium" of guerrilla warfare. But in our write-up on the 324B, we reported that its regiments crossed back into South Vietnam again in August 1967 to pressure the Marine outposts, and that this use of the border sanctuary had become standard procedure. No matter how large the forces that Giap used, the tactic was to hit and run, hide and refit, and come back again when the battlefield was to his liking.

Our OB Summaries began to accumulate enough information to reveal such tactics. And they always showed that both the NVA and VC units were able to return quickly to operational strength after battles with the Allies. I had the analysts put as much detail into these studies as possible. Other than the OB Book itself, they were the only tools we had to educate our superiors and the field units themselves about the enemy's capabilities.

I soon realized that the Monthly Wrap-Up, AKA the Composite Summary of Observations, was a vehicle to help the enlisted men update the history sections of their unit summaries. As Projects Officer, I had to prepare an activities summary for every unit identified that month. After drafting the wrap-up, I gave the pertinent pages to the analyst responsible for the unit and he held them until its summary could be updated by a typist. The enlisted man was encouraged to edit and expand my work as he saw fit. Because the OB factors in these summaries were now being placed on a new page for each subject area, their updating with new information did not require retyping and restructuring the entire document. Such a procedure seems minor, but it was vital in allowing us quickly to produce finished copy with minimum typing, which was the biggest administrative problem we had.

With each new write-up, my pride in these summaries grew. Over the months, our temporary OICs (a couple of Army majors and a Navy lieutenant commander who came and went) always fully supported the effort. As soon as the first batch of summaries was ready, I had them packaged for courier transit to the various headquarters: III MAF in Da Nang; the headquarters for Army advisors to Viet units in I Corps, also in Da Nang; the Americal Division G-2 in Quang Ngai; and the Special Forces headquarters in Nha Thrang. And I made sure my ARVN counterparts received complete copies.

I had learned that there simply was no standard operating procedure or policy in CICV or MACV J-2 requiring the exchange of finished intelligence products between the various headquarters. It amazed me. It worried me. So I sent I CTZ's best efforts to the other intelligence shops. We did not receive any products in return.

At the shop, things were smoothing out. Kernsky was more relaxed, and I was finally able to break through to the ARVNs who had been so reserved and private. One day, as I leaned back in my chair to stretch after plowing through another project, I saw the aloof Lieutenant Tri studying me from his nearby desk. As we made eye contact, this time he did not look away. Instead, he slyly winked at me and then laughed at my surprise. I returned his grin and our friendship began that day.

Tri had been careful about me. He knew, of course, that the Americans came and went, and that many were rude to the Vietnamese. But he began to trust me, I think, after I had asked him if we could rearrange the furniture so he could sit next to me and the other Viets closer to their American counterparts. Previously they had been clustered in a far corner, out of the way and largely ignored. He seemed to appreciate the gesture and we began a frequent exchange of information that was to prove invaluable.

CICV was a "combined" intelligence center because it housed us and our Viet allies. But at no time was I ever advised on how to work with the Viets or that I should develop a data exchange with them. In fact, the American policy—or prejudice—was that our data was ours, theirs was theirs. On several occasions I turned in reports relying on ARVN input; they were either rejected or I was told to add a footnote identifying the source of the data and explaining that it was all we had at the time.

There was of course always a chance some of our ARVNs were VC agents and capable of feeding us false information. But I think the reasons for our treatment of the ARVN sources as second-class intelligence went deeper. Perhaps we Americanized the war because too many of us just could not work with such different people.

But I got on well with the Viets, and enjoyed their company more than that of the Americans. On occasion I even slipped into their siesta room to grab a nap at noon, and a few times invited my counterparts to have a "33" beer with me after work. Sometime in mid-September I asked Lieutenant Tri and the other Viets if it was possible for them to help me get a captured VC or NVA flag. They huddled and replied they would try. In a couple weeks, Aspirant Qui, who spoke the best English, presented me with miniature flags made of silk: the VC's half-blue, half-red field with yellow star; North Vietnam's red flag with yellow star; and the Republic of Vietnam's with yellow field crossed by three thin horizontal red stripes. Aspirant Loi explained that Viets could not have enemy flags, so one of their wives had sewn these for me, though even this was "much danger" for them. And they had made for me one of their own flags too.

I was touched by their effort and knew it would be wise to display the RVN flag. It went under the plastic cover on my desk pad; the ARVNs noticed my gesture with obvious pleasure. The flag's field of yellow represented the riches of the ancestral land, symbolizing the golden rice grains and the metal gold. The three bands running the flag's length stood for the nation's three traditional regions, north, central, and south, and were red, the color of success. But PFC Shore had a different and too-loud interpretation, that the yellow stood for cowardice and the red for all the spilled blood.

There was a lot of that kind of resentment. Another of our EM had bitched about all the "goddamned cowboys riding around on their fucking Hondas! Why aren't they in the army? They took me out of Boston so these gooks can ride around on their fucking Hondas!" There was anger over the two-hour lunches taken by the Viets for their siesta and the weekends they went home, while the Americans worked either in the office or at a compound.

The drafted American soldier wasn't impressed by the probability that the South Vietnamese Army was now so large (over half a million) it couldn't logistically absorb more recruits—it had been increased by about half over the last four years. He knew only that he'd been yanked into a dirty little war that the nationals weren't fighting that well. He had no patience for the explanation that the people of many tropical nations slept through the day's peak heat. And he didn't realize or care that here war had always been a way of life and the Vietnamese had learned to get along with it.[5]

Because the enemy was well motivated and tenacious, we respectfully called him "Victor Charlie" (from the military phonetics for the letters) or "Mr. Charles." The rest of the Viets, the ones we were supporting, were slopes, gooks, zips, dinks. Not all Americans resorted to this outlet for their frustrations, but far too many did.

In late September I was pleased and honored when Lieutenant Tri, our other two ARVNs beside him, proudly presented to me metal pins worn on the uniforms of Republic of Vietnam armed forces to designate branch assignments. To reciprocate, the next day I gave each of them the brass insignia for the U.S. Army Intelligence branch. They bowed and formally thanked me. Our cooperation continued to prosper.

Another letter came from Swamprat. The field was quiet, he wrote, but he did have to make a nervous trip with light security out a twisting road near Nhon Troch. A week earlier an American district advisor had been killed by a booby trap on the same road. Swans said his job was interesting but often frustrating:

> Some of these fanatical Bn CO's are sending us everything but the VC—ARVN soldiers, hamlet chiefs, you name it. At times the stupidity of those people in the field seems ludicrous. Anything to get their "quota" for the month or operation. I've even heard of cases of framing civilians by putting grenades or a rifle on them and hauling them in.

Swans was amused by the guys from the Combined Matériel Exploitation Center. They came to get samples of captured VC weapons and medical supplies, and would panic each time the 175mm guns popped off. Swans said he went to sleep every night with the artillery shaking his cot. I was glad to be in Saigon.

Mail call was now bringing me advice from my father, based on his own military experience.

> We find it gratifying that you seem to take the duty in stride. Hope you are always "over-ready" for your briefings . . . don't forget the "I don't know that answer, sir, but I will dig for it and report promptly." NEVER NEVER say "I guess" or offer a guess no matter how good the odds seem. You bluff *just once* and that will be your permanent label!

In ROTC we had been given several topics to research and present, but always the emphasis had been on the graphic aid more than content and process. At Fort Holabird, we had been introduced to the fabulous "Hong Kong Pointer," an absolutely essential piece of equipment for the briefer. Cleverly constructed, it telescoped to the size of a pen so that you could carry it in your pocket, then whip it out to its full length to illustrate your lecture. And, of course, its point was an ink pen so that in one swift move you could shift from briefing to note-taking. We enjoyed the demonstration by our Holabird instructor, especially when the pen broke and splattered ink all over his uniform and his chart.

But in all the training they had never taught us how to exit gracefully from a tough question while still keeping the audience informed.

Within a week of my arrival at CICV, I was assigned as the I Corps briefing officer, each Friday giving a general overview of the week to an assemblage of Allied officers. I hated it. The preparation was time consuming, and at the briefing the audience was usually on the verge of napping. The occasional sharpshooter, almost always a lieutenant, would try to flash his own information or try to nail me on mine. More tricky was the serious question that made you sweat, and more than once I had recourse to my father's formula: "I can't presently answer that, sir. I'll check with my men and get back to you."

It was acceptable procedure only if the data follow-up was immediate. Protocol in the military was usually based on common sense, but you had to learn it by doing it.

Kernsky scored big late in September. He, or his EM, found a document that identified the location being used by the VC to launch rockets at the Da Nang air base. On 27 February 1967 the Marines there had become the first in Nam to be hit by rockets, in an attack in which some fifty 140mm rockets had hit the base in less than a minute. Later the VC converted to the more effective 122mm model, and the attacks became frequent. Two men could backpack and quickly fire a rocket by placing the 102-pound missile on a portable launcher or just a mound of earth, facing it in the general direction of their target, and letting it rip. Some ten miles away, forty-one pounds of TNT would come crashing down roughly in the area where the rocket was aimed. It was not a precise weapon, and that made it all the more frightening—especially four months later in the siege of Saigon.

Apparently field exploitation had missed this important document. Kernsky jubilantly reported the find to Colonel Mac and it was signaled to Da Nang. The site became a regular artillery and observation target and the VC had to move elsewhere. The rocketing slowed down, at least for a while.

As Colonel Morris had pointed out, CICV's role was to provide a data base, and only rarely did we see "current intelligence" such as this document yielded. Our sources offered a peek into the activity of the past few months and usually we could only perceive possible trends into the future. For what was going on *now*, like everyone else I had to rely on the newspapers, and they largely relied on what was handed out by the MACV Office of Information.

Still, a lot could be learned from the news, for instance this 15

September UPI article which declared that the B-52 bombardments of the DMZ

> have succeeded in blocking plans for kicking Americans out of the string of strong points guarding the border. North Vietnam has massed about 35,000 troops within a 15-mile corridor in the border . . . the devastating artillery, rocket and mortar barrages. . . . are taking an increasingly heavy toll at such frontier posts as Gio Linh, Dong Ha, Camp Carroll, Con Thien, and Khe Sanh.

The article referred to Con Thien as the "center strongpoint which the Communists have been trying to knock off for months."[6] Along with Gio Linh, the artillery-fire support base almost up against the DMZ some five kilometers to the west, Con Thien was the first American base to come under extended siege by the North Vietnamese Army. In their official history for 1967, the Marines estimate that by late 1967 the NVA had approximately 130 artillery pieces north of the Ben Hoi River, including 152mm howitzers with a range in excess of ten miles.

At CICV we learned that at least elements of the NVA 324B Division had surrounded the base and company-size attacks had begun. Day after day I read the Command Operations Center log reports about the heavy bombardment of these small bases dug into the red earth of isolated hills. On 25 September I counted the number of incoming rounds at Con Thien, as reported chronologically in the log: the total came to some 1,200 (on other days, only about 150 had been incoming). I shuddered to think of the fear and fatigue these men were suffering.[7]

During my next Friday briefing I mentioned the number and was immediately challenged as to my source. Colonel Mac later grumbled that I had better things to do with my time than count artillery shells. Perhaps there was concern that the press might pick up the number and use it to berate our defensive posture. I was amused later to see the figure pop up in official MACV reports (and in books written after the war).

The UPI article continued:

> The Communists have massed their greatest threat of the war along the DMZ and U.S. Defense Secretary Robert McNa-

mara has ordered construction of a barrier system to help hold back infiltration and counter the threat.

McNamara had gone public with his "electronic wall" and it received a lot of sarcastic comments from the CICV analysts. *If we can't stop 'em, we can at least listen to them as they stroll through the DMZ!* Like so many of our trial-and-error efforts in Vietnam, it was doomed to failure. "McNamara's Folly" was abandoned by the end of the year.[8]

Con Thien was the focus point of the war in September. In their official history for 1967, the Marines described the enemy attacks as a "desperate bid for a military victory, with its attendant propaganda value." According to MACV's 1967 wrap-up, our losses were 196 Marines killed and 1,917 wounded (out of a force of about 6,000). MACV declared that the USMC "killed over 1,100 enemy soldiers in one of the most costly defeats the enemy has suffered in the Republic." (In his memoirs, Westmoreland refers to "well over" 2,000 NVA killed.)

The consensus at the headquarters was that this was indeed the opening round of the enemy's major offensive of the war. At headquarters we spoke of General Giap's quest for another Dien Bien Phu, and the press was soon to include that 1954 disaster in its reviews of the current DMZ siege.

Con Thien was the first of the border battles during the fall of 1967. The ferocity of the war was vastly increasing as Giap's grand strategy moved us further into his winter-spring offensive and his master plan for Tet.

7

The September Sellout

There are three kinds of lies: lies, damned lies, and statistics.

Mark Twain
Autobiography

. . . our policy was to give Washington the most honest, accurate reports that we could.

General William C. Westmoreland
CBS interview, 27 May 1981

I saw General William C. Westmoreland for the first time on 8 or 9
September 1967 on Cong Ly Avenue near MACV. His sedan was
escorted by a single Vietnamese MP on a motorcycle, a gesture of the
general's confidence in the GVN. Seeing the four stars on the vehicle, I
snapped to and crisply saluted before heading up the gravel road to
CICV.

Westmoreland was on his way to Pentagon East, where a delegation from the Central Intelligence Agency was making its last-ditch
stand against MACV J-2, the Defense Intelligence Agency, and CINC-
PAC J-2. The military establishment was fighting tenaciously to implement its policy of "downward trending," but the CIA was sticking to its
position that the enemy army numbered at least 500,000 men. That was
a number MACV headquarters could not accept.

Since May, MACV, CIA, DIA, and CINCPAC representatives had
been meeting as the Board of National Intelligence Estimates to produce
the annual estimate of international intelligence findings. As the result
of work by analyst Samuel Adams, the CIA had developed a total estimate of VC/NVA forces of some 500,000; MACV was presenting a
total of 294,000, despite the conclusions of General McChristian, Westmoreland's head of military intelligence, and Colonel Hawkins, the acknowledged OB expert. In recent months the men under McChristian
and Hawkins had worked hard to update MACV's intelligence, and

their studies had led them to increase the estimates of the enemy force in most categories: the irregulars (guerrillas and self-defense militia), service troops, and political cadre. In May Hawkins had twice briefed Westmoreland, initially proposing a total of 429,000; on both occasions Westmoreland had rejected the new figures, though not questioning the methodology employed to reach them. Each time Hawkins returned to CICV to reduce the total, despite the evidence he knew so well.[1]

On 1 June 1967 McChristian was replaced by Davidson, and in August Hawkins found himself at the NIE conference in Washington having to defend numbers that he felt "significantly understated the enemy's strength."[2] Privately he told some of the participants that the MACV position was "crap."[3]

The NIE meetings dragged on at CIA headquarters and at the Pentagon, degenerating into bargaining sessions rather than an examination of evidence. Colonel George Hamscher of the Defense Intelligence Agency reported:

> The incident that most clearly marked the real nature of our negotiations was Graham's arbitrary wholesale deletion from the Order of Battle of entire enemy units to bring the figures under the ceiling. . . .[4]

"Graham" was Colonel Daniel Graham, then head of MACV's Current Intelligence, Indications, and Estimates Division, who had, without new evidence, cut from the OB a number of enemy combat and service units ("wiping them out bloodlessly," according to Hamscher)[5] and dropped the strength of others.

"Ceiling" was the key word. Hamscher stated:

> The term "ceiling" was used often enough that the "message" was unmistakable. . . . We all used it. I recall some comments concerning "bringing the CIA floor down to our ceiling."[6]

Hawkins, too, perceived a ceiling:

> There was no doubt in my mind before I attended the NIE conference in Langley in August 1967 that a MACV

command-imposed ceiling existed for enemy strength, that this ceiling was significantly lower than estimates indicated by the best available evidence and that the bottom line figure that was to emerge from the NIE conference was not to exceed the MACV ceiling. This requirement was not stated to me bluntly or baldly through command channels, but its existence had become clear to me after my two briefings to General Westmoreland and in light of continuing pressure from my superiors after May 1967 to reduce estimates of enemy strength.[7]

The bargaining at the NIE conference went on. Hamscher again:

There was no re-analysis, no re-examination of supporting evidence, no recourse to OB files, no respect for the work of analysts. It was a "blue-pencil" operation, and we haggled and bargained, even blustered. It progressed from unprofessional to wrongful; and it amounted to falsification of intelligence.[8]

In these August sessions, MACV began to dominate the CIA. A primary reason was the flurry of extraordinary cables and policy memos written by the military's high command that month. The first of these, sent on 15 August, was Davidson's "downward trending" memo to his deputies, shown to me in confidence by the outgoing men at CICV.

Four days later, Davidson sent another memo, this one to General George Godding of the Defense Intelligence Agency in Washington, that included the following:

2. Further consideration reveals the total unacceptability of including the strength of the self-defense forces and the secret self-defense forces in any strength figure to be released to the press.
3. The figure of about 420,000, which includes all forces including SD and SSD, has already surfaced out here. This figure has stunned the embassy and this headquarters and has resulted in a scream of protests and denials.
4. In view of this reaction and in view of General Westmoreland's conversations, all of which you have heard, I am sure

that this headquarters will not accept a figure in excess of the current strength figure carried by the press.

5. Let me make it clear that this is my view of General Westmoreland's sentiments. I have not discussed this directly with him but I am 100 percent sure of his reaction.

The height of the "ceiling" was made clear in this memo: "the current strength figure carried by the press." That number was 297,000, which the NIE participants rounded off to 300,000. That same day Godding, having briefed General Earle C. Wheeler, chairman of the Joint Chiefs of Staff, reported in a cable that Wheeler had agreed to drop the self-defense forces from the "overall total figure" and "could accept somewhat higher figures in the guerrilla and administrative services if pushed by CIA."[9]

Also on 19 August a cable was sent to George Carver, Adams's superior at the CIA, by Robert Komer. A civilian with ambassadorial status, Komer had been since May Westmoreland's deputy in charge of the pacification and Phoenix programs. In other words, he was the man responsible for "pacifying" those self-defense forces and political cadres McChristian and Hawkins had estimated at about twice the number previously carried by MACV. Komer's concern was the "ruckus" that might occur if the wide discrepancy between the MACV and CIA figures became known:

Any explanation as to why would simply lead press to conclude that MACV was deliberately omitting [militia] category in order [to] downgrade enemy strength. Thus credibility gap would be further widened at a time when in fact we are moving toward much more valid estimates.

On 20 August General Creighton Abrams, the number-two man in MACV (and Westmoreland's later replacement), sent a cable to Wheeler emphasizing the need for removing the self-defense militia:

3. From the intelligence viewpoint, the inclusion of [militia] strength figures in our estimates of military capabilities is highly questionable. These forces contain a sizable number of women and old people. They operate entirely in their own hamlets. They are rarely armed, have no real discipline, and

almost no military capacity.[10] They are no more effective in the military sense than the dozens of other non-military organizations which serve the VC cause in various roles.[11]

4. The press reaction to these inflated figures is of much greater concern. We have been projecting an image of success over the recent months, and properly so. Now, when we release the figure of 420,000–431,000, the newsmen will immediately seize on the point that the enemy force has increased about 120,000–130,000. All available caveats and explanations will not prevent the press from drawing an erroneous and gloomy explanation as to the meaning of the increase. All those who have an incorrect view of the war will be reinforced and the task will become more difficult.

Then, at Westmoreland's request,[12] the debate moved to Saigon. He offered the CIA a proposal:[13] if the agency would agree to drop the self-defense militia, MACV would increase its estimate of guerrillas by 15,000. Graham presented a "cross-over" theory, statistics that he insisted proved we were killing more enemy soldiers than were being replaced. As for the service troops, both the CIA and MACV had made projections from small samples (Adams had analyzed 14 of the nation's 234 districts, MACV had examined 3). The CIA had found a pattern in the VC personnel assignments and estimated these troops at 100,000, while MACV carried just over 25,000 (and ultimately would refuse to go higher than 38,000). Adams has since stated that each time he secured an increase, "the military would drop another category down by the same amount."[14]

On 10 September, Carver sent home to CIA headquarters the first of a series of cables reporting the stalemate:

So far our mission frustratingly unproductive, since MACV stonewalling, obviously under orders. Unless or until I can persuade Westmoreland to amend those orders, serious discussion of evidence or substantive issues will be impossible. . . . Variety of circumstantial indicators . . . all point to inescapable conclusion that General Westmoreland (with Komer's encouragement) has given instruction tantamount to direct order that VC strength total will not exceed

300,000 ceiling. . . . Root problems as we all recognize lie much more in political public relations realm than in substantive difference. . . .

In a cable sent on the twelfth, Carver reported the meetings of 11 and 12 September as "active but with little movement," and felt they were at an "impasse," although Adams had been successful in getting the estimate of guerrilla forces "appreciably raised." Carver wanted the MACV and CIA analysts to go over all the estimates category by category, "without any weather-eye on a final total." Davidson refused, Carver reported, "angrily accusing me of impugning his integrity since he had assured me he had no predetermined total. . . ." Davidson had made, he told Carver, MACV's "final offer, not subject to discussion," and the CIA "should take it or leave it." Carver saw that MACV's sticking point was the irregulars. He himself did not believe that the CIA figures were "all that firm," and would accept a "prose text" description of these forces in which an approximation of 100,000 would be presented. Davidson rejected this, and Carver had recourse to Westmoreland, with whom he was scheduled to meet the following day. In his cable of the thirteenth, Carver reported that Davidson had briefed Westmoreland, giving, as Carver thought, a

rather biased account of proceedings, noting our impasse on figures, saying he thought our paragraph written to avoid quantifying irregulars . . . unacceptable and outlining his draft cable by which General Westmoreland could advise General Wheeler of our inability to agree.

Carver also reported on Komer, who had his own agenda. He was insisting that the final estimate contain no specific numbers for the militia —the VC his pacification program had to work around. He stated his objection: "The press would add all the figures together and, hence, quantifying the irregulars would produce a politically unacceptable total over 400,000."

Carver met with Westmoreland on 13 September. To Carver's surprise, Westmoreland did not object to handling the irregulars in the "quantification paragraph." Agreement had been reached: the self-defense militia and the political cadre were to be marched out of the military order of battle into an explanatory paragraph. After that accommodation, it was all downhill. A final four hours of "brisk discussion" produced the language for the paragraph and the final set of figures, which by now had been pushed, pulled, and pummeled out of shape for five months.

Two products resulted. The National Intelligence Estimate for 1967 ("Capabilities of the Vietnamese Communists for Fighting in South Vietnam," published 13 November 1967 as a top secret document and in an edition smaller than the usual two hundred copies) included neither the militia nor the political cadre in the military OB. A range of 224,000 to 249,000 was presented for the enemy army. The final sentence of the report declared the Communists had the ability to "continue some forms of struggle—though at greatly reduced levels."

Nor did the next edition of the OB Book, for 1–31 October 1967, include the self-defense forces. The political cadre were placed in the last appendix to the OB Book and not counted in the OB total. As a result, the total military order of battle for the VC/NVA army was carried at 235,852, well under half what the CIA had declared to be the real military threat to our forces.

In early November, just before the NIE published its report, Adams prepared an eight-page memo for the record, sending copies to his CIA superiors and members of the research branch. The memo was a critique of the final NIE draft. He found it to be "less than candid," that it "conceals rather than edifies." He wrote, "Its history is one of attacks by soldiers and politicians, and retreats by intelligence officials." Finally, he declared the analysis made "canyons of gaps, and encourages self delusion."

In the end, it was no battle. The chief of the CIA delegation had been willing to deal; MACV had stonewalled; and the integrity of the intelligence process had been sold out.

CHAPTER

8

Ceilings

Each time the number of American troops increased, we were told about it. The cadres weren't afraid of telling us the truth about the enemy. They said we had to know the enemy if we wanted to defeat him.

> VC platoon leader
> Rand Corporation
> Interview File No. AG-643
> 11–12 October 1967

"I can't believe it! Lieutenant Jones, did you see this?" The analyst was looking at a new form that had just been distributed by a clerk from Admin. It was a mimeographed disposition form for sending our paperwork up through the chain of command.

At first glance the form was pretty much the usual kind of routing page with signature blocks all the way up the J-2 chain of command. There was one for the chief of the Order of Battle branch at CICV and a place for his Vietnamese counterpart, one for the Director of CICV, another for the Director of Intelligence Production, and finally the typed-in signature block of Phillip B. Davidson, Jr., Brigadier General, USA, Assistant Chief of Staff, J-2. At the bottom, under the title "Coordination," appeared a check-off or initial line for concur or nonconcur by CIIED.

Nothing wrong there. But at the top of the page was a bizarre paragraph:

Recommend acceptance in order of battle holdings subject unit. This addition of _____ in enemy strength does not increase total enemy strength in excess of that agreed upon at the September 1967 CIA/DIA/MACV Enemy Strength Con-

ference. (Present combat strength: _____; present total
strength: _____)

The shop was chaotic. "... What's the CIA got to do with it?...
What the hell is the DIA, anyway?... That's J-2 for the Joint Chiefs of
Staff... What the hell do they know about anything, we're the ones
who keep the records, no one asked us for nothin'!... If they're gonna
have these fucking conferences to decide all this shit, they don't need
us, so why are we busting our asses doing this goddamned paperwork
when it don't mean nothin' anyway... *Why don't they just send us
home?*"

I took the form and the men's complaints to Colonel Mac, who
scanned the sheet without much reaction, said he'd look into it, and
waved me off. The men, of course, wanted to know what the hell was
going on, but I couldn't offer anything more. Finally, I told them to
stop jawboning about it, there was nothing we could do. But I, too, felt
a deep distaste for this manipulation. It smelled of the Davidson
"downward trending" policy. If this conference had really set a limit on
the reportable size of the enemy army, it was amazing that the brass had
put it in writing. A few of the enlisted men and I hid copies of the form;
we were sure it couldn't last long.

And one or two days later into the shop came an enlisted man from
Admin handing out new disposition forms—without, of course, that
first paragraph. To our amusement, someone yelled, "Change one!" The
clerk told us he had to pick up all the copies of the "obsolete" DF. We
had a new OIC, a major (Lieutenant Thorny would be surprised when
he returned from his leave to find he was still just another go-fer). The
major, new in-country, asked me sharply, "Lieutenant, is that all of
these forms?"

Behind him, one of the EM who had also hid copies in his desk
was watching me carefully.

"Ah, sir, all the forms were stored in the file cabinet to be taken
out as needed."

When the major turned away, the EM and I exchanged glances.
Probably for the first time, the men in the shop looked on me as more
than just an ordinary spit-and-polish gung-ho lieutenant (although they
never entirely gave up that view). I had disobeyed, for the first and only
time, an order, if an indirect one, and I didn't regret it. Things were

starting to happen, inexplicable and destructive things, and that disposition form was too important to consign to a burn bag.

That was early in October or possibly in the last days of September 1967. The strange DF (see Appendix C) came and went but its philosophy remained in place.

At about the same time a wave of OB falsification struck. (I now believe this was the second wave of deliberate manipulations in our shop, that the first included the outgoing OIC's "project" in late August for which he had refused my offer of help. I think the captain was making the official changes in NVA and VC combat unit figures in the OB Book according to Colonel Graham's blue-penciling earlier that month.) Around the first of the month I wrote a letter home. It was drafted in a hurry and lacked clarity, but my frustration and anger came through:

> You'd find amazing the politics over here—we are now "reducing" enemy unit strengths because McNamara told Westmoreland told Davidson told us to do it. However unit X has 250 KIA's today and we identify it as being X. So we reduce its strength from 600 to 350. However in 2 weeks they're back up to strength. We know it but we have no proof. So we will be carrying low strength figures, and maybe our units will be fooled until they get hit by one of those "weak" units. I'm in the middle, but only take orders. I have proof of what I've been ordered to do, so they can't burn *me*.

The McNamara-to-Westmoreland connection was pure conjecture on my part; I presumed it was LBJ's policy to present the enemy as a deteriorating force. Certainly, *someone* was putting on the pressure to show we were winning. We had been ordered to apply reported body counts to enemy units known to be operating in the area, even if we didn't have the physical evidence required for such a linkage. "We know the battalion operates there, so reduce it by the body count!" Colonel Mac's voice would rise to its top decibel level when I protested that we didn't have any sources to support a strength change, and that there there would soon be replacements. His explosions always were intimidating and when they came I would do what he told me to do, even though I knew too well that I was doing exactly what my predecessor had warned me against.

Maybe it wasn't a sin to violate that SOP requiring document sources before you made an OB change. Maybe you could simply apply reported body counts to any unit known to operate in the vicinity of a "contact." But then you also had to add back a fair share of the replacements that would soon come up from lower VC units or down the trail from North Vietnam. If you didn't do at least that, you were ignoring —*suppressing*—all the evidence that showed active infiltration and rapid replacement. No one—not once, not ever—ordered or advised me to develop or use a replacement rate or formula, even while we were cutting presumed KIAs from the units.

My letter home also had this paragraph:

> Last night at 1700, we were all called into the Col's office to be told Gen'l Davidson (Chief of Intel) wanted a recent project re-done. It was a study of Bn's [battalions] in each corps that were once #1 and are now ineffective. I turned in 2. They were the only ones approved and the Gen'l used the one I wrote up for the guide to the others. So I got some much needed praise after a great deal of burdensome work.

Documents did show these units to be ineffective, but no one was asking how long it would take for their losses to be replaced. Davidson had come down on CICV because only the I Corps shop turned in such reports. He wanted them from the other three corps, and he used my submittal to pressure the other OICs. They made clear their displeasure with me for having provided a tool to reduce the OB further. Apparently the other shops had no firm reports on ineffective units, but now they suddenly had to produce something. At least one OIC held out and did not respond.

Defensively, I felt I had carried out my orders. The command knew what it was doing, right? If a unit was ineffective, it was *ineffective*. Right? Right . . .

Later, when we had the new OB Book, it was Shore, of course, who noted the consequences of my report. "Lieutenant Jones, remember those temporarily ineffective units we turned in? Well, their strength has been cut all to hell in the new OB Book!"

I looked at it and grimaced. We had submitted only reports showing supply and morale problems, or that a unit had disengaged for rest and refit. We had not given MACV any lowered unit numbers.

"It'll be a long time, sir, before we get documents to return these units to their real strength."

"Yeah, I know." There was nothing else I could say. I had been had. My sense of pride for having produced a "model" had turned sour indeed.

At the end of the year I read the MACV Office of Information's 1967 wrap-up on a "Year of Progress," which reported "about 30 percent" of the enemy's maneuver battalions were "considered not combat effective." But after the October exercise there had been no further studies, and CICV's report couldn't have offered any more than a handful of "ineffective" units out of the 160 VC/NVA maneuver and 41 combat support units then being carried. (Many years later I learned that on 22 November 1967 Westmoreland had declared in his Pentagon briefing that "the effectiveness of these units according to our intelligence estimates has been degraded" and that 45 percent of them were "combat ineffective.")

During this period of OB manipulations, I once went to the Caravelle Hotel downtown, where most of the press stayed. Sipping a drink at the roof restaurant, I hoped a reporter would strike up a conversation so that, off the record, I could pour out my story about the OB gamesmanship at MACV. It didn't happen. It was a fantasy.

I knew it would be "disloyal" and "insubordinate" to reveal even such shabby secrets as were current at J-2. And the press might not believe me, or would get it wrong, or would reveal me as the source . . .

I didn't seek out a journalist, nor did I write any more complaining letters home. I wanted to believe the brass was right. As we'd been told so often, signal intelligence was our ace weapon. Maybe the HQ knew more than we did from the documents, maybe replacement of losses wasn't all that easy for the Reds . . . *maybe* . . .

Always, in the end, there is that faith in the system and the loyalty and discipline that have been indoctrinated into every soldier. You believe because you want to, need to, because you have to.

The bus I rode to work also carried many of the Viet women translators to their jobs in document processing at CDEC. On that bus I met Miss My. Sitting with a girlfriend, she was giggling like a schoolgirl, hiding her face discreetly behind her hand, as she flirted with me.

I went back to say hello. Thereafter we rode together every day through the monsoon season. I always formally called her Miss My, but our courtship was like junior high school, with much flirting and laughing. Weeks passed before we touched. She saw a mosquito bite on my hand and with exaggerated attention, tenderly rubbed it. With the rain pouring outside and as the nearly empty bus passed Independence Palace, finally we kissed.

For months no more than an occasional kiss could happen, but the romance was an exquisite island in the turbulence of Saigon. But she could never take me to her home near the Phu Tho racetrack; her mother hated Americans.

Not until the Christmas holidays did she shyly tell me her friends were having a party and because of the curfew we would have to stay with them overnight. It took me a while to understand that this was what she had told her mother; she was telling me that we needed a room.

Ours became a special relationship, but as an Army brat I'd met several war brides and I knew of the high divorce rate for overseas marriages. I held my feelings in reserve, even as Miss My helped preserve my sanity during that impossible year. In the end, I left her behind. In that, also, is guilt.

On 18 October we received a tasking to provide input to the J-2 on how to improve the efficiency of the center. I responded with a blunt memo that blamed the 519th MI Battalion and CICV administrative details for consuming an incredible fifteen days a month for each enlisted analyst. These highly trained, invaluable specialists were being wasted on guard duty, training exercises, and miscellaneous details, while the compound's own enlisted men were exempt from additional duty.

I also bemoaned the tremendous duplication of intelligence and operational summaries coming from all the various headquarters. The INTSUMs, DISUMs, and advisories were largely built upon the same sources, but each summary was sent out in quantity to an army of readers. I proposed that a MACV HQ team receive all the base material and produce a single "Daily Intelligence Journal" (similar to the COC's daily journal, which was updated as needed) to reduce the flow of paper, and to provide more reliable reporting and a historical record.

The journal never happened, but there was some lessening of the demands placed on our analysts. And I enjoyed bucking the 519th.

Anyway, it was no longer my responsibility to worry about all things. I was shifting back into my Projects Officer role. After having had two majors who stayed only days before reassignment, we got one on 16 October who was to run the shop for several months. This was Major Norman House.[1] It took only a few days for us to get to know this new and temperamental OIC who, as he told us, had transferred from the Air Force into the Army for better career opportunities. Probably in his late thirties, he had graying hair and something of a gray outlook on life. I found him to be efficient, but I wrote home that he operated on a "short fuse." I hadn't had my first chewing-out yet, but he'd already accused one of the other lieutenants of being an incompetent and not worthy of being an officer. I tried to keep away from him and his temper tantrums, but as a result office efficiency suffered from poor communication.

The pace of the war was increasing and everyone's temper showed the strain. There was camaraderie in the field, but not in the Saigon puzzle palaces. There we fought our own wars against each other, and we all lost.

The 519th decided that too many of its .45s had been issued. By 23 October they were all recalled, including mine. I was assigned the responsibility of escorting them to the Plum Farm for storage. Boring duty, except that I was accountable for the handguns during transit.

Traffic was heavy, and when our truck got bogged down I got nervous. Coming up next to us was a pick-up full of black-pajamaed and blue-jeaned young Vietnamese men, nine of them, several of them with weapons. VC did not drive around in broad daylight, but a bunch of cowboys with guns was still not a welcome sight. Then I saw that not only did they have carbines and pistols, they also had guitars, drums, and bongos. This was, indeed, a strange group, even for the streets of Saigon. With the lull in traffic, I jumped out of the truck and approached them, cautiously, with my camera. They cheered and posed for some quick photos, waving as we rapidly departed when traffic opened.

Back at CICV I related this encounter and a senior sergeant said, with his most serious face, "You know what that was, don't you?"

"What?" I asked eagerly.

Without any change of expression he replied, "Why, a guerrilla band, of course!"

During the last days of October, after work several of us who lived at the Meyerkord were able to get a jeep, rarely available to junior officers. Before commuting back to our billets one evening, we heard Vice President Hubert Humphrey had just landed at Tan Son Nhut. He had come to Saigon to represent the United States at the inauguration of Thieu and Ky. Outside CICV on the continuation of Cong Ly Avenue were numerous Viet and American security forces waiting for the Humphrey delegation. Hoping to beat his convoy into town, we squeezed past a barricade, while an ARVN guard watched impassively, and pushed the jeep as fast as it would go.

A portion of Cong Ly was a beautiful tree-lined boulevard, very European in feel. The police had cleared it of traffic and the stillness was unsettling. The canopied tree tunnel aimed like an artillery bore at downtown, and we nervously kept a lookout behind us for the diplomatic barrage soon to come.

I saw a sedan shooting up on our rear and yelled, "Oh, shit, here he comes, pull off the road quick!" Like Keystone Kops, we tumbled out of the vehicle, bumping into each other, not knowing what to do.

"Ten-hut! Salute!" I improvised as the black sedan led by a strangely silent escort bore down on us at some seventy miles an hour. Front and back were motorcycles driven by the "ice cream men," the white-uniformed guards of the Viet presidential palace. As I'd noticed with Westmoreland's car a few weeks earlier, there were no American MPs in the escort.

I tried to get a glimpse of the round face of America's favorite talkative uncle, or maybe Westmoreland or Ky. But the V.I.P.s were safely tucked behind bulletproof one-way windows, shiny as mirrors. The second motorcycle driver glanced at us with a bored expression, then the bullet motorcade was gone like a puff of smoke. I suggested that we wait a little, nervously joking that we could avoid any VC ambushes that way.

A day or so later a VC ambush was a reality. Lieutenant Klcin and I were walking by Independence Palace as, inside, preparations were being made for the inauguration festivities on National Day.

The sound of *whomp-whomp-whomp-whomp* froze our steps. Mortars, we agreed. A weird silence followed, but the advisability of seeking cover never occurred to us. When I told this story at CICV, no one believed the VC could just walk into Saigon and mortar the palace. Not until we received the report in the Command Operations Center's journal was I regarded as a minor hero, the first in our shop to "come under fire." The entry reported:

> In GIA DINH Province in SAIGON at 311940H, the Presidential Palace came under mortar attack. One Australian vehicle driver killed and one building minor damaged. Fin assemblies of two 60mm Mortar rds were found on the palace grounds. The mortar pos from which rds were fired was located approximately one km from palace at 141 TON THAT TAM Street, one rd exploded in the tube killing one en [enemy]. Three other persons were observed fleeing the vicinity. One male civ (VN) who had sounded the alarm at the mortar site was killed by the en. RES [result]: FRD [friendly] —two killed (one Australian, one VN civ): one building minor damage; EN —one killed, one 60mm Mortar dest.

Charlie can't even pop off a few rounds without screwing up, I thought—how can he expect to win the war!

By no means was I immune from our arrogant headquarters disdain for the enemy.

Early in November we received an unconfirmed field report that held out the possibility of Chinese Communist troops in the boonies and repeated the old legend about VC Caucasians (Frenchmen) that surfaced from time to time. But reports on the indigenous VC irregulars were more solidly based. Down the hall at CICV in a small room at the back of the building sat Lieutenant Richard McArthur, who, largely on his own, was responsible for developing estimates of the guerrillas and the self-defense forces. I found him bitter about how his estimates were being ignored or downgraded. (This was to continue even into 1968. When he returned from R-and-R in March, McArthur found that his superiors had cut his estimates in half. He protested to his boss and was told, "Lie a little, Mac." He refused, and was soon transferred to a new position, in charge of a supply warehouse.)[2]

Numbers games were also being played with the analysts working on the political infrastructure. Lieutenant Kelly Robinson was responsible for most of this work and from him I obtained a paper entitled "What Is the Infrastructure?" This study analyzed a hamlet to demonstrate the typical VC program. It concluded that "the ultimate mission of the revolutionary forces, the control of the people, has been obtained in Quang Nhgiem Hamlet. If it can be done so quickly and so apparently effortlessly at the hamlet level, what is to stop it at the National level?"

Indeed. But early in November we received the new OB Book, the MACV Monthly Order of Battle Summary, for 1–31 October 1967, which deleted both the self-defense forces and the political cadre[3] from the military order of battle. The deletion was inexplicable to us in I Corps, even with our bias for combat maneuver units. Someone said something about that damned disposition form, the conference in September.

In the military, "change one" is a way of life. But this time the changes went beyond mere bureaucratic process. "Downward trending," as established in General Davidson's memo of 15 August 1967, had permeated all the corners of J-2.

9

Smoke and Mirrors

Major Major had lied and it was good.... Had he told the
truth . . . he would have found himself in trouble. Instead, he
had lied and he was free to continue his work.

Joseph Heller
Catch-22

From 9 to 13 September, MACV J-2 had gained the advantage over the
CIA during the final debates over the National Intelligence Estimates.
Now the last hurdle was the press, and for about two months head-
quarters carefully developed its plan of escape and evasion. Not until 24
November 1967 did MACV go public with a justification of its new OB
at the infamous "Five O'Clock Follies," the daily briefing at the MACV
Office of Information, where its chief, General Winant Sidle, presented
his optimistic interpretations of the war.

The presentation was a deft mixture of truth, partial truth, and
gross misrepresentation. It was replete with references to a "new study"
and "newest intelligence." Not only were the irregulars declared to be
declining in number, but Sidle even announced that "in retroactively
adjusting our estimates as a result primarily of prisoner interrogations
and captured documents, we now estimate that VC/NVA regular
strength peaked at about 127,000 in September 1966 and has since
declined slightly" to 118,000. This statement was made even as the
indicators of a countrywide offensive were coming in and a massive
surge of infiltration from the North was being detected. Interestingly,
Sidle had based the MACV claims on PW interrogations and captured
documents, not the precious "all-source" or "special" intelligence that
was available only to the select few.

Sidle claimed that "our new, greatly broadened intelligence base
has permitted a more realistic evaluation" of enemy strength, which he

stated as between 223,000 and 258,000. "We believe that this represents a decline in total enemy order of battle," said the general, thus completing an exercise of a classic military tactic: a plausible deviation from the truth as necessary.

An October draft of this press briefing had been critiqued at the CIA by Paul Walsh, Deputy Director of the Office of Economic Research, who called it "one of the greatest snow jobs," filled with "vulnerable intelligence judgments that cannot be substantiated at this time and promise almost certainly to lead to even graver credibility problems than the current debate over the order of battle."[1] Even George Carver, who had facilitated the September sessions, stated that the CIA had "serious substantive and procedural problems" which meant the agency "cannot support it or concur in its use."[2] But the draft was not appreciably changed.

Westmoreland himself contributed to the press relations campaign. On 11 November, the general told the press in Saigon that enemy strength had dropped from 285,000 to 242,000. He displayed a bar graph comparing enemy strength in 1965, 1966, and 1967; the numbers used for these years were 207,000, 285,000, and 242,000. (This chart —see Appendix D—had been prepared shortly after the September conference in Saigon. Secretary McNamara wanted a retroactive comparison for three years of the enemy strengths, using only the categories then to be included in the OB Book; that is, the main forces, the guerrillas, and the service units. The request went to DIA but was then taken back to Davidson in Saigon. For a full day, officers worked at a blackboard creating totals and components that were consistent with the NIE draft then being circulated. The resulting chart was based neither on archives intelligence nor battlefield realities.) Reporting on this briefing, the *New York Times* headline read, U.S. AIDES SAY FOE'S STRENGTH AND MORALE DECLINING FAST. *Stars and Stripes* also reported this new estimate.

LBJ had called Westmoreland home again for another round of speechmaking. In his memoirs the general has described the trip as "ostensibly for consultations, but in reality for public relations purposes," noting that "dissent in the press and the Congress was growing."[3] At Andrews Air Force Base on 15 November he was asked what he was going to tell the president. He replied, "I frankly don't have anything specific in mind—merely a report on the situation in South Vietnam as I see it." And his view was this:

I've never been more encouraged during my entire almost
four years in country. I think we are making real progress.
Everyone is very optimistic that I know of who is intimately
associated with the effort there.

Westmoreland spent that night at the White House and the next
morning conferred with LBJ before going to Congress to address the
Senate and House Armed Forces Committees. During dinner at the
White House, he briefed members of Congress while Johnson watched.
Assisted by Walt Rostow, national security advisor, the general used
numerous charts, which Rostow later described as "the best data available" and "evidence of progress."
Two days later Westmoreland told Steven Rowan of CBS:

The consensus is that the enemy is being weakened and our
side is growing stronger. . . . It is also evident from captured
documents and from interrogations of defectors and prisoners
of war. There is evidence that the enemy is beginning to realize that he cannot win.

He added that there was "evidence" of "manpower problems" for the
enemy in both the North and South. An article in the *Washington Daily
News* by Jim Lucas carried the headline, WESTMORELAND: THE ENEMY IS
RUNNING OUT OF MEN.
On the nineteenth, the general and Ambassador Ellsworth Bunker
appeared on NBC's *Meet the Press*. Their theme was the Allies were
"winning a war of attrition now." Westmoreland again cited "evidence"
of "very serious manpower problems" in the North and South. Robert
Goralski of NBC News challenged this, saying that the enemy had "replaced man for man all the men they have lost." The general replied
with a denial: "Actually there has been a reduction in strength of the
enemy during the past year. A year ago, of his maneuver battalions, we
considered most of them combat effective. Now we consider only about
55 percent combat effective." The program's moderator, Lawrence E.
Spivak, noted that a year ago the NVA infiltration rate was said to be
7,000 a month. Westmoreland responded that the current rate was
"5,500 to 6,000 a month, but they do have the capability of stepping
this up." (MACV analysts had been reporting a "stepping up" to 20,000
soldiers a month.)

On 21 November, the general addressed the National Press Club, saying, "We have reached an important point when the end begins to come into view," and "today he is certainly losing. The enemy's hopes are bankrupt." He saw the enemy forces "steadily declining," with the guerrilla force "declining at a steady rate." In his autobiography, *A Soldier Reports*, Westmoreland describes this as his "most important public presentation during this visit"; "I permitted myself the most optimistic appraisal of the way the war was going that I had yet made."[4]

On the twenty-second the general briefed the press at the Pentagon and quoted numbers from the MACV press release that was to be distributed by General Sidle in Saigon. A series of charts was used, including the bar graph comparing enemy-strength figures in 1965, 1966, and 1967. Westmoreland again declared that in the third quarter of 1967 "there has been a reduction," not in the number of units but in their "effectiveness" being degraded "according to our intelligence estimates." He repeated his claim that "approximately 45 percent" of the enemy force was "combat ineffective." He later added that this was "a fluctuating matter" which "can change very rapidly."

A reporter at this session—unnamed in the transcript—commented that the "question of enemy strength and what it means" was "fundamental for our understanding." Though put off by Westmoreland's claim that the study was "not fully completed yet," he persisted in adding up the omitted categories, getting a "gain in strength." But before the reporter could complete his question, Westmoreland said, "Well, gentlemen, I ask that we defer any further questions on this because of this study that I referred to which I think will clarify this and I'm afraid anything that I say now could be more confusing than helpful."

Another question asked for something to give a "greater sense of confidence" in the new figures as compared to those in the past that had "proven wrong." Westmoreland replied, "It's been an honest effort, and I stand by the figures that I have given you as the best and most honest that I can come up with. . . ."

During Westmoreland's trip, Neil Sheehan of the *New York Times* criticized the general for declining to "give detailed evidence to support his contention that total enemy forces were declining." Another writer was also unconvinced by the MACV claims. Andrew Hamilton went to an old contact in the CIA—ironically, Sam Adams—who advised him to read the release over and over again until it became clearer. In "The

Numbers Game," which appeared in *The New Republic* in December 1967, Hamilton added up all the OB categories to find an enemy army "much larger than previously suspected," some 30 percent larger. He concluded that Westmoreland's "performance" during the speechmaking tour "should be assessed as part of a political campaign, not as a candid review of the war situation."

Writers for *Newsweek* uncovered a bit more of the cover-up in a review of the war during 1967, published in the issue of 1 January 1968.

> . . . the U.S. command in Saigon believes that Hanoi has not been able to keep pace with the Viet Cong's attrition rate and that, as a consequence, total enemy troop strength has declined over the past year. Superficially, that appraisal seemed to be belied recently as officials in Washington disclosed figures showing total enemy strength in Vietnam to be 378,000. (Last year's official figure was 280,000.) All this really suggested, however, was that last year's figures had been deceptive. In November, after months of haggling among intelligence experts, the U.S. drastically revised its method of calculating enemy strength. As a result, meaningful comparisons with previous manpower estimates have now become all but impossible.

The "haggling" had been uncovered and discrepancies in reports on the enemy army noted, but these journalists had not discovered the gross falsification behind the "drastic" revision. It was only too true that "meaningful comparisons" of the order of battle were now a thing of the past. That in fact was the ultimate purpose of MACV's maneuvers, and MACV had pulled it off.

PART THREE

Pre-Tet

1 NOVEMBER 1967—29 JANUARY 1968

Nineteen sixty-seven was a year of progress. . . . By year's end, enemy strength was at the lowest level since 1965 or early 1966. And about 30 percent of his maneuver battalions were considered not combat effective.

> Military Assistance Command
> Office of Information
> "1967 Wrap-Up—A Year of Progress"

Yes, We Are Winning
(sung to the tune of "Jesus Loves You")

We are winning this we know
McNamara told us so
In the Delta we are rough
In the Highlands we are tough
But they are weak and we are strong
Heaven help the Viet Cong.

Chorus:
Yes, we are winning
Yes, we are winning
Yes, we are winning
Westmoreland tells us so.

> Author unknown

10

Thanksgiving

> The war, it would seem, is unwinnable in a much deeper
> sense than is commonly realized. It is not that our forces can-
> not defeat the enemy's forces in battle. It is that the battles
> they fight cannot decide the war.
>
> Walter Lippmann
> *Newsweek*, 1 January 1968

> We have reached an important point when the end begins to
> come into view.
>
> General William C. Westmoreland
> to the National Press Club,
> 21 November 1967

On 15 November I finally had a complete day off, my first since arrival. It was a glorious chance to sleep in until 1000 hours, take a slow
breakfast, and walk downtown with my new Canon, taking pictures of
the people, especially of the children, whose exuberance transcended
the war and poverty around them. I saw an Aussie rock show at the
USO, which I described in a letter as having "beaucoup healthy round-
eyed girls!" Then a late dinner at a fine French restaurant with Chateaubriand, a salad of fresh butter lettuce just in from Dalat, and baked
Alaska.

A letter from my father had urged me to "minimize all exposure."
Stay in, be safe! But it was not easy advice to follow. With the post-
election quiet, I was out at least one night a week. The bar girls and
their ridiculous Saigon tea were a diversion, though costly. But mostly I
enjoyed the exotic shops. A Vietnam specialty was lacquered goods
with designs often enhanced with cleverly placed bits of eggshell, and I
purchased vases, trays, and photo albums. Vietnam was a land of artists; I found some fine oil paintings, most notably, one of a young Viet
boy huddled fearfully in the corner of a hut.

Downtown Saigon fascinated me, from its fields of parked Hondas that looked like used-bike lots to the fine off-white colonial government buildings on the broad tree-lined avenues. In its core, the "Paris of the Orient" seemed less used and tarnished, still clinging to remnants of its European-style elegance. The swirl of people and traffic was especially rich around the huge roofed-over public market, an exquisite jumble of food, produce, goods and art, laced with stunning fish smells. Like all visitors to Saigon, I loved the legendary Continental Plaza Hotel, where I lounged on wicker chairs under the slowly spinning ceiling fans in its open-to-the-air restaurant behind the columned front. Sipping a gin and tonic, watching slender women in their *ao dai* and mini-skirts, you could forget the order-of-battle abstractions, the body counts. When an old legless or armless cripple, left over from one of the countless battles, tried to peddle his crudely drawn pornographic books or garish water-color-on-silk portraits of rural Vietnamese life, you could purchase his absence with a few piasters.

At one of the black market spreads, where contraband was laid out on straw mats along the sidewalk, casual as could be, was a much coveted green-and-black-swirled camouflaged poncho liner ("Liner, Poncho, DSA–100–3923"). A label warned:

> *CAUTION:* Do not fasten the snap fasteners together when used as a sleeping bag in combat areas; it cannot be opened quickly. . . .

There was a real war out there, and men had to be ready to move every second. But the Saigon Warrior could take his Renault taxi downtown to grab up a real-honest-to-God souvenir poncho liner to use as comforter on his BOQ cot or to spread under a picnic feast in a Saigon park. The men in the field had reasons for calling us REMFs—Rear Echelon Mother Fuckers.

Ironically, on my first day off, my father was writing to me about combat fatigue:

> Keep loose, soldier—try hard during work hours—then go easy and rest long hours even if sleep is hard to get—otherwise there is cumulative fatigue even in staff work—usually aggravated, not helped, by a sense of compulsion to blow off

steam somehow—usually with whiskey and parties—dangerous "safety valves"!

While sitting in the plaza of the Continental Hotel sipping a "33"
beer (the good bars removed the label so you could check for unusual
debris), I wrote in my own letter that the pressure at CICV was "profound" but that I enjoyed it "to a degree." I added that "one learns how
to balance resources and capabilities against deadlines" and concluded
that it's "quite a trick."

Even with trips into the nightlife and the occasional steambath, I
was feeling that nagging tiredness from intensive routine without
enough break. It would get much worse.

During November I came up with a better way to compile the
several overlapping monthly summaries. With the new major's support,
I issued this tasking:

Each province analyst will submit to the Projects Officer a 1
page (or more) wrap-up on his province [for the month]. This
is a "big picture" summary *including:*

1. Logistical shortages (esp. rice)
2. Info on rockets, if any
3. Decreased combat effectiveness of units, and reasons
4. ALL CONFIRMED CONTACTS
5. Possible plans for the units
6. Current known missions, if new
7. *TRENDS!*

These wrap-ups were to be placed in a three-ring binder for each
province, along with general information on shop process and the geo-
graphic area. This material would grow into a useful data base and offer
our replacements an aid in learning their jobs. The lack of such a guide
had hampered my indoctrination, and I wanted the deficiency corrected.

The emphasis on *"TRENDS!"* was timely. Increasing evidence
showed that the Ho Chi Minh Trail[1] was alive with infiltrators and that a
major build-up of NVA soldiers was in progress. For example, we had a
Rand Corporation interview, dated 15 November, with an NVA platoon

leader captured on 24 August, only days before I started at CICV. Even that early, he reported poetically, "Material and men kept coming to the south like water running in a rapids."[2]

Beginning in mid-November I got a taste of what this escalation was all about.[3] I was given the assignment of estimating how many NVA personnel were then filling the ranks of all the Viet Cong units (those units that had been created in South Vietnam from indigenous rebels). The Hanoi leadership had consistently insisted that the war was being fought solely by the southern-born VC, that it was a true "people's revolution" from within. MACV decided it was important to counter that assertion with some numbers.

It was unusual for a Corps analyst to be selected to do a country-wide study. Perhaps it had been noted that my projects were on time and of respectable quality. So, at least, I wanted to believe.

I had the job but not the methodology. Unsure how to proceed, I discussed the assignment with my ARVN counterparts. They huddled and went into their files. Then Lieutenant Tri came to me with some documents.

"Lieutenant Jones, I have way to help. These, you call unit rosters. They show, many times, place of birth."

It was so simple that it was brilliant. I jumped up and grasped Tri's shoulders, thanking him profusely. These lists of personnel were worth their weight in gold, revealing as they did strength status at the time. We didn't have a lot of them, but enough were gathered from the four shops to permit analysis. The ARVNs determined whether the village or hamlet was in the North or South, and finally we developed an average of 25 percent for the entire nation—in other words, about a quarter of each Viet Cong unit in SVN was then composed of NVA personnel. No one had suspected the percentage was so high.

Colonel Mac was impressed and asked how I had come up with the approach. Pleased, I told him about the ARVNs' contribution. When he frowned, I added that I was smart enough to recognize a good idea.

"Just like you, sir, right?" I smiled broadly.

But he had a surprise for me. After my first internal CICV briefing when I emphasized the consistency of the 25 percent finding across three of the four war zones (there was a lower percentage in IV Corps, the Mekong Delta), Colonel Mac announced that we should be "conservative" in our findings.

The 25 percent became 10 percent. Perhaps the real number reflected too rapid a rate for replacement of losses. So we were to err on the side of "caution"; some call it massaging the numbers. I took the briefing up through the CICV Director, Colonel Edward Halpin; then to Colonel Morris, Chief of Intelligence Production; and General Davidson, Assistant Chief of Staff, J-2. I was scheduled at least twice to brief the COMUSMACV but the pace of the war was increasing. Westmoreland had other things to do.

My work was praised and my ego suitably inflated. After one compliment from no less than Davidson himself, I boldly blurted out, "And that's a conservative finding! We even found a report of an NVA replacement going into a guerrilla unit!" Colonel Mac glared, and outside he ordered me to stick to the script. Thereafter, I dutifully did.

Later in November MACV received the first captured attack order for the coming winter-spring offensive, this one for Quang Tin province in I Corps. It declared:

> Central Headquarters concludes that the time has come for direct revolution and that the opportunity for a general offensive and general uprising is within reach. . . . Use very strong military tactics in coordination with the uprisings of the local population to take over towns and cities. Troops should flood the lowlands. They should move toward liberating the capital city, take power, and try to rally enemy brigades and regiments to our side one by one. Propaganda should be broadly disseminated among the population in general, and leaflets should be used to reach enemy officers and enlisted personnel.[4]

VC sources frequently made grand promises and claims, probably to give their troops a sense of momentum and impending victory. We took note of them only when they started to accumulate and could be called true indicators of the enemy's intentions and capabilities.

They would soon begin to pile up, and we would report our findings. But it all would be for nothing.

"Qui, today is American holiday—Thanksgiving."
"Yes? Thanksgiving?"
"Yes."
"What is this?"

"Well, a long time ago when the U.S. was new, the men who just came from Europe to be Americans invited the Indians—you know, Indians?"

"Yes, yes, like Montagnards."

"O.K. They invited them in for a big number-one dinner with beaucoup turkey-bird, and corn and potatoes and pies. You know, number-one dinner."

"Yes, number one."

"And this dinner was for peace and brotherhood and good relations."

"Yes, very good. What happened?"

"What happened?"

"Yes."

"Well, after that we spent the next couple of hundred years killing them all off, that's what happened. Like the movies, you know? Cowboys and Indians?"

"Yes, I know. You zap Indians."

"Yeah, for sure. We zap Indians. All finis."

He paused. "I think ARVNs don't go to dinner with you!" We laughed, but it wasn't just a joke. There was a lesson there, and Aspirant Qui seemed to have caught it. Later in conversation the extent of the American commitment to Vietnam came up and I suggested to my counterparts that we would not be here forever, that the GVN was going to have to carry the load itself someday. The ARVNs seemed distressed and apparently passed the view into their chain of command and it came back down through ours.

"Jones, what the hell you been telling the ARVNs? That we're gonna pull out and leave them on their own?"

Embarrassed, I replied, "Well, isn't that the idea, like Westy says, an ultimate phase-out?"

"Don't worry about phase-outs—just take care of your OB, all right, Jones?"

"Yes, sir." Sure. Wasn't my problem.

Early in November, on the third, the fighting around the small town of Dak To—and the Special Forces camp nearby—in the Central Highlands of II Corps began in all its fury, the most costly of the "border battles"[5] that preceded the Tet offensive. On the day fighting began, an NVA sergeant came over to us and laid out in detail the plans of his division to hold the terrain and inflict major losses on the Allies.

The II Corps personnel read the detailed PW interrogation with surprise and suspicion. The defector gave so much, so readily, that the analysts were sure he was a plant. Still, his information matched other indicators: the North Vietnamese were dug in to stay and fight, no matter what we threw at them. This engagement was to be a conventional-warfare set piece, not the usual hit-and-run VC tactics. It almost seemed that General Giap was making sure we knew where he was, wanting us to come after him. We shook our heads in wonderment that the enemy would so foolishly expose himself in a position vulnerable to our tremendous firepower.

Dak To was one of the hardest, bloodiest, and most controversial battles of the war. For twenty brutal days, it seemed like Korea and Porkchop Hill all over again. Our troops fought inch by inch up steep slopes rising to 1,300 meters. Under double and triple canopies, the dense vegetation and gloom concealed the tunnels and bunkers which the NVA 1st Division had been preparing for up to a half year; nearly every key feature of the terrain was heavily fortified with bunkers, trenches, and supplies. The dug-in enemy engaged the U.S. and ARVN force of 16,000 men until 23 November, Thanksgiving Day. The heaviest fighting began on 19 November as elements of the 173d Airborne assaulted Hill 875, which had a more gradual slope and less dense tree cover than other hills in the area. But Hill 875 may have been the enemy's most thoroughly entrenched defensive position. In five days some 300 NVA were reported dead, with 158 U.S. dead and 402 wounded. On the twenty-third, the advancing Americans met little resistance. The NVA had used their tunnels and caves to pull out during the night.[6]

At CICV we heard that the division's band had marched down the streets of Dak To village to reassure the frightened Vietnamese even as the fighting raged. The story seemed bizarre enough to be true.

It was all a parade, and we marched to a cadence that was not our own. At CICV and MACV, removed from the physical agonies of those hill battles, only one refrain was heard: Giap was finally moving into the classic form of conventional warfare, seeking his Dien Bien Phu of the Second Indochinese War. It was so clear to us at headquarters that at last Giap had begun his long-planned third phase of "counteroffensive," following "contention" and "equilibrium." This was what Westmoreland had always wanted. Now we could pour our massive fire down on the enemy with effect and engage him in place.

The border locations of these intensive battles surely demonstrated that Giap was looking for victories at the outer edge of our control, where supply and evacuation were the most difficult for us and easiest for him. It seemed we now knew what to expect in I Corps and across South Vietnam.

So we thought and so Giap wanted us to think. Step by step, he led us into the Tet offensive.

Saigon was quiet at Thanksgiving and I got my holiday dinner at a decent feast put out by the compound. I didn't mind going back to the French Foreign Legion for good food, and the military always tries to do right by its troops during holidays, as was described in a MACV publication of the period:

> Despite battles raging from the North to the South of this war-torn nation, the 1st Logistical Command delivered 57,000 whole turkeys and 325 tons of boneless turkey meat plus all the fixings of the traditional Thanksgiving feast. The impressive figures included 28 tons of cranberry sauce, 15 tons of nuts, 8 tons of candy, 11 of olives and 33 of fruitcake. Grateful troops paused in battle to give thanks to God for their blessings and enjoy the bounty of a free nation.

But on Hill 875 the remnants of the 173d Airborne were too exhausted to pause to give thanks for any blessing but simple survival. To mark the end of the carnage at Dak To, our men had their hot turkey Thanksgiving dinners airlifted in by American helicopters. In a few days we would withdraw from the hill; in the end, the battles were *not* like Korea. MACV would report a total of 1,641 NVA dead and 289 Americans and 73 ARVNs killed in action.

The enemy KIA report was as valid as any other. But the friendly-loss report was, I came to understand, an unmitigated lie.

One night in the week of Thanksgiving, I was OD (officer of the day) at one of the 519th's supply depots. Waiting for my ride the next morning, I walked over to a warehouse the GIs called the Red Ball Express. The term had originated during our drive into Germany in World War II, and meant a fast, around-the-clock supply route. Maybe it was applied here because in this warehouse were stored the personal effects of our KIA until shipment to next-of-kin—death was the fastest way home.

I walked past shelves and rows of boxes. A name, serial number, and address were written neatly in black marker on each box. Shelf after shelf, row after row.

A young black sergeant approached me.

"Kind of depressing work," I offered.

"Yes, sir, it is. We don't talk much about our job after hours like other people."

I asked what was the average number of boxes processed each week. He didn't know, but since the Dak To battle had started, he said, the work load had been huge. MACV had reported our total losses as under three hundred, but in one week, the sergeant told me bitterly, Red Ball had processed some seven hundred boxes of personal effects!

I was stunned. I asked if maybe the KIA were from all across the country. He shook his head. No, they had all come from Dak To.

Could we have lost as many, or more, men than had the NVA during those twenty days? Had most of the American dead from Dak To been added to the KIA count for Operation MacArthur, which had gone on for weeks, and would for several more, and which covered much more area than just Dak To? The dead would ultimately be reported, but spread out so you wouldn't notice all those bodies on a couple of hills during another of our "victories."

The press was criticizing Dak To. Too many men had died, some wrote. But the reporters didn't know the half of it.

This time the smoke and mirrors didn't quite get me. I believed what I'd heard from that one NCO at Red Ball more than I believed the American military headquarters. I think my disenchantment began that day. Or at least I began to notice it.

On 23 November, *Stars and Stripes* jubilantly declared that the enemy army was in decline. On the day before Thanksgiving, MACV had released to the press its "latest study" on the "broader intelligence" regarding the enemy army. These were the figures brokered at the September NIE meeting.

We were *winning*. The enemy army was *down*. The "cross-over" point had been reached and Westmoreland had gone back to the States to put out the good word. The light at the end of the tunnel was shining!

The report was discussed in bemused, cynical terms at CICV. Where the hell had all the VC/NVA *gone?*

On Thanksgiving Day, I had a late afternoon call from my old classmate Lieutenant Swandby. He and a buddy were coming into Saigon and they needed a bed and some R-and-R. They'd meet me at the Meyerkord Hotel.

I waited outside and saw them roar up in a jeep. Covered with red dust, M-16s slung over their backs, sporting flakjackets and camouflaged helmets, these spooks looked like honest-to-God *soldiers*. We were climbing the stairs while I wondered where to put them up.

As we got to the second floor, coming out of a room with an ice tray was Colonel Maggie, the Old Lady of the Boondocks—AKA Martha Raye.

"Hi, men! Just in from the field? You look muddier than a rice paddy! I was just borrowing some ice from the colonel, but he doesn't know it! He's asleep! Now that I've got it, maybe you'll join me for a drink!" Her delivery was a staccato of high energy, making each sentence seem funny.

This was the second time I'd seen her at the hotel. A few days earlier I had come into the lobby to find a second lieutenant with a stunned expression saying to no one in particular, "I didn't know the Special Forces had *women!*"

I looked at him strangely until around the corner came Martha Raye in her beret and tiger suit with Special Forces insignia and a lieutenant colonel's silver leaf. Her special love of the Green Berets had earned her the honorary rank and uniform from her men. She'd even made a parachute jump with them! In her extended annual trips to Nam she was the only entertainer who went to the smallest bases way out in the boonies. She had been under fire many times and legend had it that the Viet Cong had a price on her head. For her bravery in the field, including often working as a nurse in medic tents during attacks, she was lovingly called the "Old Lady of the Boondocks." It was a title she cherished.

My guests were stunned by the encounter. I had the great pleasure of making the introductions, and I learned you did not refer to her stage name. In Nam it was only Maggie. All Irish, she was born Maggie Theresa O'Reed. "Martha Raye" was some other person who had had one of the hit variety shows during the Golden Age of television, who made movies, and who was one of the great jazz singers. Here in Nam she was mother and friend to thousands of troops just as she had been for the men in Korea (where my father had seen her) and in World War II (the movie *Four Jills in a Jeep* was based on her USO tours during the war).

Maggie moved us into the USO lounge, the closest thing to luxury my guests had seen since we had arrived in Nam, with a bar, refrigerator, TV, carpets. She stacked their weapons in a corner and proceeded to make us honored guests. The EM jeep driver, a polite country boy from the Midwest, had probably thought the Saigon trip was going to be just another drive; he wound up in Maggie's shower with a drink delivered by herself. Then he just sat in the lounge with a series of drinks and grinned. He asked me more than once, "Is this for real, sir?"

I asked Maggie where she lived and she replied, "Vietnam!" Her trips were three months out of every year (with only per diem pay of some twenty dollars for compensation), so it was almost true. She continued, "My house is in Bel Air near Beverly Hills, but I'm only there TDY!"

She arranged food and beds and offered to give up her own if the men needed a nap. The evening was one of songs and laughter, but we never once left the topic of the war, the men, the military. She'd been everywhere and knew everyone and her stories were incredible. We were amazed that she had been trying to get to Dak To and, earlier, to Con Thien to be with the troops under fire. We were satisfied to be drinking booze in Saigon with the Old Lady of the Boondocks.

In late November or early December, I was walking down a CICV hall when I was approached by a sergeant I knew only slightly. He was always friendly, one of the gracious minority who did not go around under a constant cloud of gloom.

"Well, Lieutenant," he said to me brightly. "Are we winning?"

Equally brightly I replied, "Don't know, Sarge! No windows in the place, can't see out!"

He turned on his heels to stare at me, his eyebrows raised, then roared a solid peal of laughter as he continued on his way.

It wasn't funny.

It was prophecy.

CHAPTER

11

Indicators

Surprise can decisively shift the balance of combat power. By surprise, success out of proportion to the effort expended may be obtained. Surprise results from striking an enemy at a time, place and in a manner for which he is not prepared. It is not essential that the enemy be taken unaware but only that he becomes aware too late to react effectively. Factors contributing to surprise include speed, deception, application of unexpected combat power, effective intelligence and counterintelligence . . . and variations in tactics and methods of operation.

U.S. Army Field Manual 100–5
19 February 1962

"Well, it looks like we be starting off the Chinese New Year with a bang! The Viets won't be needing firecrackers this year, the VC are gonna provide all the noise they'll need!" That was a typical analyst's remark in reaction to the documents that were now coming in. Joking took the edge off the apprehension that grew with each new captured unit order or PW report on preparations for a coming offensive.

In Saigon, the monsoons had trickled to an end sometime in November. The dirt roads had dried and were again producing choking dust clouds that covered everything. But up in I Corps the monsoons had only begun to pour down, and this meant the Marines were going to have a hell of a time being resupplied in their DMZ outposts and being medevaced out. In the mud and artillery barrages, it was going to be a rough winter for the Leathernecks.

The indicators of things to come were beginning to arrive in quantity. In one captured document was this:

I am happy with the enthusiastic contents of the work of Leadership for Tet. Prepare to fight. The comrades are to organize the men to go visit and pay respects to the graves of the war dead with interrupted mourning. After that, launch the hatred for the American pirates. Use the 2 cruel prisoners. Actively fight to avenge our comrades.

I didn't know who the "2 cruel prisoners" were but the sense of hatred was clear. So was the sense of devotion to Hanoi's cause as seen in this verse from a combat diary:

> If I were a flower,
> I would be a helianthus.
> If I were a stone,
> I would be granite.
> If I were a bird,
> I would be a white pigeon.
> Since I am a human being,
> I will be a Communist.

Sometimes we tended to glamorize the Communist grunts into invincible supermen because of their discipline and adaptability. No small part of their legend derived from the agonizing infiltration march taken by the North Vietnamese soldiers. Most received a full month of training to prepare for the grueling trip. And now the troops were flowing in, almost all by foot with supplies moved by trucks, bicycles, and even elephants, but mostly by backpower and sweat. A MACV document summarized a typical trip down the Ho Chi Minh Trail:

When an infiltrator arrives at the Laotian border his North Vietnamese Army uniform is exchanged for a Lao "neutralist" uniform. He must give up all personal effects of an incriminating nature. A local guide takes him halfway to the first of a series of way stations along the infamous Ho Chi Minh Trail. There he is met by the next guide until the process has led the infiltrator onto South Vietnamese soil.

Here he receives a set of black civilian pajama-like clothes, two unmarked uniforms, rubber sandals, a sweater, a hammock, mosquito netting and waterproof sheeting. After being issued a 3–5 day supply of food and medicines, he is assigned to a unit for operation.

An NVA PFC captured in Quang Nam province on 29 September 1967 told of his one-month march into I Corps. Before leaving he was issued a rucksack, hammock, one-liter water canteen, mosquito net, shoes, slippers, and rice bags, which together weighed about sixty-five pounds. His unit also carried eighteen artillery pieces. The men traveled only in the evening from pre-dusk to midnight, resting ten minutes out of every hour. Every third day was reserved for rest, hunting, fishing, and vegetable forage. They would sleep near stations on the trail which were manned by two guides and two people who maintained the facility. One of the guides would lead the infiltrating group to the next station. These posts were linked by telephone and communication on the trail was conducted by runners. Radio use was minimized.

The infiltrators walked single file at six-meter intervals in the forests and fifty meters in the open. They covered about twenty kilometers a day, walking at a rate of four to five an hour. At twenty-minute lunch stops they ate pre-cooked rice balls, supplied at the trail stations; fires were not permitted. Out of a group of some four hundred, four or five died from malaria along the way. But during the entire march, the soldiers were neither bombed nor shelled.[1]

Another PW, captured in Binh Dinh later in 1967, reported that his infiltration packet walked from five to eight hours a day, covering ten kilometers. Their ration was three cans of rice a day, and each man carried a hundred malaria pills and two jars of insecticide. Along the way, on two occasions about a hundred men were dropped off to join their new units. This packet also was not bombed or shelled along the route.[2]

Gradually such sources accumulated in our shop and we became aware that the pace of the war was increasing and that infiltration was reaching invasion proportions. Captured documents and PWs provided indications but it was confirmed by our use of what we knew as SPARS —Special Aerial and Radio Sources. This was a watered-down version of the Special or Signal Intelligence (also called COMINT, for Communications Intelligence) that was used over in the Tank at MACV headquarters.

SI was produced by the Security half of Army Intelligence and Security, the boring half that years ago I'd been advised to avoid. It was supposed to be our ace card, and hence the ARVNs were kept at CICV, well away from the sensitive source at MACV headquarters.

Thus I was surprised that we would receive any form of SI. True,

SPARS were merely a list of coordinates with no indication of source or the actual intercepted radio message. But our ARVNs knew its significance. SPARS and SI were a poorly kept secret.

We were the only shop to map these coordinates, using colored stick-on dots to mark the spot of the signal interception. The process was time consuming, but our analysts liked the SPARS because they were current intelligence, which we all craved. Though we could not cite them as sources, clusters did suggest the location of a unit. Then the analysts could have a high level of confidence in any document that cited a base camp or engagement near the SPARS, and *that* source could then be relied upon for the current probable location.

The SPARS had been building up since at least early fall. The dots were beginning to overlap along the western edge of I Corps and through the A Shau valley. More and more radio transmissions were being picked up, revealing the increase in infiltration. This new phase was regularly noted in our recurring reports, including the PERINTREP, but could be based only on those sources authorized at our level of J-2; a typical report would offer something like, "Captured documents and PW reports continued to reveal the enemy's active infiltration along the Laotian border and through the A Shau valley." We said it so often that it became boiler-plate in our text. Perhaps the repetition and sameness reduced its impact. Intelligence reports, at least in Vietnam, were written in low-keyed language that could make even the most incredible seem mundane.

The number of troops coming through A Shau (known as "The Tube") was beyond belief, but ever since the Special Forces camp had been overrun there in 1966, we'd got used to the pattern. Bombing and artillery interdiction did little to slow the flow through this six-mile-long, one-mile-wide valley that flanked the Laotian border in southwestern Thua Thien province.

In 1963 the Special Forces had placed a twelve man "A team" in one of its Old West-styled forts, along with a Civilian Irregular Defense Group of 210 Montagnards, Laotians, and Vietnamese, plus 142 Nungs (Vietnam-born Chinese, known to be dependable mercenaries). The fortress helped slow NVA infiltration until 9 March 1966, when about a thousand men of the 95th NVA Regiment attacked. It was a miserable thirty-eight-hour battle of counterattacks and stands, as well as legendary heroism by supporting pilots. In the end we withdrew, losing five Americans and perhaps half of the CIDG force. We reported 800 NVA killed and the 95th Regiment was said to be inactive for the rest of the year. The MACV summary of 1966 gave the battle a single sentence that recognized A Shau as the enemy's "only notable success" of the year but one at "considerable loss to the attacking NVA." In the Army's slick and colorful booklet *Tour 365,* which was given to returnees in the summer of 1968, the A Shau defeat was not even mentioned in the history of the war.

I had great admiration for the Special Forces and when a Green Beret captain came to visit us in late December, I offered my assistance. He seemed disturbed by our wall map, on which appeared a number of twenty-kilometer acetate squares, each marked "SF." I explained that I'd plotted these from a listing we had recently received on potential Special Forces camp sites. I wanted to see where the camps were being planned in case we had to prepare an area analysis.

The captain looked around at the ARVNs and gestured wildly. "You've got a camp plotted in A Shau valley! You can't do that! That's top-secret information!" He declared I had compromised the Special Forces and demanded the list I had worked from. While he raved about an investigation by his headquarters, I doublechecked the list and saw to my horror that for the camp in question I had reversed the coordinates. That A-team was actually proposed for another province altogether. But from the vehemence of the captain's reaction I realized that the Green Berets *were* planning to return to the A Shau valley.

I explained my error. "Why make a big thing over it, Captain? It's just a simple mistake that hasn't gone anywhere." I reached over to the map, pulled off the symbol, crumpled it, and said, "Why, it never even happened. Just like you guys never go into Laos or Cambodia!"

I laughed. He didn't. He stormed out of the room. I sweated out the flap to come, but when news of the incident reached Major House, he was merely amused and simply advised me always to doublecheck my coordinates after posting. I breathed easier but I could only imagine the extent of my contribution to the Green Berets' view of headquarters REMFs.

In fact, the Special Forces never returned a camp to A Shau. After Tet and over the coming years we would make major sweeps through the Tube, but NVA infiltration would never be more than delayed.[3]

On 8 December I gave the NVA percentage briefing again, for the seventh time according to one of my letters. I was scheduled to brief

Westmoreland on the fourteenth, and I wrote that the "#2 man in intelligence" (probably Colonel Morris) felt the briefing was good enough to go to the press.

I was so pumped up I was even writing home about extending in Nam for six months. Not only was my duty good, but the war might even be wrapped up during my tour! My enthusiasm was somewhat diminished perhaps a week later when I heard that a shoebox of plastique was discovered on the second floor of the Meyerkord close to where Colonel Maggie lived. The rumor was confirmed the next day when the COC log included the incident and named Martha Raye as the probable target. I photocopied a page and clipped out the bomb reference. That night at the hotel I gave the copy to her.

She shook her head. It must be some kind of mistake, she insisted. Weeks earlier, when we'd heard a VC had thrown a grenade at her jeep, she had shrugged that off too, although she was still nursing some busted ribs from the crash (or possibly from the shrapnel). The Old Lady of the Boondocks was undoubtedly on the VC hit list.

A captured VC document in III Corps was another shocker. It listed Americans and Vietnamese working at CICV and CDEC and even included drawings of the interiors of the two buildings. Everyone wanted to see it, perhaps hoping secretly that he was "important" enough to be named.

I wanted to see it too, especially because a little earlier I had lost my snap-on photo ID card. Embellished with a Sphinx symbol (for the mystery of intelligence?) it showed my security clearance of "secret." Our passes were given to us each day when we entered CICV and we were supposed to turn them in when we left. One day I forgot to leave mine at CICV and it must have disappeared into a pile of dirty fatigues at the hotel. CICV admin was not pleased when I reported my card lost. When my picture was taken for a replacement, the Security Officer warned me that my face was now probably very well known to the local VC. This did not thrill me.

Later, my maid returned the ID. It was ragged and bent, as if it had gone through the wash. By then the card could have been processed to Hanoi and back by VC intelligence, so I went to III Corps OB to see if I was one of the chosen on the VC list. The top sarge told me the document had been declared off limits. Too many tourists.

"Lieutenant, you haven't been here long enough to be on any VC list. Anyway, it's not an assassination list, so relax." As I started to leave, he added with barely a smile, "Actually, I think the VC are gonna use it to give all of us a medal for helping them win the war!"

Then there was a phone call that I received toward the middle of December. I gave the standard greeting: "I Corps OB, may I help you, sir?"

A Viet voice on the other end said, "You like fuck Vietnam?"

"What?"

"You like fuck Vietnam? You like fuck Vietnam?"

"Cum biet [I don't understand]," I replied.

"You like short-time?" [GI for quickie sex.]

"Maybe you can get short-timed, Charlie!" I said.

"Goddamn you!" he said four times.

"Cum biet, Charlie," I snapped back.

"Cum biet. Thank you," said the caller and hung up.

I told Admin about the obscene VC call. Their reaction was to put me through a security questioning. What did he say, what did I say, why did he call me . . . to which I retorted, "I was the one who picked up the call, for chrissakes!"

Henceforth, I let the enlisted men answer the damn phone.

I saved a page from the 8 December issue of the overseas edition of *Time* that reported the impending departure of Robert McNamara as secretary of defense. Mr. Wizard himself, the man who gave us the Great Electronic Barrier in the DMZ and alternating statements of optimism and pessimism about the war, was going to retire to the inner sanctum of the World Bank.

On the same page was a story about Robert Kennedy's insistence that JFK wouldn't have got us into the Vietnam morass. But the article reported that two months before John Kennedy's death, he had declared that if South Vietnam went it would "give the impression that the wave of the future in Southeast Asia was China and the Communists," opening up attacks in adjacent nations.

I had once believed in the domino theory, but at Fort Holabird they had taught us enough to doubt a Red Chinese involvement. In a session on world Communism our instructor, Captain James Bond (Holabird had given him an ID numbered 007), showed us where the Chinese army divisions were located: along the Russian border and across from Taiwan. Invasion was not considered likely nor even possible. We also learned about the centuries of hatred between the Chinese and Vietnamese. Hanoi had only fear of its Communist neighbor and would not invite its participation. The list of reasons for our being in Nam kept getting shorter.

Indicators did not suggest a Chinese invasion, but there was one going on from North Vietnam into the South. By the end of December the western edge of our I Corps map was solid with SPARS symbols. Documents describing Viet Cong plans for the coming winter-spring campaign were accumulating. The next phase of the war was being called *Tong Cong Kich—Tong Khoi Nghia,* or "General Offensive—General Uprising."[4]

The exact date of the attacks was not specified, but it was clear they would occur around the time of Tet. This holiday period lasted seven days, the most important of which was the first day of spring. This year it occurred on 30 January; if there was to be trouble, it would probably occur just before or after the thirtieth.

At CICV we took note of these documents and shipped the most revealing up to the next level in the chain of command, Colonel Mac at Ground Order of Battle. They were summarized in the recurring reports, but in no more urgent language than had been used to report the infiltration activity (for instance, "Documents state the enemy's intent to aggressively initiate his winter-spring offensive around the time of Tet by conducting attacks across I Corps on military bases and urban centers").

Never did a tasking come back directing us to review all the indicators or gather them together for a strategic analysis. Headquarters' attitude was clear: the VC wouldn't dare attack during the most sacred of holidays or they'd lose public support. And the Viet Cong had neither the manpower nor the capability to conduct a nationwide attack. So we told ourselves. The command policy of "downward trending," unyielding optimism, and "light at the end of the tunnel" had given us no room to believe otherwise.

Suddenly I was given access to the select world of Special Intelligence. In the second half of December Colonel Mac told Major House that in each shop a junior officer would be cleared for SI in addition to the OIC. Kernsky desperately wanted the spot, but I was the second in rank. With some foreboding I headed for MACV to be interviewed and approved. I was pleased to learn that with this level of clearance (above "top secret") I could not be transferred to the field, since capture could compromise the system.

MACV headquarters, also known as Pentagon East or the puzzle palace, was an unimposing pre-fab two-story building with little to commend it. Perhaps as long as a couple of football fields, though wider, it was surrounded by a cyclone fence with barbed strands of wire at the top. At the corners and along the side were strange-looking towers in each of which sat an MP in a steel pillbox. A tenuous series of rungs led up the thirty-foot pole. Around the compound were doors through the fence for easy access of the office workers.

Inside, the well-waxed corridors had the fluorescent feel of an airport terminal. Both the Tank and the Command Operations Center (J-3) were at the end of a dead-end corridor in the windowless center of the rambling building. There was no traffic between them without a "need to know," the basic standard for access to sensitive information.

I signed in with the sergeant at the front desk, he pushed a buzzer, the door was unlocked, and I stepped into a small antechamber, then opened another door into the next corridor with two or three offices on the left. I was anxious to see the Tank, the brain of the fortress, the fount of all knowledge.

It was another legend shattered. I had expected electronic flashing boards, radar-like screens, cryptographic machines. But the Tank was just a big windowless room with a lot of wall maps, some of them hidden behind curtains. Around the room were desks for the four Corps areas, Cambodia, Laos, and North Vietnam. The III Corps desk was across from the entrance and I Corps was at the far end of the room. It was here at any hour of the day that Westmoreland and Davidson took their current intelligence briefings (during less intense periods, Westmoreland received his major intelligence input at the WIEU, Weekly Intelligence Estimate Update, on Saturday mornings).

On my first visit to the Tank I walked into a hornet's nest of excitement. A large group of officers was clustered around the I Corps wall map, pointing and talking with animation. I hung out on the edge of the group, trying to find out what was happening. Finally a field-grade officer heard my timid inquiries. He excitedly explained that Special Intelligence had just confirmed that a flood of NVA soldiers had crossed the DMZ and were surrounding the Marine base at Khe Sanh—and we had their designations!

For some time we'd had the 324B NVA Division and the 325th NVA Division in Quang Tri province near the DMZ, sometimes crossing back and forth or into Laos as necessary. (At the time the 324B was carried at 9,500 men and the 325th at 5,500.) Now our SI had also revealed the presence of the 304th NVA Division.

Sometimes called the 304th Home Guard, the division had been at Dien Bien Phu in 1954. That alone made us paranoid, and immediately the talk at headquarters was again of that disaster. The crowd of officers at the map spoke of similarities between the two posts. Both Khe Sanh and Dien Bien Phu were at the far western edge of the country, although the French post had been in North Vietnam. Dien Bien Phu, however, lay in relatively low land that allowed the Viet Minh to aim down on the French soldiers, who had not believed the enemy could move artillery across the rugged terrain. The two-mile-square Khe Sanh base was on high ground, carved out of a mountaintop. Some adjacent hills were higher but five of them were manned by smaller outposts.

The 304th had not come to Quang Tri alone. It was accompanied by the 320th NVA Division and the 325C Division, or at least components of them. I Corps was getting crowded, and it was clear to us that Khe Sanh was about to come under siege and major attack. This had to be the victory Giap had been seeking after his series of border battles.

After the paperwork was done—much later—on these units and they were added to the OB Book, the 304th was carried at 9,800 men. The 320th was at 7,400, and the 325C was first held at 5,500, then increased to 7,400 in the next edition. These "official" numbers suggest that the enemy force available to attack Khe Sanh could have been 39,600 combat troops, plus, no doubt, another army of coolies and porters. (Various estimates of the force have ranged from 20,000 to 60,000.)

Although I knew it was strictly unauthorized procedure, I jotted down the new units with their general locations and took the info back to CICV. The men were excited when I briefed them and Kernsky put the new designations on his map. The ARVNs were invited to do the same. This was too big to play games about the sanctity of Special Intelligence; we had to work together. All of us would be looking for any document that could substantiate the true battle situation so the OB Book could be brought up to date—and so that CICV could be part of the coming battle that was sure to be the turning point of the war.

But there was a disturbing undercurrent in our regular paper flow at CICV. Again and again the name of Hue, the imperial capital in Thua Thien province, would appear in captured enemy sources. Occasionally we reported the Hue indicators, but our mere paper sources could never get past the electronics and the COMINT "said" that Khe Sanh was the target. SI was always treated as the superior source and that preference of the headquarters was jammed down our throats more than once.[5] In the intelligence hierarchy, the CICV paper shufflers were always second-class citizens.

Neither the commanding officer of MACV nor the J-2 ever asked us at CICV to compile all the documents on Khe Sanh and Hue, or to present our best guess as to the enemy's plans. And so Giap's grand strategy moved ahead without challenge. In a month and a half it would lead, by twists and turns as devious as a VC tunnel, to the Tet offensive.

On one of my early trips to the Tank, I saw Westmoreland up close for the first time. I was going through the electronically controlled door when I heard behind me the staccato of a fast-moving contingent of men and the hurried snap-to-attention of the door guard.

"Good morning, *sir!*" came the sharply executed greeting. I flattened against the door, holding it open, doing my best stand-to-attention. The lean, mean figure in his gloriously fresh and crisply pressed fatigues swept past me, his face set in that perpetual granite-chiseled determination. Back at CICV, I embellished the story.

"Briefed Westmoreland today!"

"What? You did?"

"Yeah, as he came into the Tank I said, 'Good morning, sir!'"

Shore, as usual, one-upped me. "Too bad he didn't say 'good morning' to you. Then you could say Westmoreland briefed *you!*"

In fact, I had just held my breath and waited for him to go away. The man had that effect on people.

For Westmoreland, these were not the best of days. The war was about to break wide open and he was to face the challenge of his career. Infiltration was up, though not officially noted. The intensity of the Communist attacks was up. Most of all, the enemy soldiers were up and committed to a victory. Desertions still occurred, more from VC ranks than from the NVA, but they had decreased and there was in evidence an impressive level of discipline and purpose, as reflected by this PW:

. . . we were revolutionary troops and hardships were our daily fare. We had dedicated our lives to the realization of our national purpose; hardship couldn't discourage us and our enthusiasm couldn't be abated by the lack of comfort or food. . . . We defeated the French in the end. Our people had defeated others as well: Mongolia, China, Japan. With that glorious tradition and heritage, we can be sure that sooner or later, we will win though we may have to endure a great many hardships and difficulties. . . . Before we came South, we had studied the history of our country. . . . And so, now that we are in the South, the men would rather lay down their lives than give up their tradition.[6]

Such spirit was indeed an indicator of things to come. And things were moving fast.

CHAPTER

12

Holidays

... it was just before Christmas 1946 that an obscure Communist officer named Vo Nguyen Giap launched his troops upon a struggle that, in one form or another, has raged in Vietnam ever since. Last week, locked in deadly and unwanted embrace, the people of both Vietnam and the U.S. prepared to celebrate another wartime Christmas.

Newsweek, 1 January 1968

In the ninety-plus heat, it was jarring to see Vietnamese vendors downtown with both real and synthetic Christmas trees lined up along their sidewalk booths. Decorations were everywhere and carols blared from tinny speakers as the shopowners yelled, "Hey, you buy!", sometimes following that with "Cheap Charlie!" if you passed. I was used to Christmas in southern California, where hot weather in December was not unknown. But still it seemed strange for Christmas to come to this war, to this place.

For centuries it had, though. South Vietnam was some 10 percent Catholic, a result of the sixteenth-century conversions by Portuguese Jesuit missionaries (who thus began the era of Western intervention). I thought about going to the Christmas mass at the cathedral on Kennedy Square. But the occasion seemed too good a target for terrorists, so I gave up the idea.

As it happened, I wouldn't have had the chance anyway. Not only was I officer of the day at the compound on the night of 23–24 December (meaning I'd be exhausted or asleep on Christmas), I was also scheduled for watch duty at the Meyerkord beginning exactly at midnight on 31 December, New Year's Eve.

But the Army wanted me to have the holiday spirit. MACV sent out a Christmas card showing crossed poles flying U.S. and Vietnamese flags tied together with a pretty red ribbon, surrounded by MACV and Free World patches and the seals of our military branches. Inside, under a brightly drawn sprig of mistletoe, in both English and Vietnamese was, "Let Freedom Ring . . . Peace on Earth—Good Will Toward Men."

We also got one of those warm, personal mimeographed messages from the commanding officer, Colonel C. A. Cole of the 525th Military Intelligence Group, the next administrative level up from the 519th MI Battalion, who offered us his "Holiday Greetings":

> 2. I think there is no better time than now for us all to reflect on our role in Vietnam. We read often these days of the "Voices of Dissent" that certain people would have us believe are growing to major proportions at home. However I am sure that this "Voice" is as always the vocal minority shouting into the empty tunnel of frustration attempting to assault the walls of decency and humanitarianism which this "Voice" cannot understand or be a part of. In my own heart and conscience I see you, a soldier of the United States, again doing what he has done so well before, championing the cause of a people unable to defend themselves and doomed to the fate of slavery or annihilation if not given help. . . .
>
> 3. Today as before we are all fighting a right and moral fight; there is no shame to be felt, only pride and honor. I personally commend and thank each of you for the part you are playing. My thoughts and prayers during this Christmas season will be for you, your family, and our cause, with the firm hope and wish that this time next year may find us in the warmth of the family circle truly enjoying "Peace on Earth."

Another, anonymous, Christmas message was also circulating, this one from a contented Saigon Warrior to his friends in the States:

> Here I am in this terrible place. Forced to work long hours in this air-conditioned office. To spend my nights in an air-conditioned BOQ with only an ice-box, plentiful supply of booze, a stereo tape deck, an AM-FM stereo tuner, a TV, a stereo record player, and friends to amuse me. Forced to spend my afternoons off around a pool with plenty of booze in

a terrible temperature of 80–85 degrees. Or worse, still, to take in free movies or shows at the BOQ's or spend as much as $4.00 American for a huge steak or a complete French, Chinese, Italian, German, Japanese, Vietnamese, or Korean meal at a nightclub with live entertainment; . . . So stop a moment in the midst of your Christmas cheer . . . have a moment of silence for your unfortunate friend, who, although suffering terribly, usually from a lack of sleep, stops to wish you lucky people a cold white Merry Christmas and a damp, drunk Happy New Year.

It was the last hurrah of the Saigon Warrior. Soon the war would come to the rear echelon and even REMFs would be front-lined.

I wondered if there would be a burst of terrorism over Christmas and New Year's. On Christmas Eve, 1964, the VC had bombed the Brinks BOQ. Now I avoided it, as well as the Rex Hotel, where I had often gone for its famous steak cookouts (you did your own cooking on a huge barbecue grill) and the rock 'n' roll shows on the roof. Only higher-ranking officers, including Colonel Mac, were billeted there, and I avoided holiday visits to any prime target.

Families back home were sending holiday mailings of good stuff to their fighting boys, and some were surprising. One shipment to a CICV EM included a note saying that the sender had heard "you don't get much of this over there." The box contained fifteen pounds of ketchup and mustard. Another enlisted man received a mystery package with no return address. It contained twenty crumbled cookies, three *TV Guides*, a magazine about Maine, and an ad for the new 1968 Pontiac. The recipient had never been to Maine and didn't like Pontiacs.

Just after I began as duty officer at the compound in the afternoon of 23 December, I received a call from a Navy commander at CICV: I was again scheduled to brief Westmoreland, this time at 0800 on Christmas Eve—after overnight duty! I would have to leave the compound no later than 0615 to get into a clean uniform and hustle over to MACV. Compounding my lack of sleep were the effects of the plague and cholera booster shots I'd got that day; I was feverish and a bit disjointed.

But I was saved. Just before I inspected the guards as they went on duty, the commander called again; the briefing was on hold (and in fact never happened). I was greatly relieved and, after guard mount, I took up my usual letter-writing to get through the night. After explaining the on-again-off-again briefing, I pitched into a long diatribe against our I Corps major and what I saw as his increasing belligerence:

> The old Major is something else. Hot and cold, he blows. Sometimes he's great, other times he's the most insulting, cantankerous person I've ever known. If his temper tantrums only occurred when we were wrong, it would be ok and keep us in line. However, they're apt to explode anytime.

I wrote that I'd never be insubordinate, but it was getting very hard to ignore the sarcasm and constant "digging." I asked for my father's advice on how to deal with an OIC you can't stand. He'd had a few himself, and I hoped his experience could guide me.

That off my chest, I inspected the guard posts. From one of the towers I enjoyed the view of dusk settling on the shantytown around us. From below came a voice: "Lieutenant, are you up there?"

"Yes, what is it?"

It was the guard at the front gate.

"We've got an ARVN colonel at the front gate with a woman, and he wants to come in."

I climbed down and met the two at the front gate. The colonel, an unusually large and chubby Vietnamese, was in uniform, three silver pips on his fatigue tabs. The woman was beautiful, dressed in the graceful *ao dai*, but her face was cold and distant. He smiled and returned my salute.

"Lieutenant, you are the officer of the day?" His English was impeccable.

"Yes, sir."

"I am on leave visiting my family here in Gia Dinh, and we were taking a walk. We wondered if we could climb up your guard tower to view the area?"

This is strange, I thought. I knew of no standing orders on how to handle ARVN visitors. We had many Vietnamese in the compound every day. Anything the VC wanted to know could be had from any number of workers; there were Communist agents in every Allied base in Nam. I saw no harm in the request, and I wanted to be polite.

"Ah, yes, sir, I guess it would be O.K. for a few minutes."

I yelled up to the two soldiers in the tower that we had visitors. The colonel and I helped the lovely stone-faced woman up the stairs.

They stood looking beyond the perimeter, pointing and talking in Vietnamese. Then the colonel turned to me.

"Lieutenant, this is a motor pool? I don't see many vehicles."

Now it was getting sticky.

"Ah, it used to be. They just never changed the name on the entrance."

He gestured and frowned. "Then what is this place for?"

Really sticky. I could see the enlisted men in their combat gear shifting uncomfortably and exchanging glances.

"Well, it's simply a billet for enlisted men. They sleep here."

The colonel stared at me. I hoped he could not see I was sweating.

"But what do these men do?" he asked. "Are they infantry?"

"No, no. They just work in installations, ah, all over Saigon. Administrative jobs, you know. Typing. Filing. You know, clerks."

He looked at me a second longer, then nodded. He and the woman spoke some more and he thanked me. They climbed down and I watched them leave. I was desperately replaying the incident in my mind, worrying over what the consequences could be.

One of the enlisted men in the tower looked at me squarely and said, "He asked a lot of questions, Lieutenant!"

"Yeah, I know. Well, he doesn't know any more than when he came in."

"Yes, sir, but now he knows the layout of the compound."

"And so do all the Viets that work here. Don't worry about it!"

I got off the tower as quickly as possible and returned to my office, staring with dread at the duty officer's log. I knew I should enter this strange visit. I also knew I didn't want to. But maybe the guards would talk. Maybe the visit was innocent . . . but it was easy enough to fake a uniform and walk around asking questions. Especially of dumb American lieutenants. If I wrote this into the log, maybe there'd be an investigation, an inquiry, or worse.

So I didn't write it into the log. In the military, if it wasn't on paper, it never happened. Leave no trails, keep the files clean, and no one ever catches up with you.

After a few days went by, I concluded that the guards hadn't talked, that no one was checking the log for omissions. But in Nam, you couldn't do anything without consequences. I hoped and prayed this would be an exception.

Christmas and New Year's did not look promising, but the good news was that I was cleared for R-and-R to Bangkok for 10–16 January. I desperately needed some time off, especially to get a break from the major, who was swinging back and forth between praise and screaming fits. One day he gave me an "outstanding" efficiency report and was urging me to make a career of the Army, the next he was all over me for an administrative snafu. I went to work each day feeling ill, my stomach churning in apprehension. Just in time, the response to my plea for advice came back from Santa Barbara, my father's finest effort in putting life-in-the-combat-zone into human terms:

> Can't help you much with a boss who is no sweetheart. Seems to me that most of my bosses were that way! What do you expect? Sweetness and light all day in a war zone? . . . When you say he is getting on your nerves—that's bad because it shows you are losing your sense of humor and detached perspective—the ruckus in general and your little piece of it is beginning to get to you—hang loose—count the weeks and come back healthy—just concentrate on fighting the enemy, not the Major, too. . . . *Be patient—if you dislike this guy— wait about a month and he will be gone and in will come a guy you can REALLY HATE!*

I had to laugh, although I wouldn't have if I'd known the last sentence was prophecy. The best cushion between the major and me was the work load. I dug in for the duration.

Christmas came and went and, except for Miss My's surprise "all-night party" on Christmas Eve, I hardly noticed it. My only Christmas cards were from my ARVN counterparts and from Miss My, all Buddhists. They gave me beautiful hand-painted cards of graceful Viet women or flowers with holiday wishes inside. I carefully put each away, a cherished souvenir.

Then came New Year's Eve. At 2300 I pulled on my fatigues after a nap and then went dejectedly down the stairs to sign in, draw my .45 and put on the officer-of-the-day armband. From my room I had heard a vigorous party rocking out on the roof. All the roundeyes, including Colonel Maggie, were going to be there. I trudged up the stairs to inflict more punishment on myself by watching the party until I had to start my watch. On my arrival, everyone stopped dead in mid-dance. I realized with dismay that they thought I was there to quiet down the party.

Quickly I yelled that it was only coffee I wanted, that they should, please, have a good time! They carried on, but I felt like a jerk for having dampened the celebration. I drank my coffee and stayed in a corner. Maggie had seen me and waved. As midnight neared, the Old Lady of the Boondocks yelled at me, "Hey, you! Lieutenant! Come here!"

I jumped to it and found myself dancing with her to the applause and cheers of the crowd. Then someone announced it was midnight and she planted on me a huge Martha Raye kiss! More cheers from the crowd. Blushing red, I thanked her profusely, waved good-by to the party, and took off for my guard post on the sixth floor. I breathlessly wished my predecessor a Happy New Year and advised him to get upstairs in a hurry for one hell of a party!

About two hours later I was surprised by the approach of feet behind me. It was Colonel Maggie and her officer escort, delivering a sandwich and a cup of coffee, with more best wishes and a hug.

Nowhere, ever again, will I have such a joyous New Year's Eve.

Newsweek started off the new year with a bang of a cover photo: exhausted, wounded men, probably at Dak To, waiting for medevac out of the jungle. Its lead story was headlined, HOW GOES THE WAR? Interestingly, the article noted that the American public still supported the war, although with concerns. Polls showed that 58 percent believed the road to peace was in convincing Hanoi "they would lose the war if they continue fighting." By 62 to 22 percent they rejected a unilateral de-escalation. To the question of how goes the war, the writers gave this:

> With its massive infusion of manpower, munitions and machines, the U.S. has reversed the tide of battle. . . . The enemy has yet to win a single significant victory over U.S. troops and is suffering inordinately in the war of attrition. Communist casualties, according to U.S. intelligence estimates, are now running at the horrifying rate of nearly 1,700 dead a week. And replacements are increasingly hard to find. Infil-

tration from North Vietnam, the Saigon command asserts, has fallen from 7,000 men a month last year to 6,000 a month this year while recruitment of guerrillas in the south has plummeted from 7,000 a month to only 3,500.

How interesting that *Newsweek* had accepted without comment the assertion of the Saigon command that infiltration had fallen. How it pulled and pushed at your mind to see one thing in print and to be reporting totally opposite indicators. The magazine's review of I Corps was strangely devoid of references to Khe Sanh and even called the "situation" there "much improved."

As for III Corps, where I lived and worked, it was reported that MACV felt the area had the highest level of security in the nation. The commander of U.S. forces in the zone declared that the three enemy divisions previously ringing Saigon were then some ninety miles away. General Frederick C. Weyand declared, "The enemy can't suck me out of the populated areas by attacking an outpost. We now have the strength to respond to such attacks and still maintain control of the population."

Newsweek offered some interesting commentary on the VC's willingness to sustain enormous losses "for what appears to be no immediate advantage":

Some U.S. military men suggest that these suicidal tactics reveal Communist desperation. Others believe that strategists in Hanoi have made a conscious decision to accept vastly increased losses in order to raise the number of American casualties to a point where it may become politically indigestible in the U.S.

The magazine repeated the MACV gospel that Hanoi had "not been able to keep pace with the Viet Cong's attrition rate and that, as a consequence, total enemy troop strength has declined over the past year." What had gone up, according to the U.S. command, was the number of NVA personnel in VC units. I was annoyed to see that 10 percent figure from my altered study being given national exposure.

Then the analysis attempted to come to grips with the question of enemy strength, reporting that recently the command had disclosed figures showing a total of 378,000. The writers noted that last year's "official figure" was 280,000, but that this only suggested that "last year's figures had been deceptive." Then came this most interesting observation:

> In November, after months of haggling among intelligence experts, the U.S. dramatically revised its method of calculating enemy strength. As a result, meaningful comparisons with previous manpower estimates have become all but impossible.

"Months of haggling" was a new one for me, but I guessed it was tied to the mysterious disposition form that was issued and so quickly recalled back in October. It was all very confusing. But the final piece in the issue, addressing the "American dilemma," did get much closer to the realities. The war was characterized as "foggy" and "stubbornly resistant to firm judgments; an uncertain future for all sides." And it offered the ultimate irony: ". . . the U.S. position in South Vietnam is a good deal stronger than it was a year ago, but the position of the Communists is not crucially weaker."

The cautious pessimism of *Newsweek* could be contrasted to the guarded optimism in the 1967 summary presented in the 31 December issue of *Stars and Stripes*. It opened with Westmoreland's observation that 1967 marked the "beginning of the end" to the war in Vietnam. MACV's own wrap-up for 1967 offered massive optimism, beginning with its title, "A Year of Progress," and including this:

> By year's end, enemy military strength was at the lowest level since late 1965 or early 1966. And about 30 percent of his maneuver battalions were considered not combat effective.

It was infuriating, that statement about 30 percent of the enemy's battalions being combat ineffective. A month earlier we had scraped and dug, under considerable pressure, to find even a handful of temporarily inactive units. Yet even anger over MACV's propaganda did not stop me from making my own optimistic prediction in a January letter home:

> The war is beginning in I CTZ. The biggest battles are shaping up, as the NVA seek large American casualties to influence the home front politics. Also an element of desperation

has entered their tactics. Every major battle they've tried, they've lost big.

Later that week I wrote, "The war will reach its peak in early 1968; it seems NVN wants to win somewhere; we know where; and they'll hit with a big force. If they do, they'll be defeated." I was warning my folks of the impending attack on Khe Sanh, nothing more; for I too still believed that was what all the sound and fury were about.

Of course I didn't have the "Big Picture," the master plan of the coming offensive. But pieces of it did show that control of the war rested in Hanoi, not in Saigon nor in Washington. I did not know that the enemy's "desperation" and the big losses he was taking were actually coldly calculated steps by Giap to walk us right up into the Khe Sanh siege, the grandest of all decoys.

As we slid into January my morale was in pretty good shape. R-and-R was just days away and I had a party to look forward to. The ARVNs from I and II Corps invited their American counterparts to dinner to celebrate their coming holiday. The more cynical of our men presumed the Viets were setting us up for a new flood of requests for PX items as Tet, a gift-giving holiday, approached. The Vietnamese had much need then of liquor, cigarettes, and snacks to celebrate the coming of spring, the start of the lunar new year, and everyone's birthday celebration.

The dinner was to be held in a village beyond the outskirts of Saigon. That too stirred up a lot of talk among the cynics. What were they going to do, fatten us up for a VC reward? The ARVNs assured us the area was secure and on 7 January we convoyed out into the boondocks in a series of jeeps and Hondas. I drank in the lush green, pastoral calm of the rice paddies and the water buffalo and the farmers working as they had for centuries. We heard no sounds and saw no sights of war, only a strangely remote statue on a hill in the farmlands of a sitting Viet soldier, rifle over his knees. Some American predictably cracked that there was another ARVN sitting down on the job.

Lord, I thought, this country someday is going to be a paradise when there's peace. But there was no peace, and Aspirant Qui clarified that for me in no uncertain terms.

"Town down that road number ten!"

"Why, Qui?"

"Beaucoup VC."

"Oh! Ah, how far?"

"Six kilometers."

"*Six* kilometers?"

"Yes, we go home before dark!" Qui laughed.

The restaurant was a plain structure, a single room with the floor and walls in garish green and white tiles of checkerboard pattern, something like a train station men's room. Our ARVNs had taken us out so far into the country to escape the inflated prices of Saigon. Here was a simple restaurant they could afford.

Cheap the dinner may have been, but dull it wasn't, totally unlike the traditional upper-class Vietnamese meal of a series of beef selections ("beef in seven dishes"). Of course, the ever-present *nuoc nam* was there, and avoided religiously by the Americans. Sometimes we called this brown liquid "nuke bomb" for its punch and fallout. It was made from salted anchovies, left for days in the sun to ferment—or rot—in barrels. "Pungent" is too weak a description.

Most of the courses were exotic to us: sparrow soup, with shredded meat from the little birds; roast hedgehog; rabbit and fawn meat, maybe even monkey. And rice, of course. Some of the Americans did not eat too much but everyone was having fun, taking pictures and drinking too much "33" beer (which, instead of alcohol, was made with formaldehyde). Then came the surprise.

Across the room on a counter was a large glass vat, maybe two feet high, full of a yellow-brown liquid. I stared at the bottom. Stacked in the vat were the fetuses of animals: monkeys, swamp rats, deer, pigs. The theory, it was explained, was that they gave off animal protein to the drinker, making him "very manly."

The Vietnamese poured us shot glasses of this formaldehyde-based liquor and then sat politely waiting for us to take the first drink. Nervous jokes went around the table as the Americans eyed their glasses with suspicion. I took the leap and shot mine down. Tears began streaming down my face.

"No, no, Lieutenant Jones!" said Tri. "You must sip, like this!"

One of our party, a chubby, quiet, southern-born second lieutenant, had not touched his glass. He sat looking at the drink with an expression of revulsion. Finally he slowly picked it up and in slow motion he took a sip. There were cheers and applause; then he threw up on the table. The Viets were mortified, but most of the Americans hooted with laughter. The major wisely observed that the party was over.

Dusk was not far away and we did not want to be around for the changing of the guard. Late-night diners at Café Boondocks would be wearing black pajamas and AK-47s.

Less than a week later, I was on a flight to Bangkok. My R-and-R was probably no different from anyone else's—touring the fabulous temples, drinking, bar-girling, and buying rubies, temple rubbings on rice paper, and bronze serving sets. My taxi driver was on call for me alone all week for twenty dollars. His real profits came when he took me shopping; each store would give him kickbacks on my purchases.

One unnerving scene marred the trip. A large soldier who had come out of combat was staying at my hotel, and his drinking brought him to the edge of unreasoning violence. I tried to ease him out of it with the often-heard "Be nice," a favorite saying of Vietnamese girls to unruly Americans. He screamed back, "I don't have to be nice," and was on the verge of attacking me, even though he knew I was an officer. For the duration I avoided him. You could smell death in him and on him.

The five days were over too soon, and my mood was black as the plane landed at Tan Son Nhut. But when I called CICV, Shore's greeting was heartening. "Lieutenant Jones, boy, am I glad you're back! You wouldn't believe what's been going on here while you were gone!"

Apparently the major was operating in overdrive after taking on the projects load, and he hadn't liked it a bit. He'd stayed up two nights working and was heard to say, "This kind of thing can make or break a career!"

I asked Shore what project could have been so important. We shared a good laugh when he told me it was just one of the recurring wrap-ups that I usually knocked out in a couple of hours. After that conversation, I was able to plunge back into the paper wars with more self-confidence.

The major was very solicitous about my well-being. Was I well rested? Was I ready to get back to work? It was clear he didn't want "additional duty" either.

But he got it. Within the week, he was transferred to the Tank to be one of the three watch officers who sat in shifts around the clock at the I Corps current indicators desk. The assignment was temporary and he remained officer-in-charge of our shop, but he wouldn't be around much.

My elation over being acting OIC again was short lived. In mid-January Colonel Mac called me into his office. As usual he was direct and gruff.

"Jones, you're going over to J-2. They've set up a special team to monitor the build-up at Khe Sanh and target the B-52 strikes. You've got SI clearance and you know I Corps, so you're the CICV representative."

I tried to protest; the major was gone, who was going to run the shop? Colonel Mac cut me off, telling me the assignment was only temporary for both of us, the major would come around occasionally, and every few days I'd be rotated back to CICV for a work shift.

Before I left, PFC Shore put into my hands what may well have meant the outcome of the war.

About two weeks before Tet he came to me with that disarming grin of his and said, "Look, Lieutenant. See this nice stack of documents?"

"Yeah?"

"These are special. These are the VC's own special way of wishing us a Happy New Year."

"What's the point?"

Shore put on his sincere voice. "Well, Lieutenant, I know how overworked you are and how the major expects aggressive, accurate work from us so he can get promoted."

I settled back, anticipating one of Shore's performances.

"So what we did, Lieutenant Jones, sir, was to gather from all our provinces the best PW reports, captured documents, and even a nice agent report or two. So here is a stack, sir, laying it all out, how the VC are going to wish us all a happy and prosperous Tet by invading each and every urban center in I Corps."

"PFC Shore, bloody good work! I didn't know you were so ambitious. This could make you a sergeant major."

"But seriously, sir, is anyone preparing for this? Tet is just weeks away and nothing seems any different."

"Well, we've been seeing these things for weeks now. Maybe they're just a scare tactic."

"But, Lieutenant, there's just too many of them. A lot of these documents are specific orders on where to stage and what to hit and how to get there. So how about putting these into the pipe so we can say we did our jobs?"

"O.K., Shore, but it'll be another flap when the brass sees we're trying to one-up them. You just be here to take some of the heat."

Shore gave me an aggrieved look, snapped his heels, and offered, "At your service, sir!"

"Yeah, well, that'll be a first." But I smiled as I watched our sharpest EM return to his seat, gesturing like a winning prizefighter to the grins of his co-workers. The Vietnamese were quietly watching and listening. They really didn't miss anything, I thought.

"Lieutenant Tri?"

The Vietnamese officer's eyebrows arched, the only movement of his impassive face. "Yes, Lieutenant Jones?"

"What do you think? Is it really going to happen? Are the VC going to attack during Tet?"

Quietly he said, "Yes."

The room went stone silent. I'd never seen the Vietnamese so somber, the Americans so attentive to their counterparts.

I let out a deep breath. The silence in the room was unbroken until I asked, "What about the other Corps? And Saigon?"

Tri's voice was again softer than even his usual monotone. "Yes, all cities. All Corps. Especially Saigon."

No one in the room turned a page. Even Shore for a change was quiet, intently looking back and forth from Vietnamese to American faces. Our expressions showed that finally we all knew the shit was going to hit the fan.

I told the men to prepare an index and brief summary of the documents to use as a cover page, and, not knowing when the major would be back, took the package to Colonel Mac. He watched me with a kind of smile as I explained the collection to him. Then he said, "Yes, Jones, we've seen these before."

"Yes, sir, I know, but have we made MACV realize what's going on?"

Colonel Mac seemed uncomfortable. "They know about it over there."

"But nothing seems to be happening."

The colonel looked embarrassed. He spoke slowly. "The attitude seems to be that if we, ah, build up in preparation for some attacks, then we'll appear to be taking the enemy propaganda too seriously."

I groaned and threw up my hands. Colonel Mac gave a little laugh.

Back at the shop, the men were eager for news. They stared quizzically at me as I repeated Colonel Mac's comment. There was some muttering and then silence. Later I checked two of the other OB shops; they had the same kind of documents, but enthusiasm for resubmitting them was not high.

We did not have to worry about the VC beating us. We were doing a fine job of it by ourselves.

13

The Khe Sanh Red Watch

Over hill, over dale,
We will hit the bloody trail,
As the Khe Sanhs
Go rolling along!

Comment heard at CICV, 1968

Like the Chinese generals of
old, Giap knows the political
value of the "phantom army"
which compels the enemy to dig
in, expecting the worse.

Arthur J. Dommet
Los Angeles Times, 29 December 1969

The preliminary phase of Operation Niagara, a colossal application of American airpower on the enemy around Khe Sanh, began on 8 January 1968. Westmoreland was not going to let the base fall. He put everything we had into the air,[1] and he was prepared to put almost everything we had onto the ground. He moved over half of the U.S. combat battalions in Vietnam to I Corps, ready to join battle when necessary. And there were two very special study groups in progress, both highly confidential. Not until after the war was it learned that a team at headquarters was evaluating the use of a tactical nuclear weapon at Khe Sanh.[2]

I was made Intelligence Officer for the other task force. Its mission was to prepare operational plans for a massive multibattalion heliborne operation into Laos to attack the NVA siege forces from the rear. Some said the operation would be as big and historic as the amphibious landing in Korea, when MacArthur came in behind the North Korean forces to cut off their drive down the peninsula. My job was to determine what enemy forces to expect in the landing zone, but we knew almost nothing about the Communist order of battle in Laos. If we went in, we'd have no idea what would be facing us.

During the early planning sessions, I sat mutely in the back as the officers attacked a logistical nightmare. Surprise seemed an impossibility; the movements of men and equipment would be monitored by VC agents everywhere. The enemy would know we were coming and probably where we would land. The question of what forces we would be facing was vital, but the Saigon Warriors weren't going to supply the answer. I hoped the Marines and their air support could pull it off at Khe Sanh on their own.

While I was being pulled away for meetings of this task force, the shop had completed our new standard operating procedure for writing Unit OB Summaries,[3] and we had developed a respectable library of finished intelligence, more detailed and more accessible than anything we'd had before. Much of my carefully developed SOP for I Corps was soon adopted by Colonel Mac for use by all the OB shops.

But it was January 1968! How could it have been that so late in the war we still didn't have a definitive guide for the production of finished intelligence? We had only been playing catch-up ball, never pulling ahead. It was too late to be figuring out what the hell we were doing. In days it would be all we could do just to hold on.

The Marines were valiantly holding at Khe Sanh. Westmoreland had declared that the outpost was vital in cutting infiltration from Laos and the DMZ. The defense force on the several hills grew to 6,000 Marines and several hundred ARVNs. Just as with Con Thien, the press was comparing Khe Sanh to Dien Bien Phu. We'd been making the same comparison at headquarters since the middle of December and a Dien Bien Phu fixation had again taken hold.[4] Everyone seemed to be reading *Hell in a Very Small Place,* Bernard Fall's history of the battle. Westmoreland abhorred the parallel but was well aware that a loss of the base would be a psychological and political defeat as devastating as that suffered by the French in 1954. We would not lose; it was command policy.

But even for the COMUSMACV, implementation of policy did not come easily. Westmoreland always had been hamstrung by interservice rivalries. Scuttlebutt had it that now he and a key Air Force general weren't speaking to each other and as a result air support at Khe Sanh suffered.

"So we don't get targets confirmed," I was told.

"But doesn't General Westmoreland carry a bit more weight?" I asked.

"Yes, but it doesn't work out that way."

Targeting had been conducted in a command center at Tan Son Nhut, but because of the sensitivity of the B-52 strikes, Westmoreland had it moved over to the Tank. He put Army personnel in charge, perhaps on the assumption that ground soldiers would better recognize tactical targets. (A captain at the I Corps desk in the Tank had told me bitterly, "No pilot can support us unless he's been on the ground and knows what it's like.")

So was born the Khe Sanh Red Watch. We worked in a small room just at the inner hallway into the Tank, wall maps covering all available space. It was a round-the-clock operation as lieutenants and a major mapped the flood of information that was coming from an armada of sources. There was, of course, photo recon. There were ammonia-sniffers that detected human urine from troop concentrations. There were bizarre seismic sensors; thrown from aircraft, they stuck in the earth on steel spikes and picked up the vibrations of trucks, digging, or the marching of troops. (The electronic sensor system around Khe Sanh was called Muscle Shoals.) Acoustic sensors dropped by parachute hung in trees; a circling aircraft transmitted their signals to computers at the Infiltration Surveillance Center in Thailand: the data were forwarded to MACV, and then to Khe Sanh's fire-control center for artillery response.[5]

The Red Watch itself was much more basic. On 20 January when I joined it on a part-time status, I was put to work posting symbols and more symbols for troop concentrations, machine gun and artillery emplacements, stream crossings, and footpaths. The map was thick with them. Every day our OIC, a major with a country drawl, would gather us for selection of the next day's targets. We had at our disposal the entire fleet of B-52 Stratofortresses[6] available to Vietnam. For a selected target we would plot a one-by-three-kilometer rectangle on an acetate overlay, and the next day a cell of three B-52s at some 30,000 feet would drop on it ninety tons of bombs. Daily we were sending up to sixty B-52s into the Khe Sanh/DMZ region; three bombers were over their targets every ninety minutes (later it was six every three hours).

We were told that more bomb tonnage would be dropped around

Khe Sanh than had been used in World War II. But of course it was an exaggeration. Still, the quantity probably made the NVA units around Khe Sanh "the most heavily bombed target in the history of warfare."[7]

The Red Watch OIC worked us relentlessly. I was switched from day to night shifts and back again without any time to rest or acclimate to the new hours. My metabolism was all screwed around and I learned about a whole new kind of fatigue. On night shifts we were usually allowed to get some sleep but that was possible only if you could hide a cot early in the evening. Even senior officers could be found in mortal combat over these treasures. The desks were used around the clock so all that was left to huddle on was the floor in a corner. Having been on night and day duty back-to-back without notice, I hadn't brought in a blanket, toiletries, or a change of uniform. For days I washed in a sink using a razor and soap from the small MACV PX. Lack of sleep and poor hygiene made the tedious work all the more oppressive.

We were having a recurring problem: there weren't always enough significant B-52 targets to go around and we sometimes had trouble meeting our daily quota. We once put a B-52 strike on a single machine gun emplacement. Another time the major resorted to hitting a foot-crossing over a stream, calling it an indicator of troop concentrations. So we targeted a cell of Stratofortresses to put some ninety tons of bombs across a piddly stream and its muddy banks. The major saw my expression and angrily asked me if I had any better suggestions. I didn't.

Occasionally I was pulled away to work on the Laos operation, and finally it was time to brief Davidson. I waited anxiously for his inevitable question: "What do we know about enemy units in the area?" The head of the task force, an Air Force major, nodded at me, and I choked out a response. "General Davidson, we just don't have specific information other than what we know is around Khe Sanh."

I was sitting a few rows behind the general, who was slouching in his seat. All I could see was his bald head shining under the fluorescent lights. He turned to growl back at me, "I *know* that! But check anyway!"

I did ask around again at the Laos desk and back at CICV. Same answer. We'd have to go in not knowing what kind of resistance would be waiting.

At the J-2's briefing, the general had cracked, "The Marines aren't much for thinking, but they're great at hand-to-hand combat!" During the early morning of 21 January, the men at Khe Sanh had to prove it.

On the twentieth an NVA lieutenant had surrendered to the Marines at their base. Under interrogation, he revealed that regiments of the 325C and 304th Divisions would attack Khe Sanh that night before sweeping across the DMZ and the two northern provinces, ultimately taking Hue. When the report of the interrogation reached CICV, our analyst for the DMZ exclaimed, "This guy knows too much!" Was Giap repeating the gambit he had used at Dak To, where apparently he had wanted us to know in advance that large units of his troops were in place and ready to engage?

After midnight came a barrage, then an attack on Hill 861 by a force that was estimated to be between a battalion and a regiment. The NVA regulars were repulsed by hand-to-hand fighting that lasted until morning. Contrary to the PW's prediction, there were no other ground assaults, but a heavy barrage was placed on the main base. A 122mm rocket hit the main ammunition dump and some 1,500 tons of ordnance began exploding, putting the Marines under barrage by their own ammunition. Then tear gas went off and covered the base, forcing the Marines into gas masks that further limited their vision.

But another ground attack did not come. The Marines had lost 90 percent of their ammunition (why was it all stored in one place?) and they were immobilized by the explosions for hours. The NVA did not exploit this opportunity, and in Saigon we shook our heads in confusion. We believed that if the enemy wanted it, the base was his.

What was Giap doing at Khe Sanh? MACV headquarters with its mystical "all-source" intelligence didn't have a clue, but at CICV we again speculated that Giap's failure to follow through simply proved he did not want to overrun the base. We were convinced by then that he was freezing us in place, forcing the commitment of men, materials, and command attention to a decoy. Giap must have agonized over the hit on the ammo dump for it revealed his strategy, at least to some. But not to headquarters, which issued its stock response: our massive firepower had hurt the enemy so badly, he had lost the capability to launch a meaningful assault.

I passed on to the Red Watch major the CICV view that Hue might be the primary target, not Khe Sanh, and I suggested he consider that alternative. The major answered that our mission was to bomb the enemy forces at Khe Sanh, not to analyze their strategy. And there were plenty of NVA soldiers around the base, so get back to posting symbols. My job was clear: don't think, just do.

To complicate things further, on 23 January the Communists seized the *Pueblo,* our intelligence spy ship, in North Korean waters, precipitating an international flap. At the Tank, everyone was sure this was part of a worldwide Communist master plan to put extra pressure on the United States at a critical moment.

On 27 January I was put on full-time duty at the Tank, and I had the night shift to myself. Through the long hours I was worried that at any minute some general would want a briefing on the day's activities. The major never brought me up to speed on the recent targets and any secondary explosions (which revealed important hits of ammo or fuel dumps); I was just a plotter.

I had no visitors until the early morning hours of 29 January. While I was hunting for a cot, a full-bird colonel tracked me down and asked, "Are you the duty officer at the Red Watch?"

"Yes, sir."

"We just got these infrared photos in. They show a large-scale movement of men toward Khe Sanh. Here, they're yours." He thrust them into my hands and started to walk away.

I was stunned. I was being handed the intelligence on the opening moves of the attack! The turning point of the war!

"But, sir, what do I do . . ."

The colonel kept walking and cut off my question. "I haven't the slightest idea, Lieutenant. It was my job to give them to you, and that's what I did. Now it's your problem!"

I took a deep breath and forced myself to think it through. The first thing had to be to get out the word, get some rank involved.

I went to the I Corps desk at the far end of the Tank and showed the photos to the watch officer. He was remarkably unconcerned, saying that we'd hear from the Marines soon enough if the attack began. After all, they were on constant alert there.

Maybe it would be O.K., I thought. If it's no big deal to him, maybe they've been getting a lot of this sort of thing. (In fact, though I was unaware of it, headquarters had received an aerial reconnaissance report during the evening of 28 January. The next day's DISUM reported, "Both large and small units were moving from the Laotian border and from as far south as ten miles below Khe Sanh. All movements were converging on Khe Sanh.")[8]

Then the I Corps officer said, "Anyway, Khe Sanh is pretty much the concern of your Red Watch now, Lieutenant. Why don't you call your CO and get his advice?"

Another split in the bureaucracy. Khe Sanh was no longer part of I Corps, and the Red Watch had become its own little empire.

Nervously I dialed the BOQ for the major. "Sir, I'm sorry to wake you up but this seems important and I need your orders."

"It better be important, Jones."

The phone lines were notoriously insecure in Saigon, so I chose my words carefully.

"Sir, you know that project we're working on . . ."

"Yes, of course, Jones, get on with it!"

"Well, a colonel has just given me a source that indicates a massive move . . ."

"What source, Jones?"

"Sir, this is not a secure line . . ."

"It doesn't matter, it won't make any difference!"

"O.K., it's an infrared photo that shows a large movement of troops from previous positions. It could be the attack." Nervously I added, "I think you better come in, sir."

"You do, do you, Jones? There's nothing we can do now if they attack. The Marines are ready for them. We can handle it in the morning."

That was it.

I desperately wanted some sleep, but I was too wired. Anyway, if there were more indicators to be delivered, I wanted to be there and on the job posting my little symbols.

The morning came quietly and the major arrived. "Well, did anything happen?" he demanded.

"No, sir."

"See?" he snapped.

The major had bigger things on his mind; he gathered his staff and announced that it was a "historic day," that we were going to plan the largest single air strike of the war! We were going to bust the siege!

"Yeah, if they're still there," I mumbled and the major glared at me. But I believed those infrareds could have meant one of only three things: (1) the attack had begun—but we knew it hadn't; (2) all the coolies, porters, and low-level soldiers had put on a feint to make us overreact in Saigon; or (3) the NVA forces had used Khe Sanh for a staging area and a decoy and were then moving out for their real target —Hue!

So I had guessed, but I didn't have the position, confidence, or support to force the point home. Had the area been immediately saturated with constant infrareds and aerial recon, we could have tracked the exodus of perhaps half the NVA force as it moved southeast for the sixty-five-mile trip to Hue. Instead, we were going to saturate the Khe Sanh environment with even more 500- and 750-pound bombs.

The biggest strike of the war was a result of Special Intelligence. We had located a site of heavy radio transmissions just over the border in Laos, and J-2 was convinced it was the NVA headquarters for the besieging force. The site was believed to be honeycombed with caves and that again was a reminder of Dien Bien Phu, where Giap had orchestrated the attacks from a nearby cave complex.

What if we got Giap! What if we could zap the genius himself![9]

We identified everything that could be bombed within the area of transmissions, but did not use up all the B-52s available to us. We were called back for another targeting session, at which I suggested we hit the caves once more. There was a chance the enemy might set up shop again after the first raid, since B-52s did not repeat target drops. The major thought about it, then agreed that we didn't have anything better, and it might work.

I heard later that the Air Force had bitched like hell at having to fly the same target twice, and our selection had taken a lot of heat. But the two raids were successful. On 30 January the signals stopped after forty-five B-52s dropped up to 1,350 tons of bombs on the transmission site.

After our "historic" planning sessions on the twenty-ninth, I requested a chance to return to my billet. The major, feeling expansive, let me take off until night duty the next day. My body did not know if it was time to sleep or work, so I cleaned up and had a decent meal at the Meyerkord snack bar. Saigon was celebrating the approach of Tet with firecrackers, some as big as hand grenades, and the streets sounded like a continuous firefight.

Unable to sleep or relax, after dark I walked downtown in my usual shorts, sandals, and tee shirt to take a look at the partying, even though I knew it was not wise. At the public market the streets were packed with thousands of happy, boisterous people, and I found myself the only white face floating above a sea of little people, many of whom watched me in open amazement. As each string of firecrackers went off, I found my nerves jumping and my face wincing. The wall of noise took your breath away. An ancient mama-san saw my discomfort and, with cackling laughter, she mimicked my twitching face while her cronies pointed and laughed. Then an old man started running toward me and my heart began pounding, but he was grinning and only wanted to shake my hand. He bowed and talked in rapid Vietnamese, and I tried to return his greeting with a bow.

Then I got the hell out of there, back to the Meyerkord, where I took another shower to cool down. Sleep did not come easily and my dreams were troubled.

When I returned to MACV late the next afternoon—it was 30 January, the first and most important day of Tet—excitement was high in the Tank. There had been attacks in I and II Corps during the early morning hours. (Da Nang had been hit, but the VC had done poorly.) It seemed that the much-discussed "Tet offensive" would be only a few attacks in the northern provinces.[10] It was quiet at Khe Sanh and—more important—Saigon. It looked as if we'd coast through it.

Before my night shift began, I started looking for something to eat. The MACV snack bar was closed to let the Viet employees go home for the holiday. As dusk approached I left the headquarters to head for a nearby club on the edge of Tan Son Nhut airfield. The streets were deserted and soundless, and I found myself looking around corners nervously. The club was also empty and about to close, but the Vietnamese bartender got me a cheese sandwich. Two bar girls remained; one was watching me. Finally she said, "You no stay on streets! It getting dark, you go hurry back where you belong!"

I had trouble swallowing. The other bar girl snapped at her companion in Vietnamese, apparently trying to shut her up, and they argued. Two things crossed my mind: the second girl had VC leanings, and the friendly one had just given me a more realistic statement of intelligence than anything put out by MACV.

As I took off at double time into the approaching night, my headquarters complacency turned into flat-out fear. Secret eyes seemed to be burning into me, eyes sighting along gun barrels from each shadowed corner and window.

There was a checkpoint at a crossroads just before the MACV compound. The three MPs in their circular sandbagged hut seemed huddled in the gloom, and I gave them a quick wave as I jogged past their intense stares. The next day, I heard, they were dead.

As I headed back into the MACV compound, I studied its layout more closely than ever before, this time seeing only the wall of vulnerable windows and the single cyclone fence with unsecured gates at intervals. At this corner of MACV was one of the tall guard towers, a lone MP sitting in a steel box at the top. There were no troops on the ground.

Hustling inside I felt safer, but I knew that was an illusion. The total security force between Tan Son Nhut air base and MACV headquarters totaled four MPs.

A lieutenant walked by in the halls and, though I didn't know him, I needed to talk.

"Man, it's strange out there! All the locals, the bar dollies at the club, have cleared out! One told me we're gonna get hit tonight!"

The young officer gave me a skeptical look. "Well, now I know how you Intelligence types get your stuff! And why it's so shitty!"

I headed for the Tank to find more receptive listeners. The room was a tomb. No one was talking, the phones didn't ring, and no one moved from his desk. I took aside a lieutenant I knew to tell him what I'd seen. He, too, was scared and his fears fueled mine.

"I've got to find some brass," I said.

"Well, there's one of the heads of Intelligence, but you better be careful."

I knew I couldn't handle this by saying, "Sir, a local bar girl has just warned me we're going to be attacked tonight, so could we please get a few more men outside?" Instead I said, "Sir, excuse me, but I've been outside, we have little security and the streets are deserted of Vietnamese. It fits with all the intelligence we've received about Tet attacks . . ."

His reply was impatient and terse. The Vietnamese had gone to visit their families. And the VC may attack the outskirts but they couldn't get into the city; if we reacted to their threats by going on alert, we would be offering the enemy a *psychological victory* by appearing to take him *seriously.*

"Yes, sir," I said, "I've heard that one before." He glared at me, and I made a rapid retreat into the Red Watch room. There was posting to be done.

I knew it was going to be a long night, as Vietnam began the Year of the Monkey. It was all coming together—the arrogance, the self-delusion, and, beginning around 0300 hours, the consequences.

PART FOUR

Tet

30 January – 1 February 1968

INTELLIGENCE OBJECTIVES ESTABLISHED BY J2 MACV.
To provide COMUSMACV that intelligence required for making sound and timely decisions.
INTELLIGENCE OBJECTIVES ESTABLISHED BY THE DIRECTOR FOR INTELLIGENCE PRODUCTION.
PRIORITY 1. Maximum prior warning of impending military attack or reinforcement of enemy in an attack on the U.S. forces in areas for which COMUSMACV has responsibility.

> Colonel Charles Morris
> "Some Random Comments"
> Memo, September 1967

14

Night of the Monkey

By observing rules of courtesy and consideration, one can enjoy the season of Tet. Remember—to the Vietnamese, what a man does during Tet forecasts his actions for the rest of the year.

"Tet—A New Year for Vietnam"
MACV C#1–67

This Spring far outshines the previous Springs,
Of victories throughout the land come happy tidings.
Let North and South emulate each other in fighting the U.S.
    aggressors!
Forward!
Total Victory will be ours.

Poem by Ho Chi Minh
broadcast by Radio
Hanoi to signal the start
of the Tet offensive

I was running high on adrenaline. I posted more symbols on the Khe Sanh map, but soon I felt the little room closing in on me. I went back into the Tank, eager for any hint of what was to come. Still that strange silence.

Finally, sometime shortly after 0200, I couldn't fight my fatigue any longer and slipped a cot behind the curtain that covered the map of Cambodia, making a little tent to screen out the light. I had just begun to relax when a phone rang across the room at the III Corps desk, and in the silence it sounded like an explosion. The only noncom in the Tank snatched it up on the first ring.

A pause, then came his voice, expressionless, level, controlled, "The embassy is under attack."

It was not quite 0300. (The attacks in Saigon had actually begun at around 0130 with an assault on Independence Palace. The American embassy, a few blocks away, was hit about an hour later by nineteen members of the VC C-10 Sapper Battalion. In my recollection the embassy report was the first to come into MACV J-2, possibly because it was the first American facility to be attacked.)

I punched my way out from behind the map curtain to stand blinking from the fluorescent glare in a room of chaos. Now all the phones were ringing, people were yelling and running, and the watch officers at the Corps desks were calling out the sites of more and more attacks: Quang Tri City, Tam Ky, Phu Bai, Chu Lai, Qui Nhon, An Khe, Dalat, Ban Me Thuot, Hoi An, Tuy Hoa, Bien Hoa, Long Binh, Vinh Long, My Tho, Tan Phu Trung, Hoc Mon, Tay Ninh, Ben Tre, Soc Trang . . . and Hue.

For a while I hung out by the I Corps desk. Like many others, the watch officer had a wide-eyed, glazed look. But there were those who had come alive and wore knowing smiles that seemed to say, "Now we're at it and we're gonna kick some ass!" A major who was hustling by me slowed to grin and wink, perhaps as much amused by my state of shock as I was by his enthusiasm.

Finally the activity slowed down enough to allow me to ask the I Corps officer about Khe Sanh. He shot back, "It's the only safe place in I Corps! Hell, *everywhere* else is catching it!"

Then I remembered our security at the headquarters and stopped worrying about Khe Sanh. Just then I was approached by a lieutenant. "Hey, Jones, the *whole country* is being attacked!"

"Screw the country! We're in Saigon, remember? And the VC are outside the airport, they're coming over the golf course at the Joint General Staff compound next to CICV, and if they attacked the embassy, they'll be heading here!"

He paled. "How good is our security outside?"

"It ain't much!" I was eyeing the handgun he had strapped to his waist. "But if you loan me your .45, I'll go out there and take another look."

He was reluctant to give up the weapon. "What if the VC get into the building?"

"O.K., *you* go outside and check it out."

He handed me his pistol and urged me to hurry back. I went to the corner of the building closest to the airport and found a few enlisted men with their heads up against the glass door, staring into the night.

"What's happening?" I asked.

"There's been some shots but they're not too close."

"You're not standing in a very safe place. There's a light behind you. You can't see out; they can see in."

It didn't seem to bother them much. Finally I pushed through the gawkers and opened the door. The men protested and jumped back, as if that glass door had been some protection. I took a deep breath to shore up my own uncertainty and duckwalked down the drainage ditch that ran alongside the building. Moving low, I came to the edge of the compound, where stood the MP tower and one of the few bunkers for the building.

I yelled up to the MP but we could not understand each other so I waved him down. He quickly stepped down the precarious rungs on the pole while I held my breath. Bathed in the roof lights, he was a terribly vulnerable target. He jumped the last few steps and ran up to me. In the dusty light from a lamp over the gate, I could see panic in his eyes. He was too young to buy beer back home.

"Oh, sir, I'm glad to see an officer! What's happening? No one's told me anything!"

I tried to be casual. "No big thing yet. Just a few snipers around, so keep your ass low, and tell everyone you see the same, O.K.? What kind of security do we have, what weapons and ammo?"

"Just .45s and M-16s, a few clips each, and about fifteen guards around the building."

"Just a few clips. Damn, we've got to get more."

"There's an armory someplace in the building, Lieutenant."

"There is? O.K., you stay here, I'll go for ammo. If anyone with weapons comes out, hold him here."

I ran back to the door and found another group of sightseers. After recovering from their fright as I barged in, they deluged me with questions.

"We've got trouble and we need ammo. Does anyone know where the armory is?"

They shook their heads.

"I've got to get back out there. I want you and you to find the armory, see what they've got, bring back some .45 and M-16 ammo if they've got it. Then come and get me so we can distribute it. I'll be at the guard tower at the corner. You understand?"

The two men nodded reluctantly. I could see they were scared to hell.

"Now move out!" I ordered. As they hustled around the corner, I heard one say, "I ain't going outside!"

My resolve deflated. They were going to disappear into the anonymity of MACV.

Maybe the other MPs knew where the armory was. I ran back to the tower and was relieved to see an MP jeep. A sergeant seemed to be chewing out the guard, who indicated me as I approached. The sergeant, a short, stocky three-striper, turned on me, his face livid. "Are you the lieutenant who's screwing around with my men?"

I was stunned. I just looked at him.

"This guard has standing orders! He stays in his tower! He does not come down until he is relieved! You understand that, Lieutenant?"

"What if we need him, and you, and all the MPs, for an attack on another side of the building?"

"We have men. We'll respond to it."

"How many men, Sergeant?"

He cooled down. "We have fifteen."

"Not many for a building this size, is it? Can we get more?"

The guard spoke up. "While you went inside, a couple of men with a BAR came out. They're in that bunker now."

"Great! Sergeant, can we find more men inside with weapons?"

He nodded. "I'll send one of the men scrounging. Lieutenant, I have to make my rounds, check the other posts."

"O.K., but look, this is the point closest to the airfield and there's fighting going on there now. We've got to assume that this is the likeliest spot they'll hit. So if you hear shooting, get your men over here!"

"Yes, sir," he said without enthusiasm and jumped into the jeep. His driver took off with a spray of gravel. The guard returned to his tower post and I checked on the men with the BAR—a Browning Automatic Rifle, a light machine gun used in World War I and still a fine weapon. The two men—I think a warrant officer and a sergeant—were glad to see me and we discussed their field of fire. Some more men arrived, office workers with a diverse collection of weapons: an AK-47, handguns, a Swedish Bren gun. I welcomed all reinforcements eagerly.

The MP jeep swung around the building on another pass and then abruptly stopped. A major and a lieutenant approached the MP sergeant. I hustled over. The major waved away my salute: "Don't worry about formalities now." He introduced himself as the duty officer at the Command Operations Center and said he was checking out the situation.

Grateful for some support, I quickly explained that I had placed my rag-tag fire team facing the loudest sounds of fighting that were still coming from Tan Son Nhut.

"Lieutenant, were you officer of the day somewhere?" I could see a look of skepticism on his face.

"No, sir, I'm from J-2, working TDY in the Tank."

"Why did you come out? I thought you Intelligence types were lovers, not fighters!" He was smiling.

I laughed. "Well, it's probably safer outside than inside. But I'll be very happy to go back in if you've got some Infantry on the way or someone to give orders out here!"

He asked if I had any Infantry experience and seemed reassured when I told him about Benning. "Lieutenant, we won't get any troops until after we're overrun. There's too much going on. And we've got someone to give orders—you! You're doing fine. Check with me in the COC when you can. Carry on!"

The major saluted briskly, about-faced, and was gone before I could respond. I looked at the MP sergeant, who shrugged and said, "O.K., Lieutenant, you better go with me on my run and see how we're laid out."

"Good idea." I looked up at the lights on the roof of the building. "We're in full illumination here. The VC can see everything we're doing. We should shoot out those damn lights!"

The sergeant frowned. "That's government property. You'll have to answer to MACV."

I wanted to laugh but thought better of it. The jeep driver jammed his vehicle up to top speed along the side of the building and I asked him to slow down. The sergeant objected—he said he didn't want to present a target to the VC. I insisted. I didn't want to die in a flipped-over jeep.

A few moments later a radio message was coming in from BOQ One, about a mile away from MACV. We stopped and sat mutely listening to the shrill voice that rose above the sound of static and shooting.

". . . we're surrounded . . . there's no way to escape . . . they're killing us . . . I see the chopper . . . I've shot up a flare . . . oh my God, there's another flare . . . the chopper is passing over, he's shooting the wrong way . . . Lord, don't they know where we are . . . they're coming in the building . . . they're in the halls . . . oh my God please . . ."

Then came the sound of shooting and a wall of static. The three of us sat there in the dark without moving, the roar of a death in our ears. Without amplification the shooting now sounded distant and unreal. I felt sick. The MP sergeant said, "We're going there, we're gonna help them!"

"No, you're not." My voice was weak and didn't sound like my own. "It's all over there. You've got your orders, remember? Now we've got to defend this place."

The jeep run continued and we stopped wherever we found volunteers with weapons, telling these irregulars to group on the corner facing BOQ One. That had to be the way the VC would be coming now.

After circling the building and returning to the corner, I tried to remember my Fort Benning training as best I could and placed everyone in something approximating interlocking fields of fire. Then we settled into sweaty waiting. But not for long. Bullets zinged overhead and panic welled up in me. There were so few of us—only some six or eight men. I yelled at a nearby enlisted man, "This is it! We need help! Get into MACV and find us some more men, quick!"

He took off fast and, to my surprise, was back quickly with several more armed men, a couple of them MPs. It was like the cavalry to the rescue, and we all whooped a greeting to them. But we were still only the equivalent of a squad protecting MACV headquarters. Even if the other MPs backed us up when we were hit, we'd last only a few minutes.

The two MPs moved into a lightly sandbagged hut at the corner of the installation and I spread the rest of the men in the drainage ditch or along the fence, so that we came together in a vee-point at the corner. I got behind a concrete-filled barrel next to the hut by a gate. It was a terribly open and vulnerable position, but it was the only place I could find that let me watch everyone as well as see beyond the perimeter.

It didn't much matter. I figured that when the VC came, none of us would survive.

The men with the BAR were MACV's best hope at the moment, and I didn't want them to take the brunt of the attack. The hut would be sure to fall to grenades or rockets, so the weapon was placed in reserve behind us. I emphasized to the gun crew that they had to hold fire until the enemy was visible—in other words, when they were coming through the fence. And I told them to watch the Tan Son Nhut side of the building in case we were flanked.

"Be ready to relocate if I need you up here!" That was my final order before we settled down to wait.

That was the hardest part. I wondered how combat troops on the line could stand it, night after night, waiting for the attack to begin, waiting to hear the sound of incoming rounds, the rattle of AK-47s. We'd been told at Benning that when you hear the zip of a bullet you're O.K., because it's already overhead. It's the zip you don't hear that kills you.

The retort of rifles and the *whomp-whomp* of mortar shells seemed closer, and I prayed for dawn. Surely the VC would have to pull out then. Finally the sky lightened and, to our cheers, the orange ball of sun edged over the horizon.

The MP jeep stopped hard behind us and the sergeant yelled, "Bad news, Lieutenant. It's not over. The VC are digging in! And they're driving stolen jeeps up to our positions before opening fire! They're wearing ARVN uniforms, so be careful!"

The report was almost more than I could take. Dawn wasn't going to be the end of it.

From inside the guard hut I heard the MPs in hushed conversation. I couldn't see them but their voices were clear. "Look at that! You see that? Over there, on that roof, that old man sitting there watching the goddamn war!"

I scanned the horizon in front of us. There he was, maybe a quarter of a mile away. He was sitting comfortably, an old Vietnamese man on his veranda. Just taking in the dawn and the battle around him.

One of the MPs said, "That's fucking incredible. Let's scare his old ass and put a couple of rounds in the area!"

I was shocked into quick response. "You guys aren't going to do anything stupid, you hear me?"

There was a pause, then, "Ah, Lieutenant, we was just kidding."

"Yeah, sure, but you just take it easy and don't do anything until I tell you to!"

After another pause, the MP whispered, "The lieutenant is getting nervous."

"YOU'RE DAMN RIGHT THE LIEUTENANT IS GETTING

NERVOUS! AND YOU DON'T DO ANYTHING STUPID, YOU HEAR ME!"

I was much louder than necessary, and the MP was right. I was on a wire, on the edge. After a surge of energy that had come with dawn, fatigue now seemed to be sucking me under.

Suddenly bullets snapped through the air over our heads. Almost simultaneously came the *whomp* of a mortar round landing nearby. Someone yelled, a bit unnecessarily, "Incoming! Hit the ground!"

Either somebody said it, or I thought it: "Here it comes, here they come . . ." I was hugging the barrel, too frightened to look for advancing guerrillas. But there was only silence again. Our heads began to pop up, and we looked around in puzzlement.

And then came the damnedest sight I've ever seen.

Down a path that led to MACV came two fullback-sized black sergeants, five- or six-stripers, casually walking to work. They wore their jungle fatigues with black camouflaged insignia, but they carried only the ultimate symbol of Saigon Warriors—briefcases.

They strolled right past us, only yards away on the other side of fence, deeply engrossed in an animated conversation. They never saw us as, fascinated, we watched their progress up to the first gate through the fence.

As they opened the gate, another bullet or two zinged over us, and my dirty dozen, as one, started yelling at the two noncoms. They saw us at once and their shock froze them momentarily on the spot. Then they bolted for safety, got themselves jammed in the gate, shouldered their way through it, sprinted toward the MACV door, abandoning both briefcases midway, and got shoulder-jammed once again in the door frame. One man crawled in, the other dived over him.

We all howled with laughter, especially when one of the NCOs crawled back outside on his belly to retrieve the briefcases, then did a double-time low-profile duckwalk back into the building. The sergeant was able to grin and wave at us on his way back in.

Then I saw heads sticking out of the windows all over the building, gawking at us. I yelled at the tourists to get back in, but for every head that withdrew, two popped back out.

The sound of a vehicle moving fast outside the fence pulled me away from the sightseers. A canvas-topped jeep braked in a squeal right in front of our gate, and my heart pounded wildly.

All of our weapons were turned on the vehicle. To my terror, I saw at the wheel a Vietnamese in black-and-green-striped tiger fatigues. With violently shaking hands, I full-cocked the .45, loading a round into the chamber, and screamed, "IDENTIFY YOURSELF!"

I could feel, smell, taste, sense, a Chi-Com or Russian machine gun pointing at us from the back of the covered jeep. I waited for the string of bullets.

Why did they just sit there? I screamed again, maybe twice, for identification. Then one of the MPs ran to the gate and opened it. I dived at him, yelling, "What the hell are you doing?" His answer was incomprehensible but he was pointing at the jeep. Stepping out of it was a Special Forces lieutenant colonel, tall and powerful in his green beret and tiger suit. As he came through the gate, his lips curled in disdain while he eyed us. Then he assumed a wide stance, an M-16 on one hip and a hand on the other. John Wayne could have taken lessons.

"Just what the hell is going on here!" he boomed out. It wasn't a question.

I could not have stood up if it was Westmoreland himself. There was no more strength or resolve left in me. I leaned back against the barrel, my feet sprawled out in the roadway. The colonel just snorted as I said, "We've had incoming, sir, please hurry inside . . ."

Then another bullet cracked through the air, but as he walked past us into the headquarters the colonel did not flinch or change his pace. The Green Beret legend lives on, I thought. I could see the Vietnamese driver in the jeep, still wearing a terrified expression in memory of the arsenal pointed at him. I gave him the thumbs-up gesture and a smile of relief flooded his face.

The sound of fighting had lessened and the sun was finally warming away the night chill. At last the sensor-controlled lights around the building clicked off. I sat there a while longer leaning against the barrel, but caught myself drifting into sleep. Forcing myself up, I rallied some strength, yelled to the men that I was going into Operations to find out what was going on, and told a warrant officer he was in charge. It was, I think, something after 0800 hours.

Headquarters was filled with people going in every direction. I aimed down the middle, the forgotten but still cocked .45 dangling in my hand, and glared my way through the traffic. Generals, colonels, majors moved out of the way of this dirty, sweaty creature plodding down the polished corridors. I turned into the hallway to the COC and the Tank. It was blocked by desks. The Saigon Warriors had pushed all their desks into the hall to make a maze that had to be squeezed through. It was to slow down the VC once they got inside, you see.

I told the sergeant at the COC door that I had to report to the officer of the day to find out if outside security should remain in place. Without a word, he pushed a button that unlocked the door.

The room I stepped into was the true nerve center of the war. It seemed to me to have everything I had originally expected to find in the Tank: backlit glass-covered wall maps, electronic boards with flashing lights, men on ladders grease-penciling the shifting troop data on the maps. I was awed by the intense activity and reassured by the sense of controlled purpose.

The major who had checked on me during the night sat at a desk close to the door. I reminded him who I was and he looked embarrassed.

"Oh, you mean no one came out to relieve you?"

"No, sir."

"I'm sorry. Well, you can tell the men to come in. It's pretty much over. The VC are in pockets of resistance all over the city but they're not moving."

"Sir, you know we took some fire last night . . ."

"Yes, well, a lot of that was probably Americans in their barracks shooting at anything that moved."

"Ah, we don't have *mortars* in our barracks, sir!"

"The VC unloaded all their ordnance before regrouping. Don't worry. We're O.K. here. You can pull the men in. And, Jones . . ."

"Yes, sir?"

"You did a good job. I want to call your CO and tell him you deserve a commendation."

"Listen, you've got plenty to keep you busy. Don't worry about it."

But the major insisted and I gave him my CICV phone number before returning to the MACV perimeter.

"The war's over, men! You can pack it up. Operations says the VC are contained in pockets and we're O.K. here."

A big, beefy sergeant snapped out the clip from his AK-47. "Hell, I wish they'd come. Thought I was gonna get a chance to shoot a few of the bastards!" He grinned and swaggered back into the building.

Some of the men were skeptical about the all-clear signal and asked if they could stay in place. I told them that was between them and their CO. "But I've had it. I'm going in."

I started to walk back inside, then stopped and turned back to them. "Thanks, guys!" I yelled, wanting to say more. A few of them yelled back their thanks, smiling, and one gave a thumbs-up.

I never learned one name and their faces were, even in the morning light, shadowed by my tiredness. But I'll never forget them.

15

Coming In

In my opinion, this is a diversionary effort to take attention
away from the north [from] an attack on Khe Sanh.
General William C. Westmoreland,
speaking outside the recaptured
U.S. embassy, 31 January 1968

Back in MACV I saw near the door a group of uniforms, including a
full-bird colonel, crawling around on the floor, laughing and chattering.
A master sergeant stood watching, a bemused look on his face.

"What the hell are they doing?" I asked him.

He grinned. "MACV took a hit last night. See the window?" He
pointed and I saw a neat round hole. "They're looking for the souvenir
bullet!"

After a good chuckle, I wove my way through the desks back into
the Tank. Even there, furniture had been pushed into the corridor. The
Red Watch room was empty, but I heard a flurry of activity in the hall,
unmistakably the sound of arriving brass. Today there was no chorus of
"Good morning, *sir!*"

Westmoreland shot past, and I watched him from the doorway. His
face was strained and even sterner than usual as he huddled with some
officers. Then he turned back to glare at the desks in the hallway.

"What the hell is this?" he demanded of a nearby captain.

The officer turned red. "Ah, I think, sir, last night, some of the
men, they thought that if the VC got into the building . . ."

Westmoreland reacted to the thought of VC in his headquarters as
if he'd been slapped. His face grew darker, furrowed, and his bushy
eyebrows made a solid hedgerow.

"Get them *out* of here!" he ordered and marched over to the III
Corps desk for his first current-intelligence briefing on the Tet offen-

sive. The captain turned to me open-mouthed and shrugged; I observed that the general was having a hard day. Then I watched Westmoreland take his briefing. He stood stiffly in front of the desk, his arms at his sides, his head somewhat bowed. He was usually so controlled, but this morning his right shoulder was twitching in irregular spasms, almost as if he were trying to shake something off his back, something that plagued him. In this new year of the monkey, he had his own monkey on his back. The addiction was optimism, and the withdrawal pains had begun.

I had problems of my own. The Red Watch major was bearing down on me, the fire of his temper burning brightly.

"Jones, where the hell have you been?"

"Sir, that's a long story. I was outside with a defense force . . ."

"Skip it! No posting's been done all night! I damn near got killed coming through, and all I find is some cocky lieutenant who goofs off because of some excitement!"

"Sir, there was a war going on last night!"

"Don't bull me, boy! Nothing happened here. You left your post! That's a court-martial offense! What if Khe Sanh had been attacked last night?"

"Sir, Khe Sanh was the only place in the whole damn country that *wasn't* attacked!"

We stared at each other, then he said with a little less conviction, "I could still bring charges for it."

I was too tired, I was too burned out. "Major, you do what you think you have to, because I did what I thought I had to!"

I turned away from him and went back into the Red Watch room to make some effort at posting, if only to get away from him. Later, when we could tolerate speaking to each other, I told him I had not slept or eaten in what seemed like days. Grudgingly, he excused me to get cleaned up and scrounge some food.

I found the lieutenant who owned the .45 and returned it to him. He was angry that I had kept it so long, but I suggested that events were a bit out of my control. Then I found a distribution point for C-rations. For the next few days while confined to MACV, we ate like real soldiers. Weapons were being distributed at the armory and I got in line to draw an M-2 carbine.

As I stood in line I heard two lieutenants talking about the night before. "Those boxes of ammo sat there until morning and no one came to get them. The VC would have loved to find them!"

I couldn't let that pass. "What are you talking about?"

"Some lieutenant had the armory opened up last night, and boxes of ammo were taken out and piled up in the hall by the door. But the dumb shit never came back for them!"

"Well, I'm the 'dumb shit' and I ordered some enlisted men to get what they could and report back to me outside so we could distribute it! They never showed up!"

One of the men shook his head. "You've got to follow up on your orders. That was the first thing they taught us in OCS. You can't assume orders will be implemented."

The lecture by this ninety-day wonder was not what I needed. "We were more than a little occupied out here, Lieutenant!"

His round, shiny face took on a superior expression. "Oh, really? I heard nothing happened. You know, General Westmoreland saw all that ammo and is pretty pissed off about it!"

"Well, you tell the good general when you see him to come talk to me about it!"

I glared at them as they walked away, laughing. I had to give these clowns one more shot.

"WHERE WERE YOU BRAVE ASSHOLES LAST NIGHT WHEN I NEEDED YOU OUTSIDE?" It was all I could think of, but it worked. They stopped, looked at each other in some embarrassment, and the talkative one explained haltingly they could not leave their desks.

"Right!" I said, and walked away. The adrenaline of anger had at least pushed out my fatigue as I entertained dark and abusive thoughts about Saigon Warriors, REMFs, and obnoxious, cocky lieutenants. As if I weren't one myself.

Later we heard that the VC had indeed been heading for MACV headquarters. The VC main force at Tan Son Nhut would have kept coming if U.S. reinforcements had not reached the air base at the last minute. The snipers who had killed three MPs at their post must have been in place before nightfall. There may well have been VC eyes on me as I hurried through dusk before the attacks. Forces from within Saigon had hit not only BOQ One, but also the nearby billet for enlisted men, a structure with a design similar to MACV's. The Viet Cong had got lost and attacked the wrong building—thank God they were as screwed up as we were!

The EM had broken open their own armory and with M-14s these support troops had given a good account of themselves. Many of the bullets zinging over MACV may have been theirs, but they also stopped the VC from reaching the headquarters. I couldn't gather details; the enlisted men were ordered not to discuss the incident.

In spite of scattered firefights still taking place around Saigon, the Red Watch major chose to attempt a return to his BOQ quarters that evening and again left me on night duty. I was allowed to get some sleep but there were no cots anywhere and all the desks were in use as MACV operated at top velocity. In the hallway a large pile of burn bags, paper grocery bags jammed with obsolete classified documents and stapled closed, stood waiting to be destroyed outside in the incinerator. A soldier had stretched out a line of bags along the wall and was fast asleep on his makeshift couch. This seemed my last option, but all the pedestrians got a laugh out of the sight and relaxation was impossible. I went back to posting.

In the late night or early morning hours, Westmoreland returned for further briefings and the Tank assumed its formal, almost holy, demeanor. Even the phones were ordered to silence as each call was snatched up immediately. From across the room I watched him standing before the III Corps desks. His shoulder still twitched occasionally but less obviously now.

The Red Watch room was an information vacuum; the VC could have been attacking in force for all I knew. I stepped into the Tank to listen to the briefing being given to the general. Minutes later, Major House, my CICV OIC who was still on temporary duty at the I Corps desk, let me know that I was risking trouble; I had "no need to know" and should return to my post.

Major House did come to see me later. He noted my advanced state of exhaustion and said he'd talk to the Red Watch OIC on my behalf. The next day I was allowed to go back to the Meyerkord and on the way I stopped at CICV. My OB shop was a darkened tomb; only a few men were there, asleep on cots. On the major's otherwise bare desk was a note in Kernsky's handwriting, reporting the recommendation from the major in the Command Operations Center about the night of the offensive and my participation.

I threw it in the wastebasket, and for maybe a half hour I just sat in my chair staring blankly at the maps and all the VC/NVA unit symbols, still posted out in the boondocks, far from the cities and bases that were still burning.

Finally I headed for the Meyerkord to get a hot shower, hot food, and some glorious, healing sleep.

16

War Stories

I liken the recent Tet offensive by the leadership in Hanoi to the Battle of the Bulge in World War II. By committing a large share of his forces to a major offensive, he achieved some tactical surprise. This offensive has required us to react and to modify our plans in order to take advantage of the opportunity to inflict heavy casualties upon him. Although the enemy has achieved some temporary psychological advantage, he suffered a military defeat.

General William C. Westmoreland
AP Interview
Stars and Stripes, 27 February 1968

The VC had been entering the cities for weeks. Wearing civilian clothes or ARVN uniforms, they carried weapons in caskets (there was a surge of "funerals"), hollowed logs on trucks, in false-bottomed vehicles, and even in carved-out watermelons. Flowerpots contained hand grenades buried in the soil. There was always heavy traffic during Tet as relatives visited their families, but this year there was even more movement than usual. No one noticed. At least the Americans didn't.

Beginning in the early hours of 30 January[1] and accelerating through the morning of 31 January, the Viet Cong attacked up to 36 of the nation's 44 provincial capitals, 64 to 72 of the 245 district capitals, 5 of the 6 autonomous cities, all the major air bases (at least 6), and uncounted numbers of army bases and headquarters, including that at Long Binh. Occupation of villages and RD ("Revolutionary Development," that is, "pacified") hamlets also occurred by the score and the total may never have been fully recorded by MACV.

For Saigon it had been a very close thing. MACV later estimated that 4,500 guerrillas had infiltrated the city. Fighting continued until 5 February in the center of Saigon[2] and lasted until at least late in the month in the outskirts and surrounding Gia Dinh province. Three VC/

NVA divisions had been outside the city waiting to exploit the initial attacks by smaller units and infiltrators. Some of the heaviest fighting had been on the edges of Tan Son Nhut air base. On the field had been two companies from the South Vietnamese Army's best ranger battalion, waiting to be flown to I Corps for the Khe Sanh battle that Westmoreland believed was the true offensive. A scheduling error had left these units on the runway overnight and they absorbed the first VC attack.[3] Later an American armored cavalry unit was able to reach the airfield by following flares dropped from a helicopter by the unit's CO. VC demolition teams had failed to knock out the bridges that permitted reinforcement of Tan Son Nhut.

The response time of American units to the crisis in Saigon was exceptional, thanks to the foresight of General Frederick C. Weyand (who later became the third and final COMUSMACV when he replaced General Creighton Abrams in 1972). Weyand commanded the sector's U.S. forces and was responsible for protecting the approaches to Saigon. On 10 January he persuaded Westmoreland to shift combat units away from their forward positions along the Cambodian border and elsewhere. Some fifteen U.S. battalions relocated closer to Saigon (but not inside the city), giving the area a presence of twenty-seven maneuver battalions.[4] These units were not in place to ambush the invaders or repel the initial assault, but their rapid counterattack was vital in discouraging follow-up by VC reserves.

The enemy army, declared by MACV in January to be at "the lowest level" since early 1966 and to be about 30 percent "not combat effective,"[5] was all over the country, attacking at will. The bloodshed was terrible. MACV estimated that in the first three days of battle, the Communist death toll was "over 10,000."[6] The huge civilian losses would not even be estimated for weeks to come.

The most brutal and protracted fighting was in the imperial city of Hue in Thua Thien province, I Corps. This centuries-old capital of the Annam empire was Vietnam's most treasured cultural center and had been considered a neutral zone that few Americans were allowed to enter. The inner city, the Citadel, was protected by a great square wall ranging in thickness from sixty to over two hundred feet and standing some sixteen feet high. The enemy force, largely North Vietnamese units augmented by local VC sappers and political cadre, was scattered throughout the city and well dug into the Citadel's walls.

House-to-house fighting and finally assaults on the awesome wall itself lasted until 24 February, when the Citadel was retaken. ARVN troops entered to hoist their yellow and red flag, while U.S. Marines, who had borne most of the assault, watched in fatigue and some disgust. The entire city was not secured until 2 March[7] and perhaps up to 80 percent of it was damaged,[8] although the sacred Citadel remained largely intact.[9] Surprisingly, part of the Communist force was able to escape.

Hue was not the only city held for an extended time. Parts of Dalat remained in VC control until 9 February and 20 percent of the city was destroyed.[10] Portions of Cholon, the Chinese suburb of Saigon, were in contest until mid-February, and the Phu Tho racetrack, at which were located a VC headquarters and field hospital, was not retaken until late February.

By the end of the month, the MACV estimate of enemy killed had grown to 25,000.[11] During the tactically brilliant month-long counterattack by the Allies, we reported 2,371 American KIA, 11,664 WIA (of whom 5,500 returned to duty without hospital stays), and 155 MIA.[12] The SVN forces losses were less well documented, as usual, perhaps reaching 5,000.[13] At least 14,000 civilians died, about 20,000 were wounded, and according to Westmoreland's sources over half a million were made homeless.[14] But GVN officials reported 1 to 2 million people were refugees by March 1968, and some Americans felt the number might be as high as 4 million.[15]

The number of Communist attackers was unclear from the outset and has been violently debated ever since. The MACV-sanctioned number was around 84,000[16] and was cited as proving that, for an "all-out effort," the enemy army did not exceed our OB Book estimates (then 225,346).

Even in the face of disaster, the optimism continued unabated. Major House reported a case in point when he returned to CICV from the Tank. Just after the offensive he was assisting Colonel Daniel Graham, head of the current intelligence branch, on a briefing to Westmoreland. The major told us that Graham had said, "When the smoke clears in a day or so, we'll learn that there were really only a few enemy units out there, and then we'll all have a good laugh."[17] (Ironically, by 1975 when he appeared before the U.S. House of Representatives Intelligence Committee, Graham —by then a lieutenant general and head of the Defense Intelligence Agency—had revised his wartime estimate of a "few units" up to an attacking force of 165,000 soldiers.[18] But during his tenure at MACV J-2, Graham never wavered. In the period of 23–25 February he briefed the chairman of the Joint Chiefs of Staff, General Earle Wheeler, and declared that we had just "destroyed" the enemy in Vietnam.)[19]

In the weeks after the opening attacks, American casualties continued to rise. In the pre-Tet period of late 1967 and early 1968, our KIA rate (as announced by MACV) had rarely gone above 150 a week. After Tet, each week's losses were reported as follows (this source apparently did not include deaths from non-hostile sources, a soft category that was no doubt often used to absorb many combat-related losses): 3 February —367; 10 February—295; 17 February—481; 24 February—413; 2 March—490; 9 March—435; 16 March—287; 23 March—303; 30 March—294; 6 April—230; 13 April—312; 20 April—259; 27 April —265; 4 May—345; 11 May—480; 18 May—480; 25 May—480; 1 June—348; 8 June—344; 15 June—286. Thereafter the figures began to return to the pre-Tet averages.[20]

The VC/NVA army was *not* destroyed nor made ineffective during the Tet attacks. In the first six months of 1968, in spite of losses of up to 120,000 men,[21] the enemy carried the war to us and for months most of our operations seemed more defensive than offensive.

The rationalizations began at once. Arriving at the U.S. embassy minutes after it was secured at about 0915 on 31 January, Westmoreland declared to the skeptical press that "the enemy's well-laid plans went afoul." Later that day he declared the city attacks to be a "diversion" for the "main effort" to come in I Corps. The next day he refined his position to place the Tet attacks as the second stage of a three-phase campaign (the first had been the border battles of September–November). Westmoreland was sure that the Quang Tri–Thua Thien campaign would yet come, but that the current offensive was "about to run out of steam."[22]

At a press conference on 2 February President Johnson[23] called the offense "a complete failure" and declared, "We have known for some time that this offensive was planned by the enemy," and that it had been "anticipated, prepared for, and met."[24]

Westmoreland's first major pronouncement on the offensive came in late February when a reporter from the Associated Press submitted written questions for his response. On 27 February the two-page piece was printed in *Stars and Stripes,* evoking much comment from the men at CICV. Westmoreland did admit that the enemy had achieved "tactical surprise" even though we "had intelligence that there was to be an offensive." And he conceded that the enemy's ability to conduct such an offensive had been "underestimated." He believed American forces were only "temporarily on the defensive" after killing "more than 40,000 of the enemy." He declared, "I do not believe Hanoi can hold up under a long war. The present enemy offensive attitude may indicate that Hanoi realizes this also." He did think it "conceivable" that the enemy's build-up at Khe Sanh was a "feint," but he didn't "believe this was his intention"; our heavy air attacks had possibly forced a change in enemy plans. Westmoreland stated that Hanoi's "ability to pursue a protracted war has been reduced by the losses that he has recently suffered."

Also on 27 February, General Wheeler gave his report to President Johnson after a three-day visit to the war zone. It included this:

> Although many of [the enemy's] units were badly hurt, the judgment is that he has the will and capability to continue. . . .
>
> The enemy is operating with relative freedom in the countryside, probably recruiting heavily and no doubt infiltrating NVA units and personnel. His recovery is likely to be rapid; his supplies are adequate; and he is trying to maintain the momentum of his winter-spring offensive. . . .
>
> The initial attack nearly succeeded in a dozen places, and defeat in those places was only averted by the timely reaction of U.S. forces. In short, it was a very near thing.

As to how the enemy had been able to mount such a wide offensive, Wheeler estimated that the enemy force "peaked" just before Tet to a total of 240,000 "by hard recruiting, infiltration, civilian impressment, and drawdowns on service and guerrilla personnel." Losses were said to be "one-fifth of his total strength."[25]

On 6 March the Central Office of South Vietnam, the Viet Cong headquarters, published its own critique of the offensive. As usual, COSVN grossly overestimated losses inflicted on the Allies, then conducted the traditional Communist exercise of self-criticism[26] of its efforts, especially regarding the failure to "motivate the masses" to rise against the Americans and their "puppets." COSVN did claim success in forcing its enemy into a "purely passive and defensive position" with his forces "dispersed on all battlefields."[27]

On our side, the official analysis was conducted by the Washington bureaucracy well into 1968. On 16 April, the president's Foreign Intelligence Advisory Board, chaired by General Maxwell D. Taylor, issued a memorandum entitled "Intelligence Warning of the TET Offensive in South Vietnam." Attached was a DIA-prepared analysis of pre-Tet reports, which contained the following: for Saigon "only three warnings" were received, including those from a PW and from a captured document; there were "five warnings" regarding Hue; for Da Nang the enemy's plan "was known to U.S. forces as far back as 1 September 1967"; for Bien Hoa there were seven agent reports; for Phan Thiet and Can Tho, two agent reports each; Nha Thrang had four captured documents and three agent reports; Dalat, three agent reports; and Kontum received "fourteen warnings." (Given the quantity of reports we had for I Corps, this survey seems conservative.)

Of all the major cities, Pleiku was the recipient of the most attack warnings. On 5 January we obtained the VC attack plan and on the twenty-third the commanding officer of the 4th Infantry Division convened a strategy session of his commanders to prepare for the attack. Effective steps were taken[28] and of the battles in the cities, the Pleiku defense was the most successful. However, that effort caused the destruction of about half the city.[29] The devastation there was second only to that inflicted on Hue.

The Taylor memo concluded that although many warnings had been provided, "the intensity, coordination and timing of the enemy attack were not fully anticipated." And it included the most basic of all findings:

> . . . most commanders and intelligence officers, at all levels, did not visualize the enemy as capable of accomplishing his stated goals as they appeared in propaganda and in captured documents. Prevailing estimates of attrition, infiltration and local recruitment, reports of low morale, and a long series of defeats had degraded our image of the enemy. The general picture presented was an enemy unable to conduct an offensive of such scope and intensity.

The command policy of "downward trending" had come full circle. The September sellout had its payback.[30]

In the halls and offices of CICV and MACV the official proclamations of victory were less than persuasive. The cocky talk was over, replaced by a sense of depression, even desperation. Within days we had begun hearing the horror stories of human loss and suffering. These were some of them.

Bodies were strewn all over the golf course near CICV. Some were Americans with hands tied behind their backs and neat holes through their foreheads.

Somewhere in Saigon two heads of Americans were found stuck on top of fence posts. The VC left a note saying they were killed because they had been living with Viet women.

Across the city, women who had lived with or worked for Americans were killed and mutilated in hideous fashion. Heads cut off and placed on display. Parts amputated. Poles shoved up vaginas.

And I made this note toward the end of February:

A maid turned in her badge today. She said the VC found her pass in her home. They cut her baby's head off. She came in and said, "I work no more for Americans." She walked out without another word. The other maids told us what happened. We'll mail her pay to her home. There's nothing else to do.

All across the city, men who had only administrative duties were thrust into life-or-death situations. After Tet I learned about one of the most dramatic of these. The press version, based on a release from the American authorities, reported that at the closing moments of the suicide attack by nineteen sappers on the embassy, only one wounded VC was left, on the ground floor of an annex building. An unarmed civilian was trapped in his living quarters on the second floor and appeared at a window where a .45 was thrown up to him. The end of the embassy attack came when he shot the last VC on the stairs.

Or so it was reported to and by the media. Weeks later I met the secretary who worked for this embassy official. She told a different story. The handgun had not done the job—either it jammed or the official missed all his shots. He had to struggle with the VC, finally strangling him to death.

Some of the stories had more humor than horror. During the attacks, Colonel Mac had also been trapped in his room at the Rex Hotel in downtown Saigon, where he listened to the shooting outside and waited for the VC to come busting in. He unpacked his only weapon, a souvenir Montagnard crossbow that he planned to hang on his study wall at home. After loading a little wooden arrow, he sat across from the door, waiting for his one shot. Luckily no one came to visit him that night.

The residents of the Meyerkord Hotel were trapped for several days by fighting at the edge of the grounds of Independence Palace, only two blocks away. On Nguyen Du Street, which ran past the hotel, the palace, and the Korean embassy, was a partly constructed apartment building on which work had been abandoned. It stood facing the southwest corner of the palace, one block from Cong Ly Avenue, which connected downtown to Tan Son Nhut.

For weeks, the VC had been surreptiously moving ammo and weapons into the building. Neither the white-uniformed elite presidential guards nor even the ever-watchful Korean MPs had detected the activity. Neither had I as I walked past that building every day to get a ride to work.

The VC hid in the building until around 0130 on 31 January, then linked up with other forces and attacked the front of the palace, announcing they had come to liberate it. The guards, however, offered enough resistance to drive the attackers back into the half-constructed building. For at least two days the VC held out, never getting into the palace grounds but pumping a lot of ordnance into it.

The MPs at the Korean embassy were largely responsible for holding these VC in place and the shooting was incessant. Everyone on the embassy side of the Meyerkord was moved away from the firing to the back of the hotel, but many of the residents went up to the roof to watch the fighting through drainage outlets in the parapet. Some with weapons chose to join battle, and with carbines and handguns they popped off in the general direction of the enemy. Unfortunately, the target was out of range for most of their weapons and the bullets were falling on the Koreans. The Koreans did not like this and finally turned around to shoot back at the Meyerkord. The hotel's senior officer soon banished all snipers and tourists from the roof.

In the early morning of 31 January, CICV was in turmoil. VC were attacking the ARVN headquarters next door, but there were no weapons in the building other than a box of hand grenades. Kernsky described to me the defense drills the men practiced in anticipation of attack. Since there were no windows in the building, the main point of vulnerability was the front door. So, one guy was assigned to stand there and yank it open, while from around the corner another Saigon Warrior would heave out a grenade; then the door monitor would slam it closed.

This would continue until (a) the VC were blown up; (b) the CICV detail ran out of hand grenades; (c) the VC blew up the front of the building; (d) the doorman decided he was not in a tenable position.

Pick one or more of the above. If you picked (a), you are qualified to run the next war in Southeast Asia. Fortunately the VC limited their attention to the headquarters next door.

I had been anxious to find out how the compound, the 519th MI Battalion, had fared after my misadventure with that inquisitive "ARVN colonel" and his lady weeks earlier. Some of the heaviest fighting had been in Gia Dinh and entire blocks had been flattened and burned out. But at least two complexes had been untouched, the compound itself and a nearby whorehouse known as "Two Story."

The 519th became an important communications center for U.S. forces during the battles across Gia Dinh and our enlisted men were impressed into patrols with full combat gear. These men, trained as analysts, had minimal infantry boot-camp experience, but they fared well on their urban search-and-destroy missions.

Colonel Flakjacket seized the moment to overcome his fear of the outdoors by running resupply convoys to his various warehouses and scattered troops. At one point he had to link up with elements from the 1st Infantry Division. Having read his manuals on VC ambushes, the colonel chose not to use the roads but instead drove his convoy through a swamp on the edge of the city. Amazingly, he got through.

Colonel Flakjacket's finest moment came after he learned that his men at the Combined Military Interrogation Center near the Phu Tho racetrack were trapped without supplies. He geared up a convoy of armed jeeps, trucks, and a water tanker that charged right through the enemy fire to resupply the men at CMIC. Then he moved on to other installations under the 519th's administrative wing. After the smoke cleared, Colonel Flakjacket got his Silver Star. And for a cut from barbed wire at the compound, a Purple Heart as well.

Before the convoy had reached CMIC, two U.S. lieutenants on night duty there (my roommates at the Meyerkord) got a call through to their commanding officer at his BOQ. They reported that three VC battalions were in the area and that the ARVNs believed the interrogation center had been targeted for attack.

"What do we do, sir? Can you come in?" asked the lieutenant.

The colonel carefully replied, "We're confined to quarters and can't move unless we get MACV orders. Lieutenant, take over and do what you can. Keep me posted."

The phone clicked off. An ARVN major, the ranking Vietnamese at CMIC, asked, "Is the colonel coming in?"

The lieutenants looked at each other, embarrassed. "He can't make it. He's confined to quarters."

The Vietnamese officer looked steadily at them. "I see. How many of you? How much supply?"

There were seven men with nothing on hand.

The ARVN major nodded. "We will bring you food and water. We have Tet party food. We will share it. All my soldiers have come in. We are forty. Now we may be overrun. I wish we always could work together. Maybe we learn this time."

After the major left, the two lieutenants first returned to their paperwork but then decided they should check the perimeter. The Vietnamese soldiers were in place, silently watching for the enemy. Then a jeep roared up to the compound. Every ARVN weapon was activated and aimed until the men saw their major stand up in the vehicle. He delivered a basket to the Americans.

"I could find no establishment open. This is from my home. It is water and beef. We will get more tomorrow. Another jeep will supply my men." The major paused and glared at the Americans, then declared, "This is my compound!"

One of the lieutenants smiled. "Yes, sir, I believe it is!"

"And I will supply everyone!" The ARVN officer marched away. The Viet jeep-driver gestured toward the perimeter. "Beaucoup VC!" Then he grinned and pointed at the front of the vehicle. There were two bullet holes.

One of the lieutenants said to the other, "I'm beginning to feel like shit. The S.O.B. went to his home under fire to get food for us. After the way we've treated him."

"Well, I know one thing," said his colleague.

"What?"

"It *is* his compound, now. For sure, GI!"

Some time after the offensive I ran into one of my Benning-Bird classmates who had got stuck out in the field with an ARVN unit. He was in the Phoenix program, an assignment he handled by largely staying in his quarters and sending vague reports up the chain of command. The VC had easily overrun his post's perimeter early in the Tet attacks. The Americans jumped out of bed and into the dug-in bunker connected to their wood hooch.

In the fighting their hut was set on fire. While the flames trapped them in the bunker, they also stopped the VC from coming in. They could hear the enemy walking above them. At last there was quiet and they peered out to see an empty, destroyed compound littered with bodies. Only that elusive Nam phenomenon—pureblindluck—had saved them.

And so it was, for all of us.

The last reference to the Tet offensive I saw before returning to the States was in *Tour 365*, the booklet the Army gave us when we out-processed. The summary of the war ended just after the offensive, an unintentional observation on the watershed nature of the event. It defined the status of the war thus:

> To the soldiers of the United States Army, Vietnam, there was much work left to be done. New sand bag emplacements were strengthening defenses at base camps. More operations would be conducted. But we had withstood the enemy's best effort and won. Our Vietnamese comrades-in-arms had fought well and bravely with us. A new respect had grown through the blood letting that had occurred. The living would continue the struggle, the dead and severely wounded were done fighting, but the Republic of Vietnam is still free.

There was indeed "much work left to be done." In the coming months we would try to do it, under siege both by VC rockets and by our own doubts and bitterness over opportunities lost forever.

PART FIVE

Siege

FEBRUARY—MAY 1968

We were all a part of the War Effort. We went along with it, and not only that, we abetted it. Gradually it became a part of all of us that the truth about everything was automatically secret and that to trifle with it was to interfere with the War Effort.

John Steinbeck
Once There Was a War

17

Body Counting

You can kill ten of my men for every one I kill of yours. But even at those odds, you will lose and I will win.

Ho Chi Minh to the French, late 1940s

...concealed within strength there is weakness and within weakness, strength.

Strategy Since 1954
CICV study, April 1967

I got a letter off quickly on 1 February to let my folks know I was all right. I described my "defense" of MACV, emphasizing that the head-quarters had not been hit—"Why, I don't know"—and added, "If they do now they won't get in, but on the first night 3 squads could have."

Later in the day of the attacks, a company from the 25th Infantry Division had come to secure the headquarters. A little late, but they'd had plenty to keep them busy. In my letter I gave my estimate of the situation, that the enemy was aggressive but was being hurt. I predicted the offensive would be "militarily over in two weeks, favorably, for us."

The letter back from my father on 5 February was full of concern and sharp observation:

We were relieved to hear from you, although I'm afraid you are not out of the woods even yet. Seems to me that Saigon will be pretty unpredictable for a long time. There will be rapid and unexpected attacks most any night or day anywhere from suicidal types seeking "vengeance" or a sure berth in their heaven....

Sounds like you used your head on that defense situation (which doesn't speak well for the headquarters—but I've seen the same scarce protection in the rear areas before!)

We Americans sure are cocky and optimistic!

As an ex-Infantryman, I cannot see defending a building from close to it or inside, or an airstrip from its edges! Or gas tank farm from its edges, or an ammo dump. The perimeter has to be out and away—and that takes a lot of men—even with two fast-moving reserves (not one reserve—it's too easy to fake one reserve to the wrong side of the perimeter!). . . .

Catch cat naps when you can. Over-tired and you can make mistakes. Do you have some good men that are staying cheerful under pressure? Usually are some.

Best of luck—we want you back. Please, no extension!

He enclosed a Herblock cartoon showing a building in ruins, its off-center sign reading "HEADQUARTERS SAIGON." A four-star general is crouching under a busted-up desk, cranking a mimeograph machine. Pages flying from it declare, "We now have the initiative . . . The enemy offensive has been foiled . . . Besides, we knew about it in advance." The general is speaking on the phone: "Everything is OK—they never reached the mimeograph machine."

Copies appeared everywhere. Senior officers immediately ordered them down. I was a little embarrassed by the cartoon's optimistic statements—I was fairly prolific myself.

And I did it again in my next letter home, wanting to reassure my folks (just after scaring them to death, no doubt, with a request for a .38 Smith and Wesson because "sure as hell, they'll take our weapons away again!"):

Got your justifiably worried letter. I hear the US press is really blowing this up. There's no shooting in Saigon now—it's in Cholon, the Chinese "suburb." It's very tight security here—24 hour curfew for the last 2 weeks and 100% alert. So we're ready for more trouble—it could come, but I don't think so, in Saigon. The rest of VN is in for it, though. "Phase 3" as Westy calls it.

News for home consumption. I did not put my increasing cynicism on paper.

At MACV headquarters, the Red Watch major was less intense after our confrontation about my "absence" from my post. The evening after the attacks, we were alone at the watch and he showed a new side of himself.

"Quiet tonight, I guess," I suggested.

"We killed two hundred and fifty at the end of the runway a couple of hours ago," the major said.

"No kidding?"

"No, that's not kidding. And an air strike on a textile factory a few kilometers from here killed a hundred and fifty earlier."

"I knew about that one. Guess it's not so quiet tonight."

"It is for four hundred men. I hate seeing so many die. The bastards don't even know what they're fighting for."

I stopped posting the symbols. "Don't get philosophical, now, or it'll drive you crazy."

"Somebody's got to."

"Sure, but wait till it's over. Then we can think about the killing. Today it's good news. Especially because four hundred VC can't get in here."

The major said nothing. We worked the rest of the shift in silence.

The curfew was total. We could move only between our work and our billets. The city had turned into an armed fort with soldiers, armored personnel carriers, tanks, sandbagged bunkers, and coils of barbed wire everywhere. Even CICV became a fortress with new sandbagging and a monster .50 caliber machine gun placed on the roof. Our Viet counterparts became the post guards, armed to the teeth in full combat gear. For them, intelligence work was now a low priority. The ARVN military headquarters next door had come under a load of heat during Tet, and the Viet brass was not going to let it happen again.

A sense of excitement was in the air, every day likely to offer new surprises. We experienced that thrill of being "in it" but still not quite in mortal danger, or even serious discomfort. When the hot water heater for the hotel broke down and no one came to fix it, we bitched like hell. How could we be expected to take cold showers every day! And the chow in the snack bars and at the messes was *not* up to standard . . .

Meanwhile, the battles for the Phu Tho racetrack and Cholon continued. Snipers had remained active around Tan Son Nhut for some ten days, but there had been no firing in the MACV–CICV corridor that I traveled for my alternating duty shifts.

The Khe Sanh fixation continued well after Tet, though some senior officers were now hazarding the opinion that the attack might not come. But one had seemed very possible indeed through 7 February, when the Lang Vei Special Forces camp fell to an NVA regiment that overran the wire perimeter behind thirteen Russian-made PT-76 tanks.[1]

Tanks. In October 1967 I had submitted my report suggesting that the NVA planned to bring armor into the northern provinces. No response. Now we had too many dead and a base overrun while the Red Watch continued to send B-52s to bomb the NVA remnants around Khe Sanh.

But it was becoming less my worry as I returned more often to CICV and my old job. Little work was being done as everyone engaged in boisterous storytelling that didn't quite hide the tension we all felt. We knew we weren't out of it yet.

Especially on edge was the MP at the hotel guard post who swung an activated M-16 on me when I approached him from behind one evening. Then a jeep screeched around the corner and, on the verge of panic, he had his fellow MPs in the sights. My suggestion that he had to lighten up a little brought a red-eyed stare. He snarled, "They killed a lot of MPs and I ain't gonna be one of them!"

More than a few accidental rounds were put out by support troops who had to learn overnight the business of the front lines. Even the usually unflappable Koreans at the embassy next door accidentally set off a Claymore mine one night and scared hell out of us. After that I tried to avoid walking past their bastion, though one night I had to when my ride refused to take me past the Koreans. I walked down the middle of the road, whistling as if in a graveyard, and turned to wave at the guards. They had their weapons aimed at me and their expressions were hard and suspicious. Thereafter I made sure to get to the hotel before dark.

On 17 February, Colonel Mac told me I was back at CICV to stay. He had even better news: Major House was being transferred to a new advance headquarters at Phu Bai. "Better him than me," I thought happily. Later I learned that I'd almost gone with him. In March I would see this Phu Bai headquarters, and CICV would look like heaven to me.

Westmoreland, it was said, was continuing to lose confidence in the Marines. The ongoing antagonism had exploded when the Marine colonel at Khe Sanh refused to implement a standing rescue plan as the NVA were attacking the Lang Vei Special Forces camp. The Marines had radioed that weather and their own pressures made reinforcement impossible. Westmoreland had been furious.

Since April 1967, after upgrading Army units in Quang Ngai province into a full division, the Americal, Westmoreland had been cutting down on the Marines' TAOR (Tactical Area of Operational Responsibility). Part of his motivation was the increased enemy pressure on the DMZ, but a key factor, I believed, was the historic distrust between Army and Marine Corps.

And now we were going to have a new empire in I Corps as the Army (which ran MACV) shoved its command structure into Marine territory. A whole new work load would fall on my shop along with all the other post-Tet pressures as we supplied material for the new bureaucracy. Worse, the same work would be repeated at CICV, the MACV Tank, the III MAF headquarters, and now the new MACV advance unit. There were just too many damn chiefs.

The day after Major House left for Phu Bai a new shop OIC arrived, a Navy lieutenant commander who was coming off submarine duty. A pleasant sort with a boyish face and manner, he didn't know much about dry-land order of battle. Much of the time he was at the officers' clubs and the golf course.

But he was around enough to conduct his own war game. At the headquarters complex a Special Services outlet dispersed recreational goods to units for use by the troops: Monopoly, volleyball, checkers, Ping-Pong, and so forth. Every week the commander would take shop personnel, one by one, over to this outlet. There he had the soldier sign a voucher, then bring back over a hundred pounds of the goodies for the enlisted man to box up and ship stateside to the commander's home.

The enlisted men complained to me about how they were being used. Then it was my turn. After a trip to the Tank, the lieutenant commander delivered me to the Special Services office for another collection. All I could do was to make him declare that it would all go to the 519th, but the Viet woman at the counter knew it was a lie. "You come too often!" she complained. But I signed the paper. I'd learned to go along.

The political pressure was on again and we were hit by the third wave of OB manipulations. Again, I was told to bring the numbers down to show the thousands of enemy killed during the Tet offensive and our counterattacks. We had "won" and were to show it by dropping unit strengths in the OB Book.

MACV was reporting some 10,000 NVA soldiers killed along the DMZ, but we had no documents or PWs to confirm this number. Colonel Mac caught me in the hall and told me to put in the unit changes; bring 'em all down, he ordered.

I had grown numb from pressure, tension, and long duty without rest. Above all was the demoralizing knowledge, no matter how MACV tried to rebut it, that the war was no longer, if ever it had been, in our control.

But there still was a little fight in me. "Sir, if the losses were that large, surely we'll soon have PW reports or captured documents. There's so much material that's been captured and so many PWs. Can't we wait until some of that starts coming in?"

His predictable response was that there wasn't time to wait. The pressure was on from the press and the politicians, and we had to show that Tet and Khe Sanh had been fine American victories. The deed would be done. The only issue was the size of the cuts.

I was able to resist the 10,000 figure and apply instead a 4,000 KIA. I think that number had come from an early journal report from the Command Operations Center and I used the mimeographed page as a "source" to be appended to our change submittals. I made the argument against deeper cuts by insisting that to reduce the units further was insane, given the ease with which replacements could cross the DMZ. "We can't be carrying the elite units of the North Vietnamese Army at a strength that makes them look ineffective!"

In the end, the convenient lie was not so large as it might have been. I rationalized that at least it would satisfy my bosses without damaging the OB too seriously. (However, that modest deduction of 4,000 reduced the OB Book's total for the entire VC/NVA combat maneuver and support units by some 3 percent; in I Corps, the drop was about 10 percent.)

Having made my accommodation with the brass, I came to the hard part: convincing the enlisted analysts to go along with the program. I told them to apportion the 4,000 across all the units known or believed to have been in the DMZ/Khe Sanh area. They immediately argued that the losses would be quickly replaced, and I had to give these men the same impatient response that had been put to me. "Right, yes, I know, it has to be done. The numbers can be changed back later with new sources. *Do it, damn it!*"

"Is that a direct order, Lieutenant Jones?" asked an EM coldly.

"Yes," I said, looking away. It was like a kick in the stomach.

For a couple of days the men labored, crunching the numbers, and finally brought a pile of papers to me. I didn't let them explain their work, nor did I read any of it. I signed in each appropriate space on the disposition form and had an EM deliver the papers to Ground Order of Battle.

Each of these sellouts took a personal toll of guilt and bitterness on all of us. We were no longer doing the job we'd been trained to do. We were no longer trying to understand the capabilities and the intentions of the enemy. We were just going through the motions.

The motions were not good enough for our senior sergeant. He was a new arrival, a bit of a celebrity as the primary author of the Army training manual on "The Aggressor Order of Battle." This mild-mannered NCO finally exploded in anger during these cuts. "This is not the way it is supposed to be done, when we wrote the manual!"

Defensively I welcomed him to the real world, and the sergeant sullenly retreated into his paperwork. I'd lost his support for the rest of his tour.

I had one last conversation with a superior about more reductions to the OB. A colonel from somewhere up the chain of command said there was pressure for even more cuts. I pointed out that 4,000 was already too much and we could not do more without documents. He nodded and said he'd do what he could. I heard no more about it. The waves of forced and arbitrary OB cuts finally came to an end.

But there was another kind of deception going on, one perhaps even more damaging to our war effort. The headquarters was not eager to put newly discovered VC/NVA units into the OB Book, even when our submittal was backed with two hard sources.

Not long after Tet, the flood of reports on PWs and captured documents started coming in, providing more and more indicators of new and previously unknown units. In I Corps the brass had no choice but to accept the new NVA regiments that had conducted the siege of Khe Sanh. But many of the smaller units never were recognized by MACV. For instance, our submittal of a unique frogman sapper unit was rejected by J-2. The Marines were denied our knowledge of this new threat operating along the coast and rivers of Quang Tri province. Did friendly troops and civilians die because no one knew that NVA sappers could surface from the water to lay their charges?

Our work load was building at a fantastic rate. MACV wanted after-action reports on each major attack during the Tet offensive. In the shop we felt this interest in the cities was running several critical weeks too late, and that made the work all the more bitter for us. I could see it in the face and changing attitude of PFC Shore. He'd done outstanding work that had been ignored, and now we had to study and document the bloody consequences. But still the enlisted men poured it on, trying to do their jobs as analysts in spite of fatigue from their after-work duties at the compound as security forces in Gia Dinh.

Then the analysts presented a stunning conclusion: not only had most of the North Vietnamese units been held out of the offensive (Hue and Khe Sanh were the major exceptions) *but even the NVA members of many of the Viet Cong–designated units had been held back in reserve.* The Tet offensive had been designed by Hanoi as a Viet Cong initiative to prove the strength of the southern movement. We were impressed in the shop; it was amazing that just part of the "people's liberation army" could have pulled off such a broad offensive. Just how big was this army?

Now the NVA percentage study I'd done months earlier was all the more important. If, as according to the MACV revised form, only 10 percent of the VC units were northerners, then the reserve was not too significant. But if, as according to my original findings, the number was more like 25 percent, we'd been damn near beaten by well under half of the available military force.[2]

When the after-action reports were well along their way (and they showed the VC had also committed their share of blunders), I asked PFC Shore how well what we knew now stacked up against that extraordinary package of documents he'd put together before the offensive.

"Well, they hit a few more places than we knew about. But the attacks stuck pretty close to what our documents indicated. We could have been waiting for 'em."

On 18 February the enemy conducted a nationwide offensive by fire and most of the Tet targets were hit by mortars and rockets. Saigon received the first 122mm rockets of many to come, and the siege took on a more visual and immediate quality. From the roof of the Meyerkord, gin and tonics in hand, we watched those torpedoes of the sky come lazing over the city, completing a great arc with a *whiz-chrump-zing*. It was the *whiz* as the rocket roared in, the *chrump* of the explosion, and the *zing* of the shrapnel flying off.

The next day a group of soldiers at Tan Son Nhut were waiting for the aircraft to return them to the States. A 122mm rocket slammed into the terminal, killing one poor son of a bitch and wounding twenty-one. That was the nightmare of every soldier, to be hit on his last day in Nam.

The nightly light show of B-52 bombs, 'chute flares, tracers from gunships, and falling rockets was one form of entertainment. But then we heard that the VC were trying to hit Independence Palace next door and that they were using the tall radio tower with its red blinking light, only blocks away, as the aiming point. The minimal accuracy of rockets made the Meyerkord highly vulnerable, especially since its eight-story height was unmatched in our area.

This made me nervous. I asked the hotel's senior officer, a lieutenant colonel, why we had no bunkers in the building. He suggested maybe I'd like to put the sandbags in myself. I laughed it off, saying that's EM work. But, as the colonel noted, we had none and all Saigon EM were now learning how to be infantrymen. Anyway, if a rocket hit, it would probably be the only one and you'd never know it was coming. Get under your mattress on the floor to absorb some of the blast. That was all you could do.

The next day at CICV the excited troops told me a 122 had just hours before swooped over the building with a hell of a roar, landing in the Viet headquarters next door. That evening, or the next, I was shocked to see a fine French colonial building across from the Splendid BOQ torn open. I had my meal at the BOQ with a lieutenant who had barely had time to crawl under his jeep as the debris fell around him.

Returning from night duty at CICV, I was further dismayed to find that two of the damned 122s had bracketed the Meyerkord. One had blown up houses across the street and the other had landed at the very edge of the hotel, ripping open a house and killing an old man.

This sort of thing could get to you. Finally it did.

My sleep was uneven, coming in waves as I tossed uncomfortably on my cot. Suddenly, rockets! The *whiz-chrump-zing* was all around the hotel.

I'd practiced the move in my mind. Grab the edge of the mattress on the side toward the windows, roll away, pull the mattress over onto my body, and fall to the floor under its cover, safe from the shrapnel and flying glass.

I rolled, but the mattress stayed in place. My hold slipped and I fell flat out on the concrete floor, right on top of my carbine rifle, its operating handle digging into my buttock. I limped to the window, which was still intact.

Silence. No buildings were on fire or collapsed around the hotel. No *whiz-chrump-zing*. No rockets. The skyline was peaceful. I realized I had been dreaming.

In the midst of all the after-action reports, sending data to Phu Bai, submitting new-unit write-ups, and reading all the incoming documents, one of the analysts exclaimed loudly, "I knew it!"

What was it he knew, I asked.

"This document was picked up near Hue and it's signed by an NVA general who was CO of one of the divisions supposed to be at Khe Sanh!"

I told him about the infrared photos I'd seen just before Tet and my suspicions then. Other analysts chimed in, citing other indications that much of the Khe Sanh force had moved to Hue. But it was like talking about last weekend's football game; finally we just shrugged it off.

On a visit to the I Corps desk at the Tank I did, however, mention our belief that Khe Sanh was a feint for the Hue attack, and that we'd found a document supporting that finding. The watch officer reacted in surprise and even anger. He said it didn't matter now, that we should leave it to the military historians. But as I was about to leave, he asked me to bring in the document.

At CICV we tried unsuccessfully to find it in our files. I had a couple of the EM go next door to CDEC, the documents center, and track the damn thing down through the microfilm files that were supposed to contain each processed report. They came back tired and frustrated, bitching that the bureaucracy and disorganization at CDEC was worse even than at CICV. The document could not be found and my dreams of jamming some evidence about the Khe Sanh–Hue debacle up the Tank disappeared.

One postwar analysis stated:

The battle of Hue proved a sobering experience for the allied command. . . .[D]espite forewarnings of a possible multibattalion attack at Tet, American and South Vietnamese forces had been taken by surprise. Even more disturbing was the discovery made by the 3rd Brigade of the U.S. 1st Cavalry Division after the battle had begun. Fighting their way eastward toward the Citadel, the brigade ran into unexpectedly intense resistance from elements of three NVA regiments: the 24th Regiment, 304th Division; the 29th Regiment, 325C Division; and the 99th Regiment, 324B Division. According to allied intelligence, they weren't supposed to be there. They were supposed to be at Khe Sanh.[3]

Not until the end of the month was Miss My able to get back to her job at CDEC. She had been trapped in hiding for weeks in her home near the Phu Tho racetrack, where fighting had been intense. VC had occupied her neighborhood and even lived in some of her neighbors' houses. She had hid her CDEC identification card, afraid she would be killed immediately if it were found. She had stayed hidden all the time so that any neighbors with VC leanings would not identify her to the VC as an employee of the Americans. She refused to say anything more: "I tell you about VC, you must report it, then it is too much danger for me!" My protests were ignored, and she never spoke of it again.

Toward the end of February things seemed quieter, and a couple of lieutenants and I decided to make a PX run to Cholon. But at the turnoff, a few White Mice—city police—were guarding a barrier and waved us away. We were about to argue when two trucks of well-armed ARVN troops came from opposite directions to converge on a street across from us. We watched as the soldiers unloaded from both trucks and marched single file to the corners. They moved with discipline, hugging the walls. Shots rang out and the line of ARVNs began to open fire into the houses. We moved quickly back into our jeep, just as another deuce-and-a-half came roaring past us. Looking back from our accelerating jeep, we saw bodies stacked in it, stiff arms and legs sticking up at grotesque angles.

One of the lieutenants said shakily, "Maybe they were only wounded." Maybe.

The war was still not over in Saigon, nor in Hue. By early March we began to hear of the atrocities in the imperial city. Estimates of murdered civilians ranged from 2,000 to over 5,000. We heard that the Viet Cong went from door to door, clipboards in hand, reciting the names of governmental employees, educators, foreigners, members of the upper classes, then killing them cruelly, burying some alive.

After regaining control, the South Vietnamese sent in their own assassin teams to kill those who had aided the Communists. The city suffered dreadfully.

A senior sergeant who been in Hue during the fighting told us at CICV that his unit had found NVA soldiers tied to their guns so they could not retreat. As the Marines fought their way in, they killed anyone or anything that moved in front of them, no questions asked. The fighting was so intense and his unit so isolated that they went eight days without chow (finally a chopper reached them but it carried only seven reporters and two cases of C-rations). He estimated the NVA had suffered some 5,000 KIA; "they'll count them as they bury them." I never saw an estimate of friendly losses and after my visit in November to the Red Ball Express warehouse, I wouldn't have believed it anyway.

February was for body counting and justifications. On the twenty-seventh, Westmoreland's AP interview appeared in *Stars and Stripes;* he stated that "the enemy's ability to pursue a protracted war has been reduced by the losses that he has recently suffered." *Stars and Stripes* also reported on comments made by General Earle Wheeler after he made a trip to Saigon during 23–25 February: "the enemy failed to gain either a surprise military victory or a 'psychological and propaganda victory.' " The general "denied there had been a failure of U.S. military intelligence in advance of the widespread attacks." Further, the paper reported, "Wheeler said intelligence warned that the attacks would be made but could not say where, when, or the size. 'That would be a commander's dream,' Wheeler said."

It never ended, the smoke and mirrors.

My first involvement with generals on fact-finding missions came on 2 March when officers from all four of the Corps Tactical Zones were hurriedly gathered for a briefing at MACV to Major General Grover Cleveland Brown, chief of production for the Defense Intelligence Agency in Washington. As usual, the lieutenant commander was not in the office and I had to fill in for him. The general proved to be a pleasant grandfatherly type, easy to talk to, and after we gave the standard overviews, he asked if we had any personal views on the war.

After an uncomfortable silence, I offered an opinion that the cities were under control but that the countryside had been left wide open and our pacification efforts had to be in trouble. I added I had no hard data but the conclusion seemed inevitable.

The general nodded seriously. "Thank you, Lieutenant. I'll pass that on to the president with our request for more troops." (I was to learn that about three days earlier, General Wheeler had delivered the same message to LBJ.)

Then the major from II Corps, a quiet man who let his lieutenants do most of the work while he maintained a supervisory presence, announced, "MACV is not accepting our submittal of new enemy units in II Corps!"

There was silence. I glanced over at the MACV colonel in charge of the briefing; he was bright red, his mouth open. The general appeared confused, and the silence continued. To ease the strain, I made some complaint about how the CICV library never informed us about important secret documents that could not come to our shop because of the ARVNs. As the briefing began to deteriorate into a bitch session, the MACV colonel broke it up and got us out in a hurry. I was afraid some ass was going to be chewed and I only hoped the II Corps major would take the brunt of it.

A day or so later I briefed General Chester Peterson, J-2 for CINCPAC, the next level of the chain of command from MACV to the Pentagon. This one was uneventful, but the next round had me worried. We were still completing that invasion-of-Laos-relief-of-Khe-Sanh project that was now clearly obsolete. We had to fly in a small two-engine VIP airplane to the advance headquarters at Phu Bai to brief General Creighton Abrams, who replaced Westmoreland later that month. Phu Bai was next to Hue, still the most threatened piece of terrain in Nam. At least six NVA regiments were still in heavy engagement in the area. I really didn't care to visit the advance headquarters. (Neither, I think, did Colonel Halpin, Director of CICV, because we landed at about 1000 hours and were out of there by 1445.)

In a small room our team of some five men set up the briefing maps and waited for Abrams, the old tank commander who had served under Patton in World War II. In he came, a stocky man chewing his

·igar, head down, plowing ahead like one of his tanks. With him were Major General Willard Pearson (a past brigade commander in the 101st Airborne Division and now the assistant chief of staff for the Phu Bai headquarters) and Lieutenant General William B. Rosson (Westmoreland's and later Abrams's chief of staff). Rosson saw my extreme ramrod stance of attention and came over to smile and shake hands. Then he shook hands all around like a politician on the campaign trail while Abrams waited.

The project OIC gave the briefing for our fabulous airborne leap into Laos, then asked, "Are there any questions, sir?" This was where I got nervous, afraid I'd again have to confess our ignorance about Laotian Communist forces. We held our breath, awaiting Abrams's answer, waiting for an indication of history to be made.

The four-star general gestured at the base map and spoke. "Ah, next time you give the briefing, use less acetate. Fewer overlays. It's too shiny, I can't see the map."

That was it. So much for an invasion of Laos. The generals thanked us, shook hands, and swept out of the room. The briefing was never given again. (In early April the Army convoyed up to Khe Sanh on Highway 9 from within Quang Tri province and relieved the Marines without major incident; beginning 17 June, the base was dismantled and abandoned.)

Then we visited the advance headquarters G-2 shop that had been creating so much work for our I CTZ analysts at CICV. They'd been calling us almost hourly for classified information over the insecure lines until I finally complained to Colonel Mac about the security risk and the calls diminished. But it was clear they needed all the help they could get. Seeing their living and working conditions quickly created sympathy for my old boss Major House and his associates. Three men lived in a single Conex box (a metal box for storage and transport of goods). The windowless cube was dug in and sandbagged to resist the rocket and mortar attacks that were coming every few days. It was a hot hellhole that was swamped by mud with every storm. The box held only two men, so a pair had to hot-bed one of the bunks. They worked twelve hours on and twelve off, straight through the week.

The Phu Bai group was supposed to be an advance point for the processing and analysis of intelligence, but the documents were coming in by the ton, so many of them that the G-2 shop couldn't keep up. They were "laying them on the rafters, unopened," I was told.

How could another set of readers working in the most primitive of conditions accomplish anything that the organized and relatively efficient teams in Saigon couldn't? It was another insane screw-up, this "Phu Bai advance headquarters."

On 6 March General Pearson cabled General Davidson from Phu Bai about our Khe Sanh "pattern analysis," saying it was "greatly appreciated" and that both "Generals Abrams and Rosson commented on the adequacy of the material." Davidson wrote on the cable, "This is probably as good a compliment as we're ever likely to get—but I say —Damn Well Done!" The questionable praise of our "adequacy" was escalated in a memo on 7 March from the Director of Intelligence Production to the Director of CICV:

> The fact that this briefing was so well received is ample evidence of the extensive research and thorough preparation that went into this important project. Please accept my congratulations for a job well done and extend my sincere thanks to all who participated.

Not to be outdone, Colonel Halpin wrote his own memo of congratulations and sent it to all of CICV, declaring that the generals' "satisfaction" with the briefing, which was "a valuable intelligence tool," should be a "source of pride to us all." We had proved the "capability of CICV to measure up to the most stringent demands in a difficult situation."

The submarine lieutenant commander was pretty impressed by it all and put me in for a Bronze Star. Why not, I figured. It was one way to get my hero's badge.

One more long memo came down to CICV from Phu Bai on 28 March. Colonel Charles Roberts, the G-2 there (and the past head of J-2 production at the Tank), reported that by the end of February MACV believed "the military situation had been brought under control" and we were "prepared to resume the offensive." The forward headquarters, which had opened on 10 February, was evolving into a provisional corps to "assist" the Marines in managing U.S. forces in the two northern provinces. The colonel thanked us for our administrative support and supply of OB workbooks, terrain studies, special-patterns analysis, photo readouts, and the telephone communications (which he called "as vital to our success as were the finished studies"). He declared that he could not have accomplished his mission without our assistance and added:

> It is impossible to quantify the number of Allied lives you saved and the number of casualties you inflicted upon the enemy, but I am convinced that you made a significant contribution to our combined effort.

Once again Colonel Halpin added a footnote that recognized how we seldom received such deserved thanks for our "valuable and often repeated efforts to get timely intelligence to the people who need it."

We were losing the war, but our memos of congratulation were outstanding.

18

The 38th VC Battalion Incident

One of the most critical areas in the RVN today is Quang Ngai Province. A division is required there to maintain continuous pressure on the enemy...

> General William C. Westmoreland
> Cable to CINCPAC
> 18 March 1967

Throughout its time in I Corps, the Americal Division has had excellent results. . . .

> Military Assistance Command
> Office of Information"
> "1967 Wrap-Up—A Year of Progress"

During the period 16–19 March 1968, a tactical operation was conducted into Son My Village, Son Tinh District, Quang Ngai Province, Republic of Vietnam, by Task Force (TF) Barker, a battalion-size unit of the Americal Division. . . .

The infantry assault on My Lai (4) began a few minutes before 0800. During the 1st Platoon's movements through the southern half of the subhamlet, its members were involved in widespread killing of Vietnamese inhabitants (comprised almost exclusively of old men, women, and children) and also in property destruction. Most of the inhabitants who were not killed immediately were rounded up into two groups. The first group, consisting of about 70–80 Vietnamese, was taken to a large ditch . . . and later shot. A second group, consisting of 20–50 Vietnamese, was taken south of the hamlet and shot there on a trail. Similar killings of smaller groups took place within the subhamlet.

Members of the 2d Platoon killed at least 60–70 Vietnamese men, women, and children, as they swept through the northern half of My Lai (4) and through Binh Tay, a small subhamlet about 400 meters north of My Lai (4). They also committed several rapes. . . .

Casualty figures cited for My Lai (4) were developed by this Inquiry solely on the basis of statements and testimony of US personnel (numbering 175–200). Separate estimates (by others) indicate the number of Vietnamese killed in the over-all area of Son My Village may have exceeded 400.

> Report of the Department of
> the Army Review of the
> Preliminary Investigation into
> the My Lai Incident, Volume I,
> "The Report of the
> Investigation," 14 March 1970

MACV headquarters' contribution to the cover-up of the My Lai atrocity had already begun by late March. A major stuck his head in the door at my OB shop and yelled, "Jones, the colonel wants to see you. Now!"

Some of the men laughed; the lieutenant was in for it again. I took a deep breath and quickly followed the officer down the hall to a conference room. I was not allowed into the room, but I could see that a highly charged meeting of a half-dozen men was in progress. Some of the officers were still involved in heated argument, but they stopped when they saw me. Colonel Mac came to the doorway. His face was bright red and he spoke sharply.

"Jones, I've got a job for you and I want it now!"

"Yes, sir!" I cheered up. I wasn't in trouble for a change. "What's it about?"

"The 38th VC Battalion was caught in Quang Ngai province on R-and-R and got surrounded by troops from the Americal Division at a coastal hamlet. They were wiped out. We have to drop that unit to zero."

"Hey, we won one for a change!" I said brightly. A nearby major swore in disgust. I was taken aback by his reaction. Colonel Mac ordered him to move on and my confusion increased.

The colonel said sarcastically, "That's right, we won one! Now do the paperwork!" He handed me a slip of paper with the map coordinates of the engagement.

"Yes, sir, what else do you have for me? A PW report?"

"There were no prisoners! They're all dead! We don't have any documents. Just put in the damn change!"

"But, Colonel Mac, how can I prepare a change without a citation?"

The colonel was getting more excited and I was afraid his blood pressure was really going to blow. "We know the 38th operates in that area!"

Again it was that damned proximity trick. The major who had come to get me spoke up. "He's right. We have to give him something more to go on."

"Did we get any Special Intelligence?" I asked. I presumed this push for an OB change was coming from headquarters in its quest to log victories for stateside consumption; the unit identification must have come from a radio intercept. Colonel Mac seized on my suggestion, apparently with relief.

"Yes, that's it. And you can also add that we had a direct verbal communication from the field."

A couple of officers had been watching all this closely. I took a deep breath and plunged on, knowing I had to recite our gospel.

"Sir, my men feel very strongly about reducing unit strengths when we know replacements come so quickly and we'll wind up carrying a reduced unit too low for months." The colonel was getting tense again, so I hurried on. "So, will you support us if we find even just one source saying the 38th is active again so we can bring it back up to full strength?"

Colonel Mac relaxed and said that would be all right, but I felt I had to reinforce the point. "Even an agent report, Colonel!" He snapped an affirmative at me and told me to get to work.

What the hell was going on? I headed back to the shop deeply distressed. An OB change without any kind of written evidence, just a verbal report and a suggestion of "all-source" intelligence, was a terrible precedent. I knew I was really going to have my hands full this time; the analyst for Quang Ngai province was PFC Shore.

"Hey, Shore, got good news and bad news for you! You've got one less unit to worry about, but it's your favorite one!"

We had a game of picking the VC or NVA unit that was the most interesting to us. Shore had selected the 38th Battalion (known to the Marines and the Americal Division as the 48th) because of its high morale, the Ho Chi Minh patch its men sometimes wore, the songs sung on the march, and the unit's effectiveness, which was unusually high for a VC local force unit. The men called themselves the Ho Chi Minh Brigade after their hero and although they were only a local force unit, they were a bit heroic in their own way. Shore had even developed a football cheer for the unit: "Maneuver east! Maneuver west! The 38th's sappers are the best!" When I heard that, I told him that he'd been in Nam too long.

I repeated the annihilation story to him. He looked absolutely dumbfounded.

"R-and-R? That doesn't make any sense. Whole units don't go on rest and recreation together. They let a few guys off at a time just like we do."

"Yeah, maybe, but they identified them with SI," I said, lowering my voice so our ARVN counterparts, who had been listening very closely, couldn't hear. I went over with Shore the concession I'd obtained regarding a return to full strenth with any source.

Shore didn't like it, not at all, and he protested again.

"But what's the hurry, Lieutenant Jones? They probably haven't had time to gather any documents from the bodies, much less translate and process them. Why can't we just wait until the documents get here?"

"Because that's not what I was *told* to do, Shore! They must want this one for the newspapers, to show a U.S. victory, so they want it *now.*"

Shore's voice was angry. "They don't have to change the OB Book to tell the press about some big deal victory."

Finally Shore did the paperwork and I signed it, again without inspecting the product. I just wanted to get rid of it. The change went through all the levels of the chain of command without a hitch. It was always easier to delete from the OB Book than to add to it.

When the lieutenant commander got back to the shop, he quickly learned about the OB change and he jumped all over me for having put it in. I said I would have been very happy not to have done it, but since he had not been around—I almost said "as usual"—I had to follow the orders. Our OIC looked at me. "You know, I wondered why I had been sent over to MACV. There was nothing going on there. They wanted me out of the building. What does that tell you, Jones?"

It told me a lot, but I didn't want to think about it. Especially later, when Shore came to me with the rumors. Even before the new OB Book came out with the 38th Battalion carried at zero, Shore had heard about the incident from the enlisted men of the 519th MI Battalion who were stationed in the field. They said it was a *destroyed village* that had given up the bodies. The Americal Division had committed an atrocity, a war crime, and our games with the OB Book were part of a cover-up.

I was stunned. I told him I couldn't believe it, that mass killings were what the VC did, not Americans. Shore insisted that the men in the field thought it was true. I said weakly, "Let me know if you hear more."

Sometime later I asked him if there was any new information; he told me that everyone still believed the story, but no one was talking about it now. He also noted that no documents had ever come in from any VC battalion on that date and at those coordinates. If a whole battalion had really been caught, he said pointedly, there would have been documents on some of the bodies. He was right.

Even more disturbing was the fact that our ARVN counterparts had not made a change of the 38th's status in their own copy of the OB Book. In theirs I saw the unit penciled in at full strength. Forcing a joking manner, I chided them for the error. I got back a sharp "No" and a shaking of the head from Lieutenant Tri, as he averted his eyes from me. Our relationship had temporarily gone cool.

I couldn't let it alone. After discussing some routine business with the colonel, I said, "You know, Colonel Mac, there's rumors that the 38th Battalion was really a village of dead people. The ARVNs think so, too. Do you know anything about that?"

He said nothing, but his face went pale and that painful grimace took over. He gave a little negative shake of his head. I left without further comment. This had to be worse for him than for me, because he'd known from the start what the change meant.

I rushed through the approval process the first information we got on the 38th, either a PW or an agent report. It showed that the entire battalion was alive and well with no mention of an ambush or a rebuilding. MACV accepted the change and in the next OB Book the unit was restored to perhaps a strength of two hundred.

The incident was over. At least for then.

19

"Peace Is Hell"

... the engagement of U.S. forces in the towns has rendered
more acute the U.S. shortage in mobile forces in the field . . .
the rear of the U.S.-puppets has been turned into the most
dangerous battlefield for them. . . . U.S. and puppet troops
have desperately tried to strengthen their defenses around
urban centers, especially Saigon . . . the revolutionary war has
been firmly planted in the towns.

Radio Hanoi
13 May 1968

At CICV we listened to the Armed Forces Radio transmittal of President Johnson's first speech on Vietnam since the Tet offensive, heard in the States on 31 March. A lieutenant from II Corps said, "It's just more politics, turn it off." But I sensed something coming and asked to keep it on.

"Tonight I renew the offer I made last August—to stop the bombing of North Vietnam. We ask that talks begin promptly, that they be serious talks on the substance of peace. . . . I call upon Ho Chi Minh to respond positively, and favorably, to this new step toward peace. . . . "[1] He announced an increase of 13,500 U.S. troops and modernization of the Viet army.

Then Johnson spoke of his thirty-seven years of public service and how he had "put the unity of the people first." He went on, "What we won when all of our people united just must not now be lost in suspicion, distrust, selfishness and politics among any of our people."

"He's quitting!" I yelled.

"Believing this as I do, I have concluded that I should not permit the presidency to become involved in the partisan divisions that are developing in this political year. Accordingly, I shall not seek, and I will not accept, the nomination of my party for another term as your president."

The room was full of excited questions about what it meant to the war. Quietly, Lieutenant Tri came to me and asked, "Does this mean your president will end America in the war?"

I tried to be reassuring. "No, no, Lieutenant Tri! He is not popular and he will not again seek office. Soon there will be another president and we will continue to fight." But I had my doubts.

To everyone's surprise, within a few days of Johnson's speech, Hanoi responded that it would meet for peace talks. Then on 4 April Martin Luther King, Jr., was assassinated and urban riots broke out across the nation. Portions of more than 150 cities were in flames.

The war intensity and the domestic unrest were taking their toll on the home front. Earlier in March my father had complained that because this war didn't take and hold ground, there were no real "progress reports" in the media. There was "only a lot of kill statistics that are now belittled as unreliable—and of course they are." He noted that people had the "exaggerated notion that there is fighting everywhere every hour" and that the papers only reported failure.

On 30 March he sent me the editorial page of the *Santa Barbara News Press* with three columns on the war. His note at the top was, "This is the daily diet in the US!" An arrow marked a piece on MAJOR FAILURES IN VIETNAM by Jack Anderson, who wrote that "our policy makers have been basing their war plans on faulty intelligence." Anderson cast doubt on a "pre-Tet document" that MACV offered as "evidence that the southern-born enemy is rapidly losing heart for the war" and that Hanoi "has not sent south enough men to offset his losses during the past several months." As usual, MACV had concluded that "the tide has turned and the enemy's strength is on the decline."

There was also a surprise. Anderson repeated a story he had run in November 1967 that General McChristian had been transferred out of his J-2 job "because his bosses in the Pentagon didn't like his pessimistic estimates of Communist infiltration and recruitment." The columnist added, "They preferred to believe lower, more comfortable estimates of enemy strength." Anderson asserted that today intelligence experts "generally agree that McChristian was right" and that our official figures on the VC/NVA army were "as much as 130,000 short."

After reading that, I saw the confusing days of last August in a clearer light. General Davidson's "downward trending" was a massive departure from his predecessor's position and reflected the "more comfortable" approach to analysis of the opposition.

To my father's concerns about how Saigon was protected, I wrote this in mid-March:

> The US takes the outer ring, the Viet forces have the inner. From there, it's a building by building defensive plan. Each US installation has at least one MP in a concrete observation post out front . . . surrounded by concrete filled barrels, so an explosive laden car can't be run up to the building. Then the BOQs etc post their own guards. We have 3 on all night. So you wind up with many circles of resistance, many interlocking. When combined with ARVN and Korean installations, there's a lot of area the enemy cannot travel through. But there are approaches he can infiltrate. Sweep operations and MP/National Police patrols hopefully catch that.

But those "interlocking circles" had proved sieve-like during Tet. About the time of my letter the curfew was moved to 2000 hours. The enlisted men were allowed to go downtown but they could no longer wear civilian clothes. And they had never been permitted to wear fatigues in Vietnamese establishments. Nor could khakis be worn in a war zone. The Army had done it again.

Most of us stayed in our billets willingly. Boredom was preferable to risks on the streets, and we passed time as we could. One evening just past dusk I was looking at the Saigon skyline from the top of the Meyerkord. Across from me was a two-story building with a concrete shed on the roof. Its door opened and a hand appeared, holding a stick tipped with a burning red coal. The incense stick was shaken deliberately three times, then an old woman in a long black dress stepped out of the shed. A white concrete wall, the side of the adjacent building, carried her shadow, cast by the blue-white illumination of a parachute flare.

The tiny hunched woman, her gray-black hair in a bun, turned to her right and shook the burning stick again three times. Then more quarter turns and shakes brought her around to face the door. Invisible B-52s started dropping their strings of bombs in the jungles outside Saigon. The old woman was oblivious to the concussions rippling across the city, and she shook the stick a last three times before placing it on a rafter above her head. She repeated the pattern, shaking her clasped hands. A Phantom jet fighter ripped overhead, unusually low as it climbed from its Tan Son Nhut take-off, but the woman ignored its shrill roar as she completed her prayers. She disappeared into the doorway just as the rumble of the big bombs stopped.

Then I realized that a couple on the roof of the Meyerkord, self-consciously huddled in a far corner, was trying to hide from the light of the flares. I turned away and left. There were few places and moments to be alone.

At CICV we were still writing after-action reports on the Tet offensive and it seemed they would take us the rest of the year to complete. I was putting together a detailed report on Khe Sanh; for some unclear reason the request had come from J-5, the civil affairs section of headquarters. I was writing the document even as the siege ended on 8 April after seventy-seven days.[2] Army, Marine and ARVN elements advanced up Route 9 across Quang Tri province and, without major incident, relieved the Marine force. Army personnel took over the base; another MACV slap at the Leathernecks.

On 17 April, the lieutenant commander left for the States and I was again shop OIC. Now I was able to see the flow of paper on new units being detected in I Corps. To expedite production of finished intelligence, I directed the men to start a Unit OB Summary for each newly discovered organization. Not only would this provide more information for the HQ to evaluate for acceptance of the unit in the OB, but we'd also have a summary ready for distribution immediately upon acceptance.

We scanned each new monthly OB Book to see which of our submittals had made the list. Many did not, enough to make the men angry. So, if the analyst believed his sources were sound, we submitted the rejected work-up again. Soon Colonel Mac came to me and asked, "Haven't we seen these before?"

"Yes, sir, they're still valid. Just because MACV doesn't recognize them doesn't mean they're not out there."

By pure perseverance, we squeezed a few more units into the OB Book. And even when MACV did not accept a unit as "confirmed,"[3] we still sent the write-up to the appropriate field headquarters with a disclaimer about its unofficial status. And I came up with one more way to fight "downward trending." In the case of the 38th VC Battalion, we'd got the unit back to its operational strength with a single source; now I told the men that henceforth we would make recommendations on a single document if the analyst found it credible and consistent with other indicators. We also appended agent reports as a substitute for a second hard source. By such measures we tried to keep the OB Book honest, but it was only piecework.

This period of extended siege had a surreal quality. Strange scenes followed on one another. A contingent of officers was bused beyond the edge of Saigon, guards were posted, and we conducted our annual weapons qualification, firing .45s at paper targets while enlisted men watched for an attack by Charlie. Then we turned in the weapons before we left.

Then there was a dinner at the Splendid BOQ while an American in civilian clothes watched me. At last he came over, showed me a photograph, and asked, "Lieutenant, do you know how I could find a soldier? He's been here I think two months and no one's heard from him. My wife and I want to know what happened to our son." The headquarters and the embassy could not help, and now this middle-aged civilian was walking the streets of Saigon, looking for his lost boy.

Another evening at the Splendid with a dinner companion, also in his middle years, who finally admitted he was CIA but would not tell me his last name. To my questions he put a finger to his lips and looked around; "You never can know what's bugged."

By at least early April the restaurants and stores had reopened and we could move around downtown again. But Saigon was a duller city now, for President Thieu had instituted an austerity program that closed the rock 'n' roll bars and various other manifestations of Western decadence. But the crackdown did not include the French restaurants, so all was not lost.

On 14 April I was heading for the Continental Plaza Hotel when I saw a Buick Riviera, followed by a national police jeep, coming the wrong way on the one-way street alongside the hotel. The Buick was driven by Nguyen Cao Ky, vice president, senior Air Force general, and past premier. Ky parked and stepped out and a crowd began to gather. With his mustache, an uncommon Vietnamese feature, he was handsome and striking in spite of his height, short even by Asian standards. Always impeccable and flamboyant in his uniform with neck scarf, today Ky wore tight silver-gray sharkskin trousers with a wine-colored pullover shirt buttoned to the neck. Tucked into his waistband at the back was a small silver pistol. He went into the hotel and in a few minutes returned with Madame Ky, who was leaving a reception. They walked hand in hand to the Buick. She was as beautiful as reported, and smiled graciously at the crowd of admirers.

Ky and Thieu were in increasing conflict, and Ky was now openly criticizing the Americans as we pushed unilaterally for peace talks. He had said, "I have to fight not only my enemies but also my so-called friends." Ky was the only politician in South Vietnam who inspired a following, but he was not in Washington's favor, and Thieu was gradually easing him out of power.

Through April and into May, Hanoi and Washington debated through the world press over where the peace talks would be held. Finally Paris was selected, even though it provided the VC propagandists with a political connection between the two "colonial powers" that had tried to control Indochina. The meetings began on 13 May and took on another echo of the Korean conflict, where the Communists and the Allies had debated for months over the size and shape of the conference table while the battlefield continued to take lives. But the debate wasn't empty; it reflected the core issues of whether Hanoi would recognize the legitimacy of the Republic of Vietnam and whether we would acknowledge the National Liberation Front as a separate entity or merely as an adjunct of the Lao Dong Party of North Vietnam. (Not until 8 December were all four delegations finally included in the sessions; the seating and recognition struggle would continue until 25 January 1969. A circular table was finally selected, but to symbolize that there were only "two sides" involved in the war, two rectangular tables for support personnel were placed parallel at opposite sides of the central table.)

The peace talks were regarded in Saigon with great skepticism, for it was standard Communist practice to "talk-fight" and never give up anything at the conference table. That had been the experience in Korea, and it would happen again in Vietnam. We were getting sources on the next phase of the VC winter-spring campaign, another offensive to be conducted in May, fresh on the start of "peace talks." Some officers doubted another major attack could be mounted after the Tet losses, but now there were a lot more believers in the MACV headquarters.

In late April I convinced Colonel Mac that I desperately needed time off. He let me take some leave and on the twenty-eighth I got the first flight to anywhere that was available. It turned out to be Singapore. On the bus ride from the airport, the briefing officer apologized in advance to the WAC major with us for his remarks and then explained that the R-and-R program had ensured that bar girls of the highest quality worked at each hotel. They had weekly medical check-ups and each had a number; if we came up with V.D., we should report it to our unit R-and-R officer.

My seatmate, an old master sergeant, said to me, "Keeping GIs out of whorehouses is like shoveling shit against the tide." So it might as well be organized. At the Newton Towers, a modern hotel thrown up to profit from the influx of GIs, we were gathered to meet the girls and select the week's companion. The U.S. Army ran a fine whorehouse.

Singapore is a city-state on an island about half the size of Los Angeles in the South China Sea just off the tip of the Malay Peninsula. Britain granted its independence in 1959 but still retained a role as protector (its last troops were removed in the seventies). The city was 80 percent Chinese, and they exclusively ran the government. Prime Minister Lee Kuan Yew was creating a self-dependent, nationalistic society (I saw in a rural elementary school over the blackboard the motto, "United we stand, divided we fall") with a modern, universal-service army advised by Israelis. Singapore had the highest standard of living in Southeast Asia, including drinkable tap water.

This I learned from Siwa, an English literature student at the University of Singapore. He was a tall, handsome Indian who played lead guitar in a nightclub rock band. Siwa told me how GIs would ask for pop tunes in pidgin talk: "Hey, you play number one song?" He'd let them go on, then would answer in the Queen's English. When his band took a break I joined a couple of black soldiers on stage to put out an impromptu "My Girl" by the Temptations. Late into the night I hung out with Siwa and his friends at an open-air bazaar, drinking and listening to a capsule history of his tightly controlled society.

I hoped my absence from Saigon through the first of May would keep me out of the VC's second offensive. I'd sent my folks a telegram to let them know I was out of harm's way, and when it arrived it scared them to death—they were afraid it was announcing my own. But the VC waited until 5 May to launch what many called "Little Tet."

It wasn't so little. Some 119 attacks occurred, mostly by mortar and rocket fire. There were also a few serious ground attacks. Elements of the 320th NVA Division launched a three-day attack on Dong Ha; a Special Forces camp in II Corps was overrun by the 2d NVA Division; and, of course, Saigon was hit again.

On the day before the attacks I had gone swimming with a group of lieutenants during lunch at an officers' club next to Tan Son Nhut. Almost daily for months I had been jogging before a swim and on this day I found myself running along the edge of the airfield. The dusty streets and the Viet houses were silent and deserted, always the indicator of imminent problems. Again I had that creepy feeling of being intensely watched by hostile eyes. I did my best time back to the O-club, especially after an MP stopped his jeep to advise me I shouldn't be out there. I passed an old French cemetery where the next morning our troops were fighting Charlie from tombstone to tombstone.

On 6 May I wrote home that this was only a "little one" and that we were "working like normal." But at CICV we could stand at the front door and watch fighter planes launching rockets at dug-in enemy troops around the airfield. It was disconcerting; Tan Son Nhut was so loud and brassy with its constant air traffic, it seemed invincible. But now VC were again in the complex.

The May offensive had begun at 0400 hours with a barrage of mortars and rockets into downtown Saigon. Bombardments occurred throughout May into June, and we were again locked into full curfew as fighting continued in Cholon (where VC flags were flying), near the Phu Tho racetrack, at the Y Bridge, and in the northeast edge of the city. On the twelfth, from the hotel roof I watched in morbid fascination the shower of tracers from M-133 Miniguns fired from gunships into Cholon. Entire blocks were being flattened by the avalanche of slugs—6,000 a minute—from these modern Gatling guns. By the next day, as the Paris sessions began, this wave of attacks had receded. They were renewed by fire on 19 May, Ho Chi Minh's seventy-eighth birthday.

I was awakened around 0100 by explosions and saw fires about a half-mile from the Meyerkord. Two rockets swooped overhead, one landing in the palace grounds and another hitting the public market. In all, about twelve rockets landed within a mile of the hotel, almost in a circle. On the twentieth I was standing on the roof with a small battery-operated tape recorder picking up a GVN propaganda lecture being broadcast from a truck when the generator kicked on again after being down for days. The hotel's residents had been getting increasingly spooked sitting in the darkness waiting for the next barrage with no place to go when it came. Then I saw toward Tan Son Nhut a string of huge explosions that lit the sky with a blue-green glow. I'd never seen a B-52 strike so close to the city and our installations.

There was still extensive enemy movement in Saigon. On the

twenty-fifth VC and NVA troops again came into Cholon and the northeast edge of the city. Some areas weren't cleared until 6 June and on that day there was a battle only a mile and a half from the Meyerkord. By any accounting, May produced America's heaviest losses in the war: more than 2,000 KIA. This toll was taken by an enemy army that was supposed to have been dwindling before Tet and then "destroyed" during the offensive.

On the first day of the May offensive, a major strategy change was put into motion in Hanoi, signaled by a speech delivered by Truong Chinh, the third-ranking member of the Politburo and North Vietnam's most militant Marxist-Leninist theoretician. He called for a "shift to the defensive to gain time, dishearten the enemy, and build up our forces for a new offensive." He declared that it was time to again "grasp the motto of long-drawn-out fight." By the end of the summer this policy had begun to shift the war back into the guerrilla and sapper hit-and-run tactics of earlier days. Large units did not return in more conventional offensive attacks until Tet of 1969 and then the massive Easter offensive of 1972.

In Saigon, the American intelligence agencies had completed their own battlefield evaluation about three weeks ahead of Hanoi's. At the request of the Director of Central Intelligence, the intelligence community met from 10 to 16 April to address again the CIA's position that estimates of the enemy forces were understated and too restrictive in scope. It was a repeat of the NIE conference that had culminated in the September sellout of 1967. However, this time the CIA, again urged by Sam Adams, did not back down. Under the leadership of Colonel Daniel Graham, the MACV, DIA and CINCPAC teams once more resisted the CIA and the Department of State positions. For pre-Tet, MACV held to a 305,000–340,000 spread while the CIA advocated an estimate of 440,000–660,000. For post-Tet, MACV held to 278,000–328,000 while the CIA stayed with 440,000–590,000. Some agreements on bookkeeping methodology were made, but neither side would budge on overall numbers.[4]

Once again U.S. intelligence experts were reduced to debating form, not substance. MACV's failure to accept the OB realities precluded any critical analysis of what the enemy's capabilities meant to our strategy. The Communists proved to be highly flexible in adapting their strategy to the changing battlefield, even while their tactics remained static because of poor communications and unyielding prior planning; on the other hand, American mobility and communications gave us vastly superior tactical adaptability, but our strategic decision-making never was in tune with the battlefield realities. Not until General Abrams assumed command of MACV would we alter our approach to the war, but that change would result more from the politics of withdrawal than from the strategies of victory.

On 19 May, Ho's birthday, we were tasked with a project that would make a swell birthday present for the people's president. The first days of the peace talks had become stuck on a single issue: who was conducting the real aggression in South Vietnam. Our delegation was insisting that the North Vietnamese Army had to get out of the South before there could be a settlement. The Hanoi delegation was insisting North Vietnam had honored the 1954 Geneva Agreement and only southern-born patriots were trying to overthrow the U.S. imperialists and their Saigon puppets.

Now our diplomats wanted documents from J-2 to demonstrate the NVA presence in South Vietnam. We were ordered to turn over all our Order of Battle Summaries on each NVA regiment recognized in the OB Book. In sum, we were going to hand to the Communists the total of our finished intelligence that we had been laboring on all year. Hanoi would know exactly what we knew about them.

This was the last straw. The analysts were disgusted and angry. Once again I marched down to Colonel Mac's office. He listened with sympathy and replied that we had to follow instructions coming from the embassy (the ambassador was technically Westmoreland's immediate supervisor). Finally, I struck a deal with him. We would not turn over the entire OB Summary, just the history section, which addressed the infiltration process and dates.

We cut the histories down to their bare bones. Unfortunately, this meant we could not just recycle our existing material. Production of new pages kept all of us busy often past midnight until the end of the month. I put up a sign in the shop saying "Peace Is Hell." Colonel Mac immediately ordered it down.

Our work was made especially difficult because of the developing manpower shortage: we had become seriously and permanently understrength. By 9 May I was writing in my letters that we'd lost seven men and had only six left. It seemed that Johnson's de-escalation of the war had begun with CICV, for we were told not to expect replacements. I had to find ways to simplify procedures and focus our available time on the most crucial missions. The SPARS were the first to go. The enlisted analysts grudgingly admitted that the electronic symbols were expendable, so I recommended to Colonel Mac we discontinue their mapping. He had no objection; he didn't know we'd been doing it.

Change was also occurring in another section of CICV where the computers were kept. I was walking down the hall when a young and very upset sergeant approached me, almost in tears.

"Lieutenant Jones, I can't believe it, they're making us throw out our entire computer program and replace it with all new information. I've been working days and nights for the last year and now they say the work was all wrong and I have to put in a new data base!"

His complaint had a familiar ring. I could offer no way out but I wanted him to feel better. "Well, Sergeant, your work was used successfully by the headquarters for the entire year, so it certainly wasn't wasted. And maybe this new system will be even better."

My words seemed to help, and he thanked me. I hadn't believed a word of what I'd said.[5]

After watching VC rockets burn downtown, I came into CICV on 19 May to find our ARVN counterparts in something of a social gathering. I asked what was happening.

Aspirant Qui explained, "Lieutenant Jones, today is the birthday of Ho Chi Minh. He is the father of our country."

I just stared at them. *Bac Ho*, he was called; Uncle Ho. The father of Vietnam. And the president of the Democratic Republic of Vietnam. But still the people's hero, everywhere.

There was no hope for us.

PART SIX

Short-Timer

June—August 1968

The Light at the End of the Tunnel

What's that up ahead?
A light? Can it really be?
After all this darkness
And pain and anguish.
Is it really there?
It can't be a mirage this time.
It's a light, alright.
I'll blink and close my eyes
Then look again.
It's there, not as bright, but it's there.
The tunnel plays tricks on you.
You can't be sure.
I saw the light before
And it wasn't there.
But this time, it has to be.
There isn't much time left.
The light's still there, but it flickers.
Then it fades and comes back.
It looked so bright at first
But now it's not so bright.
Wait. It's gone. The light's out.
Now it's back.
It's a light.
It has to be. It has to be.

Author unknown
Grunt magazine, 1968

CHAPTER

20

Burn-Out

The dissatisfaction of those U.S. and Allied troops forced to come here, and the anti-war movement in the U.S., added to our attacks, political struggle, and initiative gained on the battlefield, will certainly conduct the U.S. Imperialists to an ignominious defeat.

Captured Viet Cong
training document

"So you're a captain now," a co-worker observed.

"Yeah, Uncle Sam in his infinite wisdom chose me before thee," I replied.

"Right. Isn't he the guy that did the Bay of Pigs, the Tonkin Gulf Resolution, and the War on Poverty?"

"Same guy, another disaster. You got it."

On 8 June 1968 I became a captain in the New Modern Action Army with a raise pushing my salary up to $630 a month, plus the $65 combat pay. To get my twin tracks I had to agree to serve a full year at my new rank, which meant three months added to my basic two-year commitment.

I even got a swell mimeographed letter of congratulations from Colonel Flakjacket, who declared that my "advancement in rank is well deserved and indicative of exceptional service, sincere devotion to duty and demonstrated outstanding abilities." It was amazing that anyone who had been on active duty just barely over a year and was still in his first assignment could receive a "well deserved" promotion to 0-3. In the U.S. Army of Vietnam, they gave away rank and ribbons like candy kisses.

But even getting a semi-automatic promotion didn't come easy. A captain from Admin told me my papers had arrived and I asked if I should just put on my bars.

"Sure," he said with a shrug.

So I cut off the sewn-on black cloth bar from my collar and pinned on the new silver bars from the PX (I'd asked my father for his, but he said they were too corroded).

When he saw me, Lieutenant Kernsky was not thrilled but offered his congratulations. Shore stage-whispered, "A captain! He's gonna get worse." But this was the last time he played it for laughs. He was acting very strangely. In fact, our best analyst was about to become a problem.

The next day the same captain from Admin caught me in the hall and told me angrily that the CO of CICV was really pissed off at me because I had pinned on my bars before "the ceremony."

"What ceremony?"

"The ceremony where the CO pins on the new bars for promoted captains."

"You didn't tell me about any ceremony."

"There's always a ceremony, but now there won't be one because you pinned on your bars."

The CICV commanding officer did send for me within the week. He was new, and he was a big chunk of an Army full-bird colonel. I asked the messenger why I was being summoned.

"He heard you're planning to extend."

True, I had picked up the papers, but I had maybe two more weeks before I had to decide. Why would the CO care?

At the door I waited until his adjutant announced me and ordered me in. I stopped midway in the office to deliver my salute and to announce, "Sir, Captain Jones reporting as ordered"; I was cut off midway with, "Sit down, Jones."

The colonel silently studied my file. I shifted uneasily in my chair.

"Jones, you're thinking of extending."

"Yes, sir, my job is a pretty good one, and if I could stay in it . . ."

"You'll serve according to the Army's needs, Jones. Wherever you're needed. No guarantees."

"Yes, sir."

There was a long pause. I thought I'd better cover my bases. "Sir, I guess I owe you an apology. I was not advised about the promotion ceremony, so I pinned the bars on myself. I meant no disrespect."

He grunted and finally turned to look at me. "Jones, do you plan to marry your Vietnamese girlfriend?"

It was sudden and unexpected, and I just sat there staring at him. Finally I answered, "She wants to, I don't." After another long pause I added that we hadn't talked about it in months.

"They can put a lot of pressure on. The Army does not approve of war brides."

I laughed. "Yes, sir, I come from an Army family and I've heard that one before."

He looked at me critically, no doubt wondering if I was mouthing off. My reputation had probably preceded me.

I really wanted to talk about my extension, thought better of it, and when he told me that was all, I left in a hurry, not even stopping to salute. Back at the shop I threw my extension papers in the trash and went back to work, aware that I was now officially short.

There was still plenty to do. On 25 June I wrote home that we had to "research and accept about a 1000 new units in CTZ." The VC were apparently taking good advantage of the bombing pause, but we may have only been finding out about the invasion force that had flowed in before and during Hanoi's winter-spring offensive. Some portion of these unit submittals were summarily denied (or lowered to the innocuous "possible/probable" categories). How many, I didn't know. We just read the reports and pumped out the recommendations. What the brass did with them was their problem.

Dissent was growing everywhere. On the home front, out in the field, and even within CICV itself. Especially painful to me was what was happening to Shore; our best analyst was losing his hold on the program. By late March, after the 38th Battalion incident, Shore's sly humor and brazen satire had become black cynicism and mean sarcasm. He conducted a loud and cruel monologue on "slopes" and the condition of "slopeness." He noted that I had found the Vietnamese to be "gentle," then asked why they were so good at killing: "All of them, both sides, they do it so well!"

He deeply embarrassed the Viets and me, but reprimands barely fazed him. His conversations became rambling, sometimes near-manic, and he began wandering around the room, interrupting and disturbing everyone.

His tour would be over in June and he was too short for formal discipline. Finally it was his last week. I needed one more project out of him, but each morning via an EM he sent a message that he was having to outprocess at the compound. For a couple of days I let it ride while sending back reminders that he owed me work. Then one day he didn't show and no one knew where he was. In other words, he was AWOL.

I told his enlisted buddies to get him in right now or the MPs were going to do it. In an hour I learned he had appeared and was filing a complaint in Admin. I yanked him out and chewed him royally. I told him he was close to an Article 15 and only his shortness and my work load were saving him.

"But you *have* blown your medal and your efficiency report! You understand?"

He looked hurt. "I've worked hard for you, Captain Jones. There were all those OB Summaries and those Tet documents . . ."

"Yes, Shore, for most of the year you were outstanding, but for the last month you've made my job very hard. Now get in there and finish that project!"

He put in a couple of hours and turned in a paper that was a shadow of his best work.

"O.K., Shore, now clear out!" I ordered as he began talking with one of the men. He walked slowly to the door, and his long face under his sparse blond hair looked old and tired. The silence held on for hours. The enlisted men were sullen but I told myself I had had no choice. Since Shore had been so blatant in pushing the system, the reprimand, as low-grade as it was, had to be done publicly.

But I felt like hell. Shore had a bad case of short-timer's disease. I understood that, because I was catching it too.

Just after my promotion I mailed a letter I had been planning since 7 May when a first lieutenant who lived on my floor at the Meyerkord had given me an insane jeep ride to CICV. One of the "Nine Rules" that Westmoreland wanted us to observe was always to give the Vietnamese right of way on the road. It was a rule in constant violation; vehicles seemed to amplify intolerance and arrogance (I had even had to discipline an enlisted man who intentionally drove over dogs with a deuce-and-a-half).

This officer drove at extreme speeds, honking and weaving wildly, forcing pedestrians, including old women, to jump for safety, breaking through intersections with blasts of his horn, forcing local traffic to swerve for safety, cursing the inferiority of the Vietnamese all the way. To his commanding officer I wrote that he was going to kill someone and that "I believe appropriate action should be taken to halt further damage to the USA image in Vietnam, as caused by this officer."

I showed the letter to Kernsky, thinking he'd support me for nailing this fool. Instead he said, "Don't send that! You'll ruin his career!" That seemed a desirable result, but it didn't happen. In a few days the lieutenant in question approached me at the Meyerkord, this time humble, his eyes downcast. He reported that his CO had had a "talk" with him. It was better than nothing. There was so much hatred and anger, you couldn't stop it and many officers didn't even try.

The grunts who fought out in the boonies were, understandably, the hardest and the coldest, but not without humor: "Yea, though I walk through the Valley of the Shadow of Death, I fear no evil, for I am the toughest mother in the Valley." But that cockiness could be transformed into brutality, as in this verse:

> Vietnam, oh Vietnam
> should be a testing site for the nuclear bomb
> we could take the pimps, whores, and American haters
> and bury their asses in the vast bomb craters
> they rob and they cheat and they scream and holler
> while making a mockery of the American dollar
> They're bad when they're born and worse when they're grown
> ain't got the guts to fight for their own
> If it's something worthwhile, the slopes will say screw it
> If there's work to be done—let the Americans do it
> The government's corrupt, the people are worse
> The country itself smells of a curse
> Well I'm tired of playing the invited guest
> What I'm gonna say now is not in jest
> We'll take every house, every building and store
> and give them a taste of Martial Law
> They do what they're told and jump when we speak
> They'll learn to be humble, obedient and meek
> and if they bitch with voices asundry
> We'll bring in the asphalt and black the country
> we offered our hand and they accepted with grace

while they squandered our money and spit in our face
when the country falls, we should remain calm
and value the lesson of Vietnam
When in the future, another Vietnam comes to pass
This time we'll go in and kick some ass.

Even worse than the hate were the indifference and emotional isolation. In April, when Martin Luther King, Jr., was murdered, the brass worried whether they should give the blacks a day off to go to church, or something. I heard this being debated in Admin and commented, "Maybe you should give *all* of us a day off." That possibility was never considered. The only concern was to avoid black political demonstrations.

Then, on 5 June 1968, Robert Kennedy was shot. The two murders and the violence at home were too much to bear in the war zone. Every time I got a copy of the *San Francisco Chronicle* that my folks had ordered for me, the headlines were of riots, murders, dissent, disarray. How could we make the world safe for democracy when we couldn't maintain peace in our own country?

After hearing about Kennedy, I went to the officers' mess and sat at an empty table, hoping I'd be left alone. Soon a captain and a lieutenant sat down. The lieutenant said casually, "Did you hear on the radio that Kennedy was shot?"

The captain said, "Oh, yeah?" He added, "That's too bad," as he got up and walked to the salad bar, filled his plate, and returned. "Damned if they don't have fresh tomatoes for a change. Where did it happen?"

"California, I don't know where."

Without looking at them, I said, "L.A. He had just given his victory speech."

The captain said, "Oh, no wonder. There's a lot of people who would like to get rid of him, especially if he was winning."

"Maybe my family even heard the shot!" laughed the lieutenant. "They live downtown."

"A little excitement for a change, eh?" added the captain.

"Yeah. After the Watts riot, it got dull in L.A.!"

I had to get out. I shoved my chair away and left the mess. I was so frustrated. The war and my future were little clearer to me now than when I had arrived at Long Binh.

I hated the Army. I loved the Army.

I couldn't leave Vietnam. I had to get the hell out.

The war was right. The war was insane.

I scorned the brass. I yearned for their praise.

They couldn't do without me. Let them find another sucker.

I couldn't understand anything, and I couldn't understand myself. All I knew was that Vietnam could twist you around and leave you spinning.

Despair was not unique to me, or even just to Americans. Reading a PW report, I had an insight into the agony felt by a North Vietnamese Army lieutenant:

> There were times I wished that the North would send an incredible number of troops to the South and let the war escalate into an incredible level so that the fighting would end much sooner. . . . Let the Front win. Let the GVN win. That I don't care. But let the war become fiercer so that it could end so much sooner. Let those who would be killed anyway, get killed. . . . The people are being pulled this way and that. The Front wants them. The GVN wants them, and the Americans want them also. . . . The people are being pulled apart and they are the ones who have to endure the most suffering in the war. Meanwhile, the war continues, and no one seems to know when it will end.[1]

Right.

21

Wrap-Up

It was an act of impulsive frivolity and rebellion for which he knew afterward he would be punished severely. The next morning he entered his office in trepidation and waited to see what would happen. Nothing happened.

Joseph Heller
Catch-22

Out of nowhere came a trip to Da Nang. On 1 July CICV sent a team of us to III MAF to coordinate with the Marines. Fine with me. Fewer days in the office.

At the Da Nang air base I had trouble handling the crack of 90mm cannons from the Marines' M-48 tanks as they performed as artillery from within the base. Greenies and rear-echelon types couldn't tell outgoing from incoming. Any *crack* or *whoosh* at least earned a jump, and I felt foolish trying to be cool, and failing, when those suckers popped off.

G-2 was in a nondescript pre-fab hut. All the Marines, even the lieutenants, were much older than I. In the USMC you could have gray hair before you got twin tracks. For the Leathernecks there was no such thing as automatic promotions. I was nervous; my youth, my service, and my assignment in MACV headquarters were not going to impress these Marine lifers.

"Good morning, gentlemen, I'm from the Combined Intelligence Center in Saigon and was sent to, ah, coordinate with you."

I faced a roomful of scowls. I sat down on an unused desk while the silence continued. Then a grizzled major growled, "Is it true you guys at MACV get a day off every week?"

I said, "Usually." There were some exclamations of disgust and shakes of heads. I didn't add that for much of my tour I hadn't had any time off. "Don't you?"

"Hell, no, all we get is two-hour lunches to run errands."

"Two-hour lunches!" I laughed. "If I had two-hour lunches, I wouldn't need a day off!"

A mistake. Any chance of "coordination" had just gone down the tubes. Hurriedly I tried to recoup. "Is there any OB you want to talk about? Have those Unit OB Summaries I sent been useful to you?"

A relatively young captain said, "Oh, you sent those? Yes, we've used them."

That was the first feedback I'd ever had. They also seemed to appreciate the directory of I Corps intelligence shops that I had compiled during the days when the OB Summaries were being sent out by courier to users. I asked them to help us update the summaries, but there was no show of enthusiasm.

The silence resumed. I tried one more thing. "Did III MAF drop the 38th VC Battalion to zero in March, like we did?"

There were glares and rumbles of anger. "Hell, no, that was Army bullshit!" a Marine retorted.

I sighed, slid off the desk, waited a moment, and said, "Thank you, gentlemen. It's been swell!"

As I was leaving, the youngish captain followed me out. "Captain Jones, I'm sorry. . ."

"Don't worry about it," I told him. "Always been that way with the Marines and Army, right?" I waved and headed for the South China Sea. I was going to the beach!

Maybe a hundred men were splashing in the beautiful clear water off the long, white beach. Most of them had on fatigue trousers. Swimming suits weren't part of your average combat load. I too stripped down and went for the waves.

Heaven could be the South China Sea, its water only some twenty degrees cooler than the 90–100 degree air. I swam and body-surfed for two hours, imagining a peaceful Vietnam someday crowded with tourists.

Finally I pulled out to shape myself up. A light-bird colonel saw me half dressed, but he just grinned at my exuberance, and I grinned right back. My jungle fatigues dried quickly in the heat and I spent the rest of the day and evening sightseeing around Da Nang, a pleasant city, the second largest in Vietnam, without the dirt, smog, and rush of Saigon. Off in the distance loomed Marble Mountain, site of a colony of monkeys and no few VC. Its marble quarries produced Da Nang's major export and store items: ash trays, boxes, anything that could be fashioned out of the slick gray stone.

The flight back to Tan Son Nhut was uneventful, and I was grateful for my all-expenses-paid vacation. I figured I could now skate through the next month on my head. To the amazement of the shop, I set up a short-timer's calendar. They were still convinced I was too gung-ho for such devices.

I was so short, in fact, that my replacement arrived by the middle of July. A captain in the regular Army, he was a lifer, which to non-lifers stood for "Lazy-Inefficient-Fuckoff-Expecting-Retirement."

This guy, a large, stout, hugely confident man, in his late twenties, hit me wrong from the first minute. Before I met him, the enlisted men had laughingly reported that almost the first thing out of his mouth was that having a major general for a father-in-law *really* didn't help his career any. I arrived to find the room rearranged. The captain's desk now rode at the top of our area with much-coveted open space on both sides of his executive position. The rest of us had been crowded together, our backs to him.

And he had jammed the Vietnamese into a tiny space in the far corner, away from the Americans. I learned he hadn't even discussed the move with them, and our counterparts were embarrassed and angry. I too was furious.

For some time I listened to him hold forth from his desk, even though he had no idea who I was. Finally I said that I presumed he was my replacement. We made our introductions. He told me that this was his second tour in Vietnam, though the first was only several months long and not in OB. I told him that we had a lot of projects to do without much time to show him the ropes. I offered him one of the recurring reports so he could get his feet wet while I was still available to answer questions.

He simply wouldn't do any of the work. He would not get involved in any of the damn projects, even though I explained that the OIC would have to engineer most of the assignments himself since the reduced staff carried no Projects Officer. He then let me know that he was due for promotion to major, that he was the new OIC, and if he wanted me to do the projects, I'd do them. In a patronizing voice he added, "Won't you?"

It was now time to deal with the issue of the ARVNs, how his reorganization had ruined a useful working relationship and cut off a valuable source of information. I also reminded him of the Asian importance of saving face.

"That's where I want them," he replied abruptly. Thereafter, the ARVNs treated the captain only a little less formally—and coldly—than I did.

I went back to work on a project that was especially interesting to me because it was my last one. I was plotting the movements over two years of enemy units in two provinces during the dry and wet seasons. Were they as mobile during the monsoons as during the rest of the year? After digging through our files to get all the past current probable locations, I plotted dry season movements in red and rainy moves in blue. The project demonstrated the need for an addition to our Unit OB Summaries that would show all the units' identified locations in a chronological list, so that their patterns of operation would be better understood.

We had erred in not having isolated this information as it came in, and now the enlisted men complained about the time it would take to pull out all these coordinates. That familiar refrain made me realize that my last contribution had to be a new, revised SOP that established our priorities, especially with a diminishing staff. I was at work on it when I heard, "Jones, I want to talk to you."

It was the new captain, Captain "R.A." as I thought of him, who lacked even the courtesy to refer to me by my rank. He told me to sit in the wooden chair next to his desk. The conversation was unfocused and I had no idea of what he wanted. I tried to be responsive but this guy made me uncomfortable. I wasn't aware that I had hooked my feet under the front rung of the chair and was nervously rocking it from pushes of my toes and the calves of my legs. Then I noticed his eyes were riveted on my feet. He wasn't hearing anything I said and his face had grown red. Suddenly he exploded, "Stop rocking that chair or I'll march you over to the major's office on charges!"

He never saw the astonishment on my face because he kept staring at my feet. I remained silent, wondering if he would look me in the eye. He didn't. Finally I said, "I'm sure you would. Anything else, Captain?"

He said, "No," still not looking at me, and I returned to my desk. I gotta get out of here, I thought.

Later Colonel Mac asked how the movements analysis was coming along. I had only begun it, but I thought the study would show more movement in the dry seasons. Colonel Mac said, "Yeah, that's what I thought, too."

Some days later, he blew up at me—for the last time—when I told him that I'd found equal mobility by the VC/NVA units in dry and wet weather.

"Damn it, I already told MACV that they moved mostly in the dry season!"

"Colonel Mac, I told you I wasn't done."

"Then you shouldn't have given me an opinion!"

"Yes, sir, apparently not!"

I saw the colonel only once more—I hadn't realized how short he was. He flew in through the doors at the shop as was his style, but this time his face was pale, his eyes distant and moist, maybe even a little wild. He came straight to me, shook my hand, and said in a choked voice, "I'm leaving. You did a good job, Jones." Then, I swear, he began to cry soundlessly. He looked around the room, then he shot out through the doors.

I hadn't said a word to him. Stricken, I announced, "Colonel Mac is going home!" No one said anything. I hurried into the hall and checked the other OB shops but he had left. It had been rough going with that old S.O.B. but his last words to me meant more than any medal could have.

Very soon Colonel Mac's replacement, an Army major, was making his presence felt. Kernsky was getting on well with the new generation. I was not ingratiating myself with anyone. I fought with both of the new officers over PFC Shore's efficiency report. How could I rate him highly if I reported an attitude problem? I argued that his skills had been marred by a temporary short-timer's syndrome. They tried to put the new captain's name, as OIC, on the report instead of mine. I got mad again. "He never even met the man!"

Then, on Kernsky's request, I put him in for some combined services commendation. But later I saw on the major's desk paperwork for Kernsky's Bronze Star. I told the major bluntly that this was not my recommendation as his OIC. He just gave me a sheepish grin, and I didn't pursue it. Colonel Mac had put me in for the Bronze with a write-up recognizing my entire tour. Hell, give them to everyone, as long as I get mine.

The work kept coming. In a letter home on 17 July, I complained about the number of projects: "You'd think I could leave this place gracefully and leave the work load behind." The shop was now down to one NCO, one EM, a new first lieutenant and the "two old hands," Kernsky and me, plus the new captain, who didn't count for much. To my letter I added, "Yeah, I'm ready to come on back."

I was doing my job, but I took every opportunity for momentary R-and-R. At lunch I ran a couple of miles, then swam while the hour slid into an hour and a half. I left work by 1800 unless there was a crisis and took off all the weekends. Now that the rockets had stopped, I was going downtown every night, roaming the streets, photographing every-thing.

I was in search of some revelation of the elusive butterfly that was the essence of Vietnam. But all I could do was repeat the same old experiences. Especially the French restaurants, where I went nightly for the Chateaubriand and baked Alaska, now available again after the long, dry siege. (Once I found "Banana Split" on the menu and decided to see what the Viets did with that American staple; they brought me a plate with a single three-inch banana, split down the middle.) Somehow, the French cooking just didn't taste as good as before Tet, but it was still fattening and I was putting on pounds in spite of the noontime runs. I was getting golden-tanned, well-conditioned, and chubby. And *short*.

Too short to be getting into trouble. I should have stayed inside and counted down the days. But my wanderlust took me on a clear Sunday to the edge of Saigon after a long pedicab ride. In a Buddhist temple I had photographed an old Viet woman kneeling in prayer under a huge, bell-shaped coil of slowly burning incense that hung from the ceiling. Outside, I walked along the temple grounds and saw a beautiful woman in *ao dai* sitting next to a young, muscular Viet man wearing a white shirt and black shorts who was kneeling on their picnic blanket. His bearing seemed military, and his apprehension was obvious when he saw me. His face turned hard and cold as he started to rise, but the woman, glancing at me, put a restraining hand on his knee. He settled back but the tension of a hooded cobra was still in him as he watched me.

I did not change my pace. Forcing a half smile, I gave the smallest of nods. His expression relaxed as he returned the gesture. After pass-ing them I still felt his intense scrutiny on my back. I was sweating profusely and finally spun around, but his eyes were again only for the woman. I breathed deeply and decided to call it a day. Not until later did I remember the .38 in the valise under my arm.

I thought back to day one in-country when I'd written in my notebook, "I hope I kill every VC I meet. I hope I never meet a VC."

Nothing was that simple in Nam.

I was still working on the wet/dry season movements study. The deadline was looming and I was pushing to make it. In through the door marched Colonel Mac's replacement, heading straight for me.

"Jones, I've got a short fuse on this project." He threw papers on my desk. He didn't hand them to Captain R.A. The project came directly to Captain Jones.

"But, Major, I've got this project that's—"

"DO IT!" he bellowed as he headed for the door.

My mouth was still open in mid-sentence and there was some laughter around the room. Then without any premeditation, I raised my hand and gave him the finger. I was stunned to realize what I had done.

The shop exploded in laughter and applause, some of the men even coming over to slap me on the back. I think it was Kernsky who yelled, "At last, he's one of us!" The major heard the burst of noise and turned with a perplexed expression, then went on his way.

I started laughing in disbelief and amazement over what I'd done and turned to see the captain's face livid with anger. I laughed even harder. Maybe I'd be called into the major's office, or not (I wasn't), but I was sure I'd blown my Bronze Star. I was too short to care.

In my last days at CICV, I was rushing to complete the SOP for a shop that was undermanned and that had an OIC who wouldn't get into the mechanics of operation. Or maybe I was just trying to extend my influence beyond my tour, unable to let go. It was a wrenching thing to give up the job that "only you could do."

The captain must have felt threatened by my SOP because when I passed out review drafts to the men, he exploded and withdrew them. He insisted I didn't have the authority to distribute anything.

Right. That was it. I was done. In the last week of July, he told me I had the option of taking some eleven days to outprocess if I wanted, but he'd be pleased to have me help with some more projects.

In minutes I was packed up. I extended my hand to this OIC of I Corps Order of Battle and said, "Good luck. You're going to need it." Then I found Kernsky and asked if he was staying another six months.

"Dunno, maybe."

He was still keeping distance between us; by then he had to know. He said something about it having been a pleasure serving with me. I thanked him for his hard work. It was true; even if we hadn't got along, he had given the job his best shot, never skating.

Then I went to my ARVN counterpart. My eyes were beginning to mist. "Goodbye, Lieutenant Tri, thank you for your help. I will write you. Take care of yourself."

Always formal, he stood and bowed slightly, said good-by and shook my hand. His English was not good enough to say more without preparation.

Aspirant Qui had been transferred to III Corps OB and by the time I got to his room, my eyes were wet. I grabbed Qui's hand, told him I was leaving, and, to his embarrassment, hugged him. Then, as fast as I could, I got the hell out of the CICV because I was crying.

With the extra time on my hands, I finished making the purchases on my shopping list of souvenirs. Outprocessing took about a day, and I ran out of things to do. At the hotel a Special Services woman asked me to accompany her downtown to get a painting on which she'd put a deposit. The store was closed and she exploded in rage.

"That son of a bitch! I'll never get it. I've gone three times to pick it up and he hasn't been there. Don't they know we work until six? They should be here so we can get our things. Damn lazy people!"

I pointed out it was Sunday and that most American stores also didn't stay open after six. That didn't matter: "They never work anytime." Her other trips had been at noon when many stores were closed for siesta. But, of course, that was unreasonable to Americans who do everything in double time.

The two cultures were, indeed, radically different. We see ourselves as action driven, our slogans "Can do!" and "Drive on!"; they seek harmony through the philosophies of tolerance and detachment. Americans are candidly blunt; Vietnamese are politely indirect. We're cowboys and engineers; they're poets and artists. Our propelling force is ego; theirs is dignity.

This war could never have been a truly "combined" operation.

In these last days I thought a lot about the war, and made some notes. I wrote that our airpower was "overrated," that the "ARVN must be built up," and that the "SVN army's role and prestige should have

253

been stressed much earlier."[1] (In fact, General Abrams had already begun moving in that direction, laying the groundwork for Nixon's too-late "Vietnamization" of the war.) I thought there should be more GVN guerrillas in their own black pajamas to match the VC at their own game. (A VC platoon leader had declared in interrogation that they were "terrified of the few Vietnamese rangers who often attacked their headquarters and caught them off-guard.")[2] Instead of sending large, noisy units into ambushes it had always seemed more logical to me to rely on small, fast long-range reconnaissance patrols to find the enemy before bringing in blocking units for a cordon. Then we could just blast them from the sky,[3] laying siege to the VC for a change. Dak To could have been a true victory in this way, not the unconscionable slaughter that it was.

But the war was no longer my business. I had only to close out my personal affairs, the most important of which was Miss My. I had told her I intended to extend, and I had not been able to bring myself to explain I was going home. On 21 July we had our last full day together. We were both invited to a wedding reception at the Majestic Hotel for one of the CICV secretaries, a beautiful and well-schooled woman who was marrying a French-educated scholar, Tran Nha. In April he had begun publishing a new English-language magazine called *The Saigon Enquirer*. His fiancée had given me a copy of the first issue and urged me to write a letter of support. In the second edition of 23 April were my comments:

> Don't feel timid about criticizing Americans. While American impatience . . . may often exasperate the Vietnamese, remember that, at the same time, we are probably the most self-critical people in the world. The Vietnamese opinion will be interesting to us, if it remains objective.

Tran Nha was making a valiant attempt to bring American and Vietnamese opinion together, guiding readers, as he wrote in his first editorial, "through the maze of Vietnamese psychology, politics and other equally puzzling aspects of life in this unhappy but fascinating nation." Given the amount of blank spaces in his first issue, left by the government censor, he had a hard journey ahead. I wished him good fortune.

Several days later Miss My and I had our last date. We had coffee and croissants at the milk bar across from the Continental Hotel. I told her it was over; she'd already known.[4]

My last purchase in Saigon was the 2 August 1968 issue of the English-language *Saigon Daily News* (whose slogan was, "Of the Nation's March Toward True Democracy"). The lead story was about the first major VC attacks since the May offensive, which were, predictably, in the Saigon area. Before I left CICV there had been more indicators of another phase of attacks to come in early August. During the jeep ride to Long Binh with my old classmate, Lieutenant Klein, I watched our surroundings very carefully. It would have been too much to have got caught in some battle in my last hours. The image of those servicemen at Tan Son Nhut, nailed by a rocket on their last day, was very much with me.

Before we boarded we were given copies of *Tour 365,* prepared by the U.S. Army headquarters, with coverage of the war up through Tet. A message from Westmoreland appeared on the inside front cover:

> Your tour of duty with the United States Army, Vietnam, is ended. May your trip home and reunion with family and friends be the pleasant, happy occasion you have anticipated. You go home with my best wishes.
>
> As veterans of this war, you can now look back with perspective on your experience and know the trying and difficult tasks inherent in fighting to protect the freedom of peace-loving people against Communist invaders. . . .
>
> People at home will want to hear your story of the war. Tell it. . . .
>
> I extend my sincere appreciation for your help in accomplishing our task in Vietnam, and my thanks for a job well done. Good luck in the future.

On the plane, I busied myself organizing a bag of photographs. The enlisted man next to me was fascinated. He'd spent his tour in a warehouse on some big base.

"I guess you had a hell of a year, huh, sir?"

"Yeah, I guess I did."

As we were getting close to Hawaii, deterioration from tropical humidity and the pressure of those pounds gained from over-indulgence in French restaurants put an unbearable strain upon the seatseam of my khakis. The back of my pants split open from my crotch up towards my belt.

I asked if any of the stewardesses had needle and thread and could help. One did and could. I took my trousers off in the tiny lavatory and handed them out to her for repair. There was no way in hell to keep such a wonderful event unknown to a hundred GIs. When the stewardess knocked on the door to deliver the trousers and I reached out, there was a huge cheer.

After we took off from Hawaii, I learned that all the senior officers had disembarked for a stay. I had desperately wanted to do that, but no one in CICV admin could confirm if it was O.K. or if there was further outprocessing to be done at Travis AFB in California. (I would learn, too late, that there wasn't any. After the landing, the officers would just pick up their bags and taxi into San Francisco. The clerks had got me again.)

I was now the ranking officer and would have to lead the men off the plane. Fine, except some fifteen minutes from California the makeshift seam popped again. I would come home literally dragging my ass behind me. Somehow it seemed appropriate, but I would stand tall in spite of my indignities. Then I would get into civilian clothes as fast as I could. Forever.

Below us were the green-oak-dotted, golden-brown hills of summertime California, and the Pan Am 707 circled for its landing.

As the wheels touched down at Travis on 4 August 1968 the men were stone-cold silent.

EPILOGUE

All the business of war, and indeed all the business of life, is
to endeavor to find out what you don't know by what you do.
Arthur Wellesley,
Duke of Wellington

Until I left the Army in 1969, I was assigned as an advisor to a wide
variety of reserve units in southern California: civil affairs, a radio station, a Special Forces company, a marching band (that had no instru-
ments), transportation, a hospital, and others. My only respite from the
tedium of the job was Colonel Maggie. I wound up living in west L.A.
near her house in Bel Air, where I was often invited for dinner and to
play Scrabble (until dawn, and she always beat me).

Each year during her stateside T.V. and stage appearances, Colonel
Maggie asked relatives of GIs to write her so that she could deliver letters
in person to their sons and husbands. I created a filing and index system
for the five hundred or so letters she had received; a single folder contained all the communications for those men stationed in or near each
base camp she was to visit. Reading those letters gave me a new insight
into the war's emotional cost; I was pleased that during her 1969 trip,
Colonel Maggie was able to find up to three hundred of the men.

To my surprise the Bronze Star did come through. My father
proudly photographed the awards ceremony in the fall of 1968. On 10
September 1969 I was honorably discharged from active duty in the
United States Army. I even got a certificate signed by General William
C. Westmoreland, U.S. Army Chief of Staff, for my "faithful perfor-
mance of duty."

On a November morning in 1969, I read in the *Los Angeles Times*
a report of the My Lai atrocity. I had never known the name of the
hamlet, but its location in I Corps and the date jumped off the page.
There could have been only one such tragedy in Quang Ngai province
in March 1968; finally to see it described in print was stunning. I cut
out the article, stared at it for a while, then threw it away.

EPILOGUE

By the end of the year the state senator for whom I'd worked before the Army invited me to come to Sacramento as his administrative assistant. I began a career in government and environmental planning.

But My Lai kept coming back to me. The Army finally released its own review of the My Lai event in 1974, although it was dated 14 March 1970 (it had been withheld while the trial of Lieutenant William Calley and associated proceedings were in progress). The author was Lieutenant General W. R. Peers, a respected thirty-six-year veteran who had commanded the 4th Infantry Division through 1967. According to the news reports, the Peers inquiry had found that a cover-up of the war crime had occurred *but had been limited to the Americal Division in the field.*

I knew that was not the truth. The newspaper report of the Peers inquiry moved me to action, and on 15 November 1974 I wrote my first letter to President Gerald Ford, requesting a copy of the Peers report and giving a general overview of how MACV headquarters had involved itself in damage control during March 1968.

Until mid-1975 letters flowed between me and Secretary of the Army Howard Callaway, the General Counsel of the Army, Charles D. Ablard, and the Acting Chief Counsel, Richard Kearney, as well as my California senators (who expressed concern but offered no follow-up). In one letter I even sent the Department of the Army a copy of the October 1967 CICV disposition form that acknowledged a ceiling had been set on the reportable size of the enemy army. There was no reaction.

In response to my allegations, the Army conducted searches for related MACV records at the Washington Records Center, the Military History Research Collection at Carlisle Barracks, Pennsylvania, the Office of the Assistant Chief of Staff for Intelligence, and other repositories, as well as making several inquiries of the Defense Intelligence Agency. (I was to learn years later, to my surprise and fascination, that none other than Daniel Graham—who as a colonel in Saigon was chief of J-2 current intelligence and was responsible for approving changes to the OB Book—had been promoted to lieutenant general and was then, in 1974–75, the head of the DIA.) Several photocopied pages from the 1968 MACV Order of Battle Summary were sent to me, but, inexplicably, the 1967 editions could not be found.

It didn't matter. The OB extracts and a letter of 6 February 1975 from the Army General Counsel finally put the cold realities clearly before me. The official file copies of the MACV OB Book no longer showed a drop in strength for the 38th VC Local Force Battalion from its operational level (around 250 to 300) to zero and back again. The official archive records had been purged of any indication that MACV headquarters had known about My Lai and had abetted the cover-up.

In his book, *The My Lai Inquiry,* General Peers referred to the "haunting problem of the destruction of records and the 'cleansing' of files." But the Peers Commission didn't know the half of it. The general also wrote:

> If by some means information of the incident had gotten out-side of the Americal Division to higher headquarters, almost certainly a proper investigation would have been conducted. . . . To this day the matter that most greatly concerns me is that so many people in command positions . . . had information that something unusual had occurred during the My Lai operation and yet did nothing about it. To my mind this has had the most damaging effect upon the image of the U.S. Army as a professional institution and has cast doubt upon the integrity of all its officers and men. Had any of these persons made their knowledge known to the proper investigating authorities, the whole blanket of obscurity covering the incident would had been rolled back and the true facts brought to light.[1]

Years later, General Bruce Palmer, who had been Westmoreland's deputy at MACV, wrote, "We—indeed, everyone except those involved—were totally ignorant about the matter [My Lai] until it surfaced a year later."[2] But the general's disclaimer can apply only to his level of command and that of the COMUSMACV. The decision to falsify the OB Book had to have been made by someone at headquarters level closely involved with the intelligence process and with enough authority to intervene. In MACV in 1968 that didn't necessarily mean a general, but in the Washington of 1974 access to nationwide intelligence archives surely required a senior officer of considerable influence.

On 9 June 1975 I wrote my last letter to President Ford, summarizing everything I had learned. But I knew the battle was over; the cover-up had, indeed, been effective. Around this time I threw away my dog tags and would not talk about Vietnam to anyone, especially men who had served there.

In 1979, when Peers's book was published, it received particular publicity locally because he lived nearby in the San Francisco Bay area. I called him.

No, the Department of the Army had never sent him my letters. Was I perhaps confused about when the 38th Battalion was in combat, since they were pretty badly beaten up during Tet? Yes, he would like to see copies of my letters, but there was nothing that could be done about it now.

I sent the package of correspondence but never heard from Peers. I wrote an article about the series of events and offered it to every possible magazine. No takers. Finally I put it all away again, I hoped forever.

On 10 June 1983 I pulled from the hold basket on my desk a newspaper article about the Westmoreland–CBS lawsuit. It had been there for months. I knew I should call CBS, but memories of being lavished with apathy in the seventies were still strong. However, I'd just resolved a major financial crisis and I decided to tie up some more loose ends that day.

My call to CBS in Los Angeles was transferred to New York, where I spoke to George Crile, the producer of the CBS documentary, "The Uncounted Enemy: A Vietnam Deception." It was this show, aired on 23 January 1982, that caused General Westmoreland so much discomfort with its declaration that America was "misinformed about the nature and the size of the enemy we were facing." Mike Wallace for CBS had described a "conscious effort—indeed, a conspiracy at the highest levels of American military intelligence—to suppress and alter critical intelligence on the enemy in the year leading up to the Tet offensive."

In the documentary Westmoreland admitted to rejecting the intelligence estimate prepared by General McChristian and Colonel Hawkins for "political reasons" and because "the people in Washington were not sophisticated enough to understand and evaluate this thing, and neither was the media." It was a startling admission for a professional soldier to make. The American military has always maintained its separation from politics, and it is, according to my 1959 ROTC manual, an "instrument of civilian authority." (That point was of course made almost two centuries before, in the Constitution of the United States.) The military does not create public or political opinion; it is controlled by it.

The show's producer seemed interested in my background and asked if the CBS attorneys could call me. In an hour I heard from Robert Baron of Cravath, Swaine, and Moore. Sam Adams joined him on an extension. Their interest in the experiences I recounted reassured me I was doing the right thing. A week later Baron flew to Sacramento to begin work on my affidavit. On the day he arrived, I found in the boxes of my Vietnam notes and souvenirs the "downward trending" directive issued by General Davidson on 15 August 1967.

In March 1982, Davidson had written to the *New York Times* challenging CBS to produce "concrete evidence" of any orders to "manipulate, suppress, or alter" enemy-strength figures. The two documents I submitted—the Davidson memo and the swiftly recalled disposition form—proved to be that concrete evidence; they were the only direct physical proof of a cover-up that came from within MACV headquarters.

My affidavit, which included my knowledge of the My Lai cover-up, was notarized in July 1983 but was not submitted as trial evidence until after Davidson's deposition in October. The CICV documents were appended to my statement and were held in confidence until they were handed to Davidson at the end of his videotaped interview. He reacted with surprise, but then and at the trial denied knowledge of them and their meaning.

The CBS attorneys supplied me with key trial documents and I read thousands of pages. Finally I was beginning to understand what the hell had been going on around me in Saigon. I began the early drafts of how my story fit into the larger context of the overall intelligence debacle.

Not until June 1984 was my deposition taken, after I had been subpoenaed by Westmoreland's attorneys. For the first session, Sam Adams flew out with Baron. He was all I expected: six feet tall, lean, dignified, a bit reserved at first, but animated when talking about his efforts to demonstrate the truth about Vietnam. Together we reviewed my notes and documents. His eye for detail was awesome. He alone had found the strings of evidence, following them until he had backtracked to the whole twisted ball. He was, in my view, a hero, a patriot who had fought at personal loss the wrongful actions of bureaucrats and soldiers who had damaged our nation.

After the first deposition, Adams and Baron said they were pleased with my presentation, especially because I was able to supply new information as questioning prodded my memory. For instance, Westmoreland's position was that there had been no increase in NVA infiltration before Tet, but I explained how SPARS, representing a flood of NVA replacements, had filled the Ho Chi Minh Trail on our I Corps map.

But in the third and final deposition session, on 10 July 1984, Westmoreland's attorney challenged me on My Lai and the 38th Battalion. The convoluted facts made it easy for the lawyer to attack my credibility by making me look paranoid, finding conspiracies at every turn. I did have the chance to retort, "I know that someone goddamn well lied, and went in there and falsified and perjured the archives records." And I called the archives OB Book a "pack of lies." Ten days later, Westmoreland's attorneys released a trial document that included five paragraphs on my testimony, which was described as "false, misleading or inherently incredible."

The trial began on 27 October 1984. I was at the bottom of the CBS witness list. Each side was allocated a hundred hours of testimony and it appeared time would run out before my turn came. One of the last witnesses was Major House, my old boss from I CTZ OB, and watching on television I was surprised to see him entering the courthouse, his gray hair now white and unmilitarily long as it blew in the wind of a New York winter. He nodded repeatedly at the crush of photographers and TV crews, a look of bemusement on his face. I saw no news account of his testimony (though I'd read his affidavit months earlier and was pleased that he reported how new enemy units had not been picked up by MACV), but I admired the old major for telling his story. And I envied him for having the chance.

On 17 February 1985 Westmoreland agreed to drop his suit in exchange for a joint statement with CBS that the network respected his "long and faithful service to his country" and never believed the general was "unpatriotic or disloyal in performing his duties as he saw them." Sam Adams did not sign the statement and was conspicuously absent from after-action comments and interviews. Most observers felt that the testimony of McChristian and especially Hawkins had given Westmoreland no option but to withdraw. The final statement appeared to many to be an inconclusive ending to a painful struggle that in its ambiguity paralleled the war itself.

But clear lessons did emerge, although they are hardly new or unknown. Most pertinent are the words of General Peers in a memo of 18 March 1970 to Westmoreland describing his approach to the My Lai inquiry:

> There can be no vacillation with the truth. Statements and reports, whether in combat or garrison, must be precise, factual, and complete, with no shading of the unpleasant or unflattering aspect of such reports. Officers who fail to adhere to this practice violate their commission. . . . Because men's lives are at stake in combat, there can be no acceptance of mediocre leadership nor mediocrity in performance of other duties relating to the support of combat.

Intelligence is a window on the battlefield, offering a view of the enemy's disposition, capabilities, and intentions; it is the core of all strategy decisions. In Vietnam that window was not cracked open until 1966, well after we had begun committing our forces. But by the work of General McChristian, Colonel Hawkins, Sam Adams, and their colleagues, we were finally beginning to get a glimpse of that invisible jungle army.

Then that window was slammed shut by a handful of senior officers and officials. For reasons of expedience, we blinded ourselves with our own smoke and mirrors. We locked ourselves into an unwinnable war without windows.

Our soldiers did not lose in Vietnam. The war managers and the military bureaucrats did when they violated their codes of conduct and were trapped by their own public disinformation.

We must never repeat the tragic blunders made in Southeast Asia. Above all, we must never again be misinformed about the risks of a foreign intervention and the capabilities of the adversary. America must be allowed to understand its enemies, the true reasons for confrontation with them, and our chances of success. Then the people and their government can decide whether to stay home or to apply the strategies of victory and fight to win.

APPENDIX A

HEADQUARTERS
UNITED STATES MILITARY ASSISTANCE COMMAND, VIETNAM
APO San Francisco 96222
Office of Information

MACOI-P   15 June 1967

MACOI FACT SHEET 3-67

SUBJECT: The Republic of Vietnam—General Description

The Republic of Vietnam (RVN) is a long, narrow, crescent shaped country which forms the SE coastal rim of the Southeast Asian Peninsula bordering on the South China Sea. The RVN extends about 575 miles north to south and is about 37 miles wide at the Demarcation Line at the north. At its widest lateral, from Tay Ninh Province to Ninh Thuan Province, it measures about 225 miles across. It presents nearly 1,500 miles of coastline. The RVN is bordered by North Vietnam in the north and Laos and Cambodia in the west. The long inland border shared with Laos and Cambodia is remote and vaguely defined.

Most of the northern two-thirds of the country consists of hills and mountains (the Chaine Annamitique), and the southern one-third is mainly a flat plain (the Mekong Delta). The highlands, which extend from the northern border to within 60 miles of Saigon, are characterized by steep slopes, sharp crests, and narrow valleys and are covered mainly by dense broadleaf evergreen forest. Most peaks are from 4,000 to 7,000 feet above sea level, and a few in the north are over 8,000 feet. In the west central part of the country, the Central Highlands or the Western Highlands, the mountains grade into rolling, generally grassy, upland plains. On the east the highlands are flanked by narrow, coastal plains which are compartmented by rocky headlands. Belts of sand dunes and, in areas with suitable soil, ricefields are common along the coast. From the crests that mark the drainage divide in the highlands, streams flow eastward to the sea or westward into Cambodia.

The population of the RVN is about $16\frac{1}{2}$ million. About 50 percent of the population lives in the area from about Saigon to the southern tip of the country—the Mekong Delta. Most of the RVN is sparsely populated or uninhabited rain forest.

The southern third of the RVN is an extensive, low, flat plain, separated from the hills and mountains to the north by a band of rolling plains called the transition zone. The zone contains dense to open forests and scattered areas of grass and dry crops. The flat plain comprises the deltas of the Mekong River west of Saigon and the Song Dong Nai east of Saigon, and their distributaries. The plain is characterized by a poorly drained surface that is criss-crossed by many streams and an intricate network of canals and ditches. Elevations in the Delta nearly everywhere are less than 10 feet; in the rolling plains they are commonly less than a thousand feet. The Delta is extensively cultivated in wetland rice and is generally considered "the Ricebowl of Vietnam" and potentially the "Ricebowl of Southeast Asia." Long stretches of mangrove swamp line the coast and parts of the lower courses of tidal estuaries, and there are large areas of marsh. The Plaine de Joncs (Plain of Reeds) is a large marsh west of Saigon containing vast areas of tall reeds and scattered scrub trees.

Through administrative division, the RVN consists of four corps tactical zones, or corps, and certain separate areas such as the Capital Military District, and Hue. They are numbered with roman numerals, I through IV from north to south. I Corps is pronounced "EYE" Corps; II Corps is pronounced "Two" Corps. Each corps consists of a number of provinces: I Corps (5), II Corps (12), III Corps (11), and IV Corps (16), 44 provinces in all. Each province is organized into districts. Districts are organized into villages with an average of 8–12 villages per district and 4–6 hamlets per village.

The seasonal alternation of the monsoons determines both the rainfall and the temperature in the RVN throughout the year. However, geographical features do alter patterns locally. Annual rainfall is heavy in nearly all regions and torrential in many. Heaviest annual rainfall occurs at Hue—128 inches. The wet season, the SW monsoon, extends from mid-May to late September. The dry season, the NE monsoon, extends from early November to mid-March. These two major seasons are separated by short transitional periods, the spring transition from mid-March to mid-May and the autumn transition from September to early November. For most of the RVN, the SW monsoon is the wet season, but the NE coast is dry during that period. The NE monsoon is the dry season for all of the RVN except for the NE coast which then experiences its wet season.

APPENDIX B

Office of Assistant Chief of Staff, Intelligence

MACJ2
15 August 1967

MEMORANDUM FOR: DEPUTY J2, PRODUCTION

SUBJECT: New Procedures for OB

    1. Now that we are getting our revised format for our revised OB squared away I want to move boldly into a new procedure for determining OB on a *weekly basis*.

    2. What we have got to do is to attrite main forces, local forces and particularly guerrillas. *We must cease immediately using the assumption that these units replace themselves*. We should go on the assumption that they do not replace themselves *unless we have firm evidence to the contrary*. The figure of combat strength and particularly of guerrillas must take a steady and significant downward trend as I am convinced this reflects true enemy status.

    3. Due to the sensitivity of this project, weekly strength figures will hereafter be cleared personally by me.

    4. This directive is effective immediately.

PHILLIP B. DAVIDSON, JR.
Brigadier General, USA
Assistant Chief of Staff, J2

cc: Col. Roberts
    Col. Morris

APPENDIX C

REFERENCE OR OFFICE SYMBOL	SUBJECT
MACJ286	

TO	FROM	DATE	CMT 1
U.S. Director, CICV	Chief, OB Branch, CICV		

Recommend acceptance in order of battle holdings subject unit. This addition of_____in enemy strength does not increase total enemy strength in excess of that agreed upon at the September 1967 CIA/DIA/MACV Enemy Strength Conference. (Present combat strength:_____; present total strength:_____)

Ch, OB Br (JGS Elm), CICV   Ch, OB Br, CICV

TO: Director of Intel Pdn   FROM: U.S. Director, CICV

Recommend (approval) (disapproval).

U.S. Director, CICV

TO: ACofS, J2   FROM: Director of Intel Pdn

Recommend (approval) (disapproval).

Director of Intel Pdn

TO: Director of Intel Pdn

(Approved) (Disapproved).

PHILLIP B. DAVIDSON, JR.
Brigadier General, USA
Assistant Chief of Staff, J2

COORDINATION.

CIIED concur_____ nonconcur_____

APPENDIX D

In his trip to the States in November 1967, General William C. Westmoreland used the following chart to brief the press (it is referred to in a *New York Times* article of 22 November 1967) and President Lyndon Johnson:

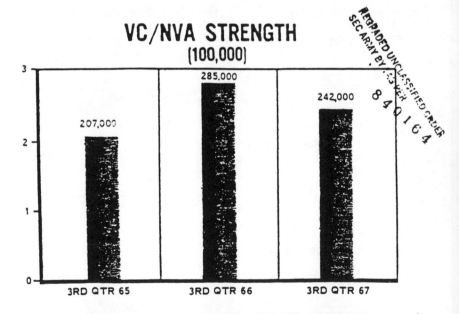

(FIGURES DO NOT INCLUDE POLITICAL INFRASTRUCTURE OF ABOUT 80,000)

NOTES

PROLOGUE

1. Adams wrote of his experience in an article for *Harper's*, "Vietnam Cover-Up: Playing War with Numbers," May 1975.
2. Colonel Gains B. Hawkins, "Vietnam Anguish: Being Ordered to Lie," *Outlook* magazine, *Washington Post,* 14 November 1982.
3. Hawkins, personal communication, 27 January 1986.
4. Major General Joseph A. McChristian, affidavit, *Westmoreland* v. *CBS,* No. 82 Civ. 7913 (S.D.N.Y. 18 February 1985), "Memorandum in Support of Defendant CBS's Motion to Dismiss and for Summary Judgment," 23 May 1984, Appendix B, 398. All affidavits and depositions cited hereafter were made in this proceeding unless otherwise noted.
5. Hawkins, affidavit, 7 September 1983, B-252.

CHAPTER 1

1. In the 1980s this is no longer true. ROTC-trained generals now compose the majority of the promotion lists.
2. In *Street Without Joy,* Bernard Fall provides an excellent, terse summary of the historic Cold War relationship between the three countries; the Indochina war, he writes, "became strategically hopeless when the Chinese Reds arrived on Indochina's borders late in 1949 and China thus became a 'sanctuary' where Viet-Minh forces could be trained and refitted. And it was lost militarily as of 1953 when the cease-fire in Korea allowed the concentration of the whole Asian Communist war effort on the Indochinese theater. The denouement of the Indochina war was, therefore, about as foreordained as that of a Greek tragedy" (17).
3. Years later, the Intelligence insignia was used on the uniforms of the crew in the television series *Battlestar Galactica*.
4. A joint operation involves at least two of the five U.S. military

services (Army, Navy, Air Force, Marines, Coast Guard). A joint headquarters is responsible for a field army or a theater of operations. MACV headquarters reported directly to CINCPAC (Commander-in-Chief, Pacific), another joint headquarters, which had its own J-2. ("J-2" can mean either the staff organization or the officer who heads it.) The intelligence function is indicated by the 2-designation; at the division level it is G-2 and at battalion S-2. Other functions are 1, personnel; 3, operations; 4, supply; and 5, civil affairs.

CHAPTER 4

1. Thieu and Ky were elected with only some 33 percent of the ballots, which, Nguyen Cao Ky declares in *Twenty Years and Twenty Days*, 157, proved it was an honest election. A captured NVA lieutenant saw the election from a different perspective: "There were [potentially] fourteen million voters in the South but only six million . . . cast their ballots. The new president received only one million and eighty thousands votes . . . in the North, if there are eleven million voters, the president received all eleven million votes." Rand Corporation Interview File No. AG-647, 23 October 1967.

Frances Fitzgerald, writing in *Fire in the Lake,* finds the election much less of a model than the U.S. embassy declared it to be (see her chapter 11). Among the Vietnam histories, this source offers perhaps the most thorough analysis of the election.

CHAPTER 5

1. Descriptions of the OB Book are based on examination of eight declassified editions from 1967 to 1968. Details of distribution and origins are taken from two sources: General Joseph A. McChristian, *The Role of Military Intelligence, 1965–1967,* and a memo sent from COMUSMACV to the DIA, dated 9 April 1968, to supply background for a briefing to General Maxwell Taylor on how document exploitation had produced the infiltration estimates.
2. During the trial of *Westmoreland* v. *CBS,* it was learned that these charts with retroactive numbers were included in the OB Book at the request of Secretary of Defense Robert McNamara, who, with his systems analysis approach to the war, had created our excessive emphasis on statistics to measure progress.

3.   The Koreans had a corner of coastal I Corps in Quang Ngai province, where the 2d ROK (Republic of Korea) Marine Brigade operated independent of III MAF control. The VC rated the Koreans as the best fighters, ahead of the Americans, and Communist units generally stayed outside the ROK tactical area of responsibility. One reason was suggested by this conversation in CICV: "I see the ROKs got 125 KIA." "Yeah, counting children, dogs, and water buffalo."

4.   Descriptions of the functions of CICV and the other combined intelligence centers are based on McChristian, *Military Intelligence,* 26, 32, 40, 45.

5.   As noted by McChristian in *Military Intelligence,* 50. He also described order of battle as "the foundation of combat intelligence" (157).

6.   McChristian, in *Military Intelligence,* 65, writes: "Capabilities and vulnerabilities of the Viet Cong infrastructure . . . were as much a part of the enemy war-making potential as was his military order of battle." He declared that the infrastructure "had to be neutralized" (13).

7.   CDEC had "go-teams" that could relocate to the field to assist in screening large amounts of documents captured during operations. But McChristian, *Military Intelligence,* 39–40, emphasizes, "Before teams were dispatched we encouraged sending such materials by special courier to the center, where document exploitation was much more efficient. . . . Experience showed that the Combined Documents Exploitation Center could, by far, provide the most rapid readouts, summaries, and full or extract translations of significant documents." McChristian further reported, "When we discovered that some units were delaying transfer of certain documents until they could complete local exploitation, we procured duplicating machines so that units could copy documents they wished to retain and send the originals back to the center. This simple measure permitted significant improvements in our document exploitation system." However, the 9 April 1968 cable (supra, note 1) noted that units conducting field exploitation, which were allowed fifteen days before forwarding documents, "are now being provided with reproduction equipment which will enable them to make copies of highly significant documents for their retention so that the originals can be forwarded to CDEC without delay." The one-year delay in delivery of requisitioned equipment may have had incalculable consequences. Hoarding of documents occurred both in the field and at headquarters. Only readily available reproduction facilities could circumvent this practice.

8.   One VC platoon leader said: "The Region always gave advance warning about the coming of the B-52s at least a week ahead and thus

we were able to move away from the target areas . . . the people were evacuated. . . . " Rand Corporation Interview File No. AG-643, 11–12 October 1967. Another reported: "I saw three or four B-52 attacks. We had been informed of their coming before they arrived. I don't know what they had at the Military Zone—might be radar—but we were told that at such-and-such a time the B-52s would fly through our area. . . . All they achieved was the destruction of the trees. . . . We were told to stay where we were . . . after the first bombing raid, we . . . should not run straight ahead, but to the right or left [in relation to the line of bomb impacts], and we would be saved. . . . If there were any casualties, they always occurred during the first bombing raid, not the second or the third." Rand Corporation Interview File No. AG-647, 23 October 1967.

CHAPTER 6

1.   COSVN was a highly mobile advance headquarters for Hanoi in the South. Its political and civilian components included some 9,000 personnel; the command center itself numbered several hundred cadre. The headquarters moved frequently and was often located in Cambodia. COSVN was a target of Operation Junction City in 1967 and of the Cambodia incursion in 1970; however, we never located it.

2.   Most sources have concluded that boobytraps and pungi sticks caused up to a third of the American casualties (a comparable figure in other wars is 3 percent).

3.   Vo Nguyen Giap was born in 1912 in Quang Binh province, just north of the 17th parallel, which would divide North and South in 1954. His father was a poor but respected scholar who had participated in an earlier rebellion against the French. At the age of twelve he attended a school in Hue established by Ngo Dinh Diem's father (and attended before him by both Diem and Ho Chi Minh). In 1926, as a student, Giap joined the "Revolutionary Party for a Great Vietnam" and in 1930 led student demonstrations at Hue over the starvation of farmers. He was jailed for several months, then returned to his studies, ultimately taking a law degree in Hanoi. Probably by March 1937 he joined the Indochinese Communist Party (formed in 1930 with help from the French Communist Party). Giap became a history teacher in Hanoi but had to flee in 1939 when France outlawed the Communist Party, both at

home and in its colonies. Giap's wife was captured by the French and died in prison in 1943; Giap escaped into South China, where he either trained at a Red Chinese stronghold or studied military tactics from history books. In May 1941, at a Central Committee meeting of the ICP, Giap met for the first time Ho Chi Minh, a revolutionary who had not been in Vietnam for thirty years. At this meeting (which created the Viet Minh front) Giap was assigned to organize a Communist military force inside Vietnam. On 22 December 1944 the first platoon of what would be known as the People's Army of Vietnam was organized near Cao Bang and two days later overran two small French garrisons at the Chinese border. By V-J Day, 15 August 1945, Giap's guerrillas controlled the rural areas of the country, allowing Ho Chi Minh and Giap to enter Hanoi. On 2 September the Democratic Republic of Vietnam was proclaimed, and Giap remained the commanding officer of the PAVN. In January 1946 he became defense minister as well. In June 1946, while Ho Chi Minh was abroad, Giap used his de facto powers to execute hundreds of non-Communist and Trotskyite nationalists across the country. In December 1949 the Red Chinese reached the northern border of Vietnam and made possible intensive training of the Viet Minh army. On 1 October 1950, Giap began a seventeen-day offensive, using battalions in conventional tactics, to overrun French positions along the Chinese border. The French suffered some 7,000 casualties, and the First Indochinese War had begun.

In time Giap became a full general holding the posts of defense minister, commander-in-chief of the PAVN, and vice premier. He was also a member of the DRVN legislature, vice chairman of the National Defense Council (headed by Ho Chi Minh), and a member of the Politburo of the Vietnam Communist Party. Giap defined the role of the People's Army of Vietnam as being "the instrument of the Party and the revolutionary state for the accomplishment, in armed form, of the tasks of the revolution."

For the facts of this brief biography I am indebted to Bernard Fall's "Vo Nguyen Giap—Man and Myth" in the English-language edition of Vo Nguyen Giap, *People's War, People's Army*.

4.   The 38th VC Battalion offers a good example of the use of AKAs. The Marines and the Americal Division preferred to use the 48th VC Battalion designation, while MACV headquarters

stayed with the 38th. Ultimately, after we went through an on-again, off-again confusion over its existence, the VC formed a 48th Battalion.

5.   When he was advocating the establishment of a combined intelligence system, General McChristian faced similar American concerns about "apathy." In *Military Intelligence,* 22, he noted that Americans in Vietnam worked a seven-day week because, as one-year visitors, we had little else to do. However, the Vietnamese "had been under the pressure of fighting a war for years" and had to raise their families as well as to soldier. But he had seen them "on the job around the clock if needed."

6.   In a volume of the Marines' official history, *Fighting the North Vietnamese, 1967,* 95, Con Thien is described as the northwest corner of the "strong point obstacle system" known as McNamara's Wall; it "overlooked one of the principal enemy routes into South Vietnam." Its capture would "open the way for a major enemy invasion of Quang Tri Province by 35,000 NVA troops massed north of the DMZ, a victory of immense propaganda value." Even though the base sat at a height of only 158 meters, it was surrounded by plains and looked down on the U.S. logistics complex at Dong Ha, some ten miles away.

The first attack on Con Thien was in July 1967; for the first time the NVA extensively used artillery to support its infantry. The Marines counterattacked with Operation Buffalo and reported 1,290 NVA KIA and 159 Marines KIA/345 WIA. The fighting was considered by the Marines more vicious than "most of the Communist operations in I Corps" to date.

7.   "The constant danger of artillery, rocket, and mortar fire, and massed infantry assaults, and the depressing drizzle and mud from which there was no escape, combined to make it miserable for the Marines there. Neuropsychiatric or 'shell shock' casualties, relatively unheard of elsewhere in South Vietnam, were not unusual. Duty on and around the drab hill mass was referred to by all Marines as their 'Turn in the Barrel,' or 'the Meatgrinder,' *Fighting the North Vietnamese, 1967,* 139.

8.   The full story of McNamara's Wall is told in *Fighting the North Vietnamese, 1967,* chapter 7. The plan created a bitter debate between General Lew Walt, backed by the USMC leadership, and Westmoreland. MACV had been ordered to implement this

scheme, which had originated in Washington as early as March 1966. The mine and wire barrier was to extend from the South China Sea across northern South Vietnam, perhaps even through Laos to Thailand. From the beginning the Marines strongly opposed any variation of the concept as a strategic blunder that could tie down their troops in static positions and remove the flexibility of mobile defense. But after MACV counterproposals to Secretary McNamara, the concept evolved into that of a "strong point obstacle system" linking northern outposts by cleared zones of mines and electronic devices. In March 1967, over continued USMC opposition, Westmoreland ordered Walt to begin the project. Resistance by the enemy was increasing and on 7 September Westmoreland asked the Marines to assess the human cost of finishing construction: the estimate was 672 U.S. KIA and 3,788 WIA. On 13 September Westmoreland approved the alternative III MAF plan of abandoning the obstacle construction until completion of the northern bases or "strong points." By the end of the year, at a cost of more than $1.5 million and, more important, 757,520 man-days, as much of the system was completed as ever would be. In his memoir, *A Soldier Reports,* 200, Westmoreland recognized that the project was abandoned, but he had wanted no formal announcement, "lest the enemy claim he had forced it." The result was not a wide swath cleared by bulldozers the length of the DMZ, but a series of clearings around the bases with intermittent barriers of wire, mines, and sensors.

CHAPTER 7

1.   Hawkins, affidavit, 7 September 1983, B-253.
2.   Ibid., B-255.
3.   Colonel George Hamscher, affidavit, 3 February 1983.
4.   Ibid.
5.   Hamscher, deposition transcript, 240. See also CBS Motion to Dismiss, 82.
6.   Hamscher, affidavit, 3 February 1983.
7.   Hawkins, affidavit, 7 September 1983, B-253.
8.   Hamscher, affidavit, 3 February 1983; Hamscher, deposition transcript, 244. See also CBS Motion to Dismiss, 82.

9.   Cable, Godding to Major General Chesley Peterson, CINCPAC J-2, 19 August 1967; declassified by DIA 18 October 1983.

10.   This argument against the importance of the militia (self-defense forces) was critical to both the 1967 debates and the Westmoreland suit. It is not supported by intelligence sources from the period. For example, a VC guerrilla who went over to the GVN on 30 August 1967 described the hamlet self-defense group as follows: "Their responsibilities were the same as those assigned to the guerrillas. That is, they had to guard the hamlet, set boobytraps, plant spikes, place land mines, grenades, and so on." Rand Corporation Interview File No. DT-237-I, 11–12 September 1967. This interrogation corroborated numerous other sources. One was none other than General Vo Nguyen Giap, quoted in CICV's *Strategy Since 1954*, 32:

> The self-defense militia forces have satisfactorily fulfilled the role of the reserve force. Under the leadership of our party and forged through realistic combat and production, the self-defense militia forces have matured swiftly and steadily, satisfactorily fulfilled the reserve force's tasks, provided the frontline with replacements, and created very favorable conditions for the expansion and development of main force units.

11.   Other "non-military organizations" which were here alleged to be comparable to the militia (self-defense forces) were educational, political, and logistical associations used by the VC to involve all the people of a hamlet or village. Included were groups such as the Labor Youth Groups, Women's Associations, Combatant Mothers' Associations, Combatant Sisters' Associations, Farmers' Associations, and other units that could produce at least a three-person cell.

12.   That the move to Saigon was on Westmoreland's directive was stated initially in a letter from Hawkins to his wife on 28 August 1967, and confirmed by Westmoreland in his 16 May 1981 interview with Mike Wallace for "The Uncounted Enemy."

13.   Confirmed by Westmoreland, ibid.

14.   Adams, "Vietnam Cover-Up."

CHAPTER 8

1.   Not until years later did I learn how the then Major House had come to CICV. He had been at the Current Intelligence, Indications,

and Estimates Division at MACV headquarters since August. There he was assigned to reading enemy documents and PW interrogations to find evidence of setbacks to the VC effort in IV Corps. Specifically he was told to demonstrate that the enemy had been forced to revert to guerrilla warfare. He found no such evidence and wrote a report to that effect. The colonel in charge of CIIED (Leon Goche, Colonel Graham's predecessor) advised House that if that was the best he could do, he would not fit in at the estimates branch. He was then transferred to CICV. Lieutenant Colonel Norman R. House, affidavit, 25 August 1983, B-262.

2. Statement of Richard G. McArthur at the Pike Committee Hearings, 3 December 1975.

3. Dropping the VC infrastructure from the order of battle listings technically meant that the political cadre were no long considered combatants and thus could not be killed under the rules of war. During his deposition, Westmoreland was told that some 20,000 VC cadre were killed during the Phoenix program. He replied that this was "wrong, definitely wrong" (deposition transcript, 968) and that he was "shocked" (dep. tr., 699) because "these were civilians" (dep. tr., 700, 1598).

CHAPTER 9

1. Memo, Walsh to George Carver, 10 November 1967.
2. Memo, Carver to Philip Goulding, Assistant Secretary of Defense for Public Affairs, 13 October 1967.
3. Westmoreland, *A Soldier Reports,* 231.
4. Ibid., 234.

CHAPTER 10

1. This amazing complex of trails, paths, and roads began in North Vietnam and wound southward, largely in Laos and Cambodia, with many offshoots leading into South Vietnam (such as through the A Shau valley in Thua Thien province of I Corps). This system is described by General Van Tien Dung, Giap's successor, in *Our Great Spring Victory,* 14. By the end of the war tens of thousands of workers had constructed 20,000 kilometers of road over which had passed tens of thousands of vehicles. Some 1,000 kilometers were built to a width

of eight meters to accommodate large trucks. Hanoi was even able to lay some 5,000 kilometers of pipeline to carry fuel to the battlefields in South Vietnam. Other sources have reported that parts of the system were paved. American veterans who observed the trail report that even early in the war (1966) trucks could be heard. Occasionally lights were seen in the night sky that could only have been helicopters. (Some reports of NVA choppers being used for logistics did come through CICV.)

2.   NVA aspirant platoon leader, Rand Corporation Interview File No. AG-652, 15 November 1967.

3.   At about this time, on 15 November, Lieutenant Colonel Everette Parkins, Chief of Special Studies, CICV, tried to submit his own new estimate of infiltration rates—a huge jump from some 6,000 a month to as much as 20,000. (The rate may have reached 30,000 before Tet.) The increased infiltration was never reported by the high command. On 19 November 1967 Westmoreland on *Meet the Press* estimated the enemy infiltration at "5,500 to 6,000 a month, but they do have the capability of stepping this up."

4.   MACV headquarters chose to release the Quang Tin document with a press release on 5 January 1968, twenty-five days before the offensive, indicating there was some concern about attacks on cities. However, there was no intelligence follow-up. On 20 January, Westmoreland had cabled the Joint Chiefs of Staff that nationwide attacks could be expected. He did relocate some units before Tet, and on 30 January, after the "premature" attacks in I and II Corps, MACV put all U.S. troops on maximum alert (*A Soldier Reports*, 323). These efforts, though, can at best be described as cosmetic or incomplete.

5.   These battles began with the siege of Con Thien in September and continued with two more attacks in late October. On 27 October an NVA regiment attacked an ARVN battalion in Song Be, Phuoc Long province. The enemy was thrown back with a reported 134 KIA. Then on 29 October the VC attacked the Special Forces camp and district headquarters at Loc Ninh in Binh Long province, near the Cambodian border. Rapid reinforcement by our 1st Infantry Division led to an intense ten-day battle in which the enemy was said to have lost 852 KIA (with 50 U.S. and ARVN dead). The engagements at Dak To began on 3 November, before the Loc Ninh battles had ended.

6.   During his 22 November press briefing at the Pentagon, held at about the time Hill 885 was being abandoned by the NVA, Westmoreland replied to questions about Dak To by noting that "sometimes we try to make it possible so that they cannot run away; that's one of the objects of the exercise. So that we can use our firepower on him."

CHAPTER 11

1. Rand Corporation Interview File No. SX-60, 15 December 1967.
2. Rand Corporation Interview File No. AG-652, 15 November 1967.
3. One of the first major American operations after the Tet offensive began on 19 April 1968, when elements of the 1st Cavalry Division (Airmobile) and the 101st Airborne Division swept into A Shau valley in what one writer (John Randolph of the *Washington Post,* in a report reprinted in *Stars and Stripes* on 30 May 1968) called a "spectacular" airmobile operation "without precedent" in size and sweep. Few engagements occurred with NVA troops but substantial stores of weapons, ammunition, and supplies were seized.
4. Achieving a people's revolution to overthrow the Americans and their "puppets" was always a major objective of the Communist strategy, as established in Party Plenum Resolution 15, 13 May 1959. This policy statement is considered to be the decision that initiated the Second Indochinese War; its first principle was "to make the people rise up."
5. In *The 25-Year War,* 167, General Bruce Palmer, Jr., who served as Westmoreland's deputy, stated that one of the reasons for our tactical surprise during the Tet offensive was "overreliance on signal intelligence":

> This kind of intelligence can be very misleading and is also subject to manipulation by the enemy. . . . Identifying and, by direction finding techniques, locating a radio transmitter belonging to a specific NVA regiment, for example, does not necessarily mean that the regiment is there too, although it is is a good indication that elements of the regiment are in the vicinity. But in actuality, a small forward communications detachment might be the only element of the regiment present. One obvious conclusion is that we did not put enough emphasis on direct human sources of intelligence, as opposed to those of the electronic variety.

6. Rand Corporation Interview File No. AG-647, 23 October 1967.

CHAPTER 13

1.   During an "average day" over Khe Sanh there were 350 tactical
   fighters, 60 B-52s, 10 RF-4c reconnaissance jets, and 30 0-1 and 0-2
   Birddogs. Operation Niagara lasted from 8 January until the siege
   "officially" ended on 8 April 1968. In 2,548 sorties the B-52s dropped
   "as much as" 90,000 tons of bombs. Other aircraft added some 10,000
   tons of bombs, and they flew some 25,000 sorties during the seventy-
   seven-day period. Supporting aircraft numbered 2,000 fixed-wing and
   3,300 helicopters. See John Morrocco, *Thunder from Above: Air War,
   1941–1968*, 178.
2.   Robert Pisor, *The End of the Line*, 37.
3.   This SOP offered an attempt to expand the traditional OB factors
   into a more useful listing. It set up the following major headings to
   organize information on each unit: unit history; contacts, mission; area
   of operation; strength; combat effectiveness and morale; training; tactics; logistics; weapons and equipment; communications; personalities;
   AKAs; sources (an attempt to make analysts cite the documents they
   relied upon, an extraordinary failure in past procedure); miscellaneous;
   and composition and organization chart.
4.   The Dien Bien Phu fixation had been with us for a long time. In
   the CICV report *Strategy Since 1954*, 10, was this:

> Giap's willingness to subordinate the military to the
> political is nowhere more effectively demonstrated,
> however, than in the pivotal battle of Dien Bien Phu.
> The French fortified Dien Bien Phu to protect Laos
> and to draw the Viet Minh into attacking a strongly
> held position which, it was assumed, would prove to
> be to their detriment. Although fighting a pitched bat-
> tle—particularly a near siege—was against the classic
> conception of Mao's doctrine, Giap accepted the chal-
> lenge. Giap suffered heavily; the French estimated his
> losses in the ten to twenty thousands. The French
> losses (estimated at 2,000, with 10,000 captured) were
> not militarily devastating to the French in Indochina,
> but the political and psychological repercussions—as
> foreseen by the Viet Minh leaders—caused Paris to
> end the struggle. There is no reason to think that Gen-
> eral Giap and the leadership in Hanoi should feel that

the outcóme of the current war will not be decided by
similar factors.

5.   For descriptions of electronic devices and processes used in Vietnam, see Pisor, *End of the Line*, 106; Nigel Hawkes, "Catalogue of
Carnage," *World* magazine, 5 December 1972; and Edgar C. Doleman, Jr., *Tools of War*, 145, 155–58.

6.   The B-52 Stratofortress was developed as a long-range strategic
nuclear bomber and added to our military arsenal in the early 1950s.
On 18 June 1965 the first "Arc Light" strike was made by the bombers
as they were used in tactical roles within South Vietnam; the first
strike on North Vietnam came on 11 April 1966. At first the B-52s
came only from Guam, a twelve-hour, 5,500-mile round trip that required mid-air refueling. Later, B-52s were stationed in Thailand and,
still later, Okinawa. The original load of twenty-seven bombs was
later increased by wing racks and a "big belly" design. By February
1968 the sorties rate per month in South Vietnam was 1,800, or 60
flights a day. John T. Greenwood, "B-52s: Strategic Bombers in a
Tactical Role," in *The Vietnam War*, ed. Ray Bonds, 198.

7.   Bernard C. Nalty, "Seventy-Seven Days: The Siege of Khe Sanh,"
in *The Vietnam War*, ed. Ray Bonds, 162.

8.   A copy of the DISUM (Daily Intelligence Summary) was included
as an appendix to the Taylor Report of 16 April 1968, an analysis
classified "secret" that was prepared by General Maxwell Taylor to
determine how pre-Tet indicators were overlooked.

9.   In *Summons of the Trumpet*, 170, Colonel Dave Richard Palmer
reports, "General Giap let out the word that he was in the field and in
personal command of the siege." In fact, Giap remained in Hanoi to
coordinate the Tet offensive. Stanley Karnow in *Vietnam: A History*,
540, suggests that nonetheless the Khe Sanh Red Watch may have
come close to "getting Giap": "Giap . . . flew to the front late in January 1968 to inspect the situation personally—and he nearly became a
casualty himself when a flight of thirty-six B-52s dropped a thousand
tons of bombs near his field headquarters." Karnow reports that the
strike had been ordered after we intercepted enemy radio messages
that indicated a "prominent Communist figure" might be in the area.

10.   The apparently premature attacks on 30 January began shortly after
midnight and included Nha Trang, Ban Me Thuot, Tan Canh, Kontum, Hoi An, Da Nang, Qui Nhon, and Pleiku. As Westmoreland
notes in *A Soldier Reports*, 323, all these targets fell under the juris-
diction of VC Military Region 5, which could have erred in ordering
the time of attack. The general and others have suggested that the

saturation B-52 attack on the thirtieth could have triggered the attacks in I and II Corps, but the timing of the two events does not support the supposition. It is possible that the early attacks were conducted to suggest that the Tet offensive was limited to the north.

CHAPTER 16

1. An attack had occurred on Da Nang on the twenty-ninth and was followed by the "premature" attacks on the thirtieth in I and II Corps. Most of the attacks across the nation occurred on 31 January.

2. Westmoreland, *A Soldier Reports*, 328.

3. Pisor, *End of the Line*, 173.

4. D. R. Palmer, *Summons of the Trumpet*, 184.

5. MACV Office of Information, *1967–A Year of Progress*, 1.

6. United States Army, Vietnam, *Tour 365* (returnee magazine), Spring-Summer 1968, 50.

7. Harry G. Summers, Jr., *Vietnam War Almanac*, 201, reports that Operation Hue was declared over on 2 March. After 24 February the fighting became a scattered mopping-up action.

8. *Tour 365*, 50.

9. Westmoreland, *A Soldier Reports*, 330.

10. Clark Dougan and Stephen Weiss, *Nineteen Sixty-Eight*, 20.

11. Estimates of enemy KIA in the Tet offensive vary from source to source. In Westmoreland's AP interview published in *Stars and Stripes* on 27 February 1968, he said the loss was "over 40,000"; in *A Soldier Reports*, 332, the general cut his estimate to 37,000 (for KIAs through February 1968). Nguyen Cao Ky in *Twenty Years*, 161, puts the losses at "over 34,000." President Johnson put the number through February at 45,000 in his memoir, *The Vantage Point*, 382.

12. *Tour 365*, 51.

13. Nguyen Cao Ky, *Twenty Years*, 161.

14. Westmoreland, *A Soldier Reports*, 332.

15. Dougan and Weiss, *Nineteen Sixty-Eight*, 132.

16. Westmoreland, *A Soldier Reports*, 328.

17. House, affidavit, 25 August 1983, B-266.

18. *Sacramento Bee* (UPI), 3 December 1975.

19. Colonel John Barrie Williams, deposition, 27 September 1983, tr. 41–42.

20. These figures, from files at the U.S. Army Center of Military History, Washington, D.C., were obtained and analyzed by Sam Adams

(personal communication, 20 August 1986). Since for three successive weeks in May the same figure (480) is given, Adams believes headquarters was able to provide only estimates for the May offensive. In Vietnam, even such statistics as American KIA reports could be confusing. A memo to President Johnson from the duty officer of the MACV situation room, dated 9 June 1968, provided different numbers; these figures may have included deaths from non-hostile sources. The reported KIAs in this memo were: 3 February—203; 10 February—481; 17 February—584; 24 February—497; 2 March—536; 9 March—520; 16 March—365; 23 March—371; 30 March—335; 6 April—290; 13 April—369; 20 April—287; 27 April—324; 4 May—374; 11 May—616; 18 May—552; 25 May—443; 1 June—459. The total casualty report for Americans during all of 1968 was 14,589 KIA and 92,818 WIA. This almost equaled our total losses in the war up to that time.

21.   U.S. Grant Sharp and William C. Westmoreland, *Report on the War in Vietnam,* 168. Admiral Sharp covered the air and sea campaign; Westmoreland reported on ground combat.

22.   Dougan and Weiss, *Nineteen Sixty-Eight,* 22.

23.   In *The Vantage Point,* 380, Johnson offered a largely dispassionate account of his reaction to the attacks. He did admit a mistake in not warning the American public about the indicators, but the president found it "one of those delicate situations in which we had to try to inform our own people without alerting the enemy to our knowledge of its plans." The impact of the offensive was perhaps more accurately described by George Christian, Johnson's press secretary from 1966 to 1969, as a "brutal surprise." Further, in his affidavit of 30 November 1983, Christian stated, "While there were intelligence reports that the enemy was planning some kind of attack, its scope and ferocity stunned Washington." He got to the core issue when he said, "We in the White House had been led to believe that the Viet Cong were pretty well defanged by that period, that the pacification program had worked very well . . . and that it was virtually impossible for the enemy to rise to the heights it did during the Tet offensive" (2).

24.   Dougan and Weiss, *Nineteen Sixty-Eight,* 19.

25.   "Report of Chairman of the Joint Chiefs of Staff Gen. Earle G. Wheeler on the Situation in Vietnam, 27 February 1968," in *Vietnam: A History in Documents,* ed. Gareth Porter, 358.

26.   Self-criticism was an integral part of Communist methodology, designed to urge all ranks to better achievement of revolutionary goals. Every action was followed by this process of *kiem thao.* Many documents read at CICV included apparently earnest and blunt confessions

of failures and weaknesses of both individuals and units. Frequently, the authors were simply meeting their quotas; yet these ritualistic confessions were often used by MACV headquarters to demonstrate morale and effectiveness "problems" in VC/NVA units. For an example of our eagerness to make this interpretation, see Westmoreland, *A Soldier Reports*, 332.

27. "Lao Dong Party Training Document on COSVN Resolution No. 6, March 1968," in *Vietnam: A History in Documents*, 362.

28. Appended to the Taylor Report on Tet indicators, dated 16 April 1968, was a memo for record, dated 28 January 1968, from 4th Infantry Division headquarters. It reported the defensive measures selected at the staff meeting on 23 January, which included these decisions: not to initiate a new plan of defense because of lack of time, but to rely on the existing scheme; to continue emplacement of gun positions in downtown Pleiku; to place an "exploitation platoon" at an artillery location; to move armor to the airfield; to reconnoiter all landing zones in advance of their use by reaction forces; to identify the most likely positions the enemy would select to block reinforcements into Pleiku; to identify units which would interdict these blocking positions, and to rehearse their actions; to locate all flareships and to fit other helicopters with flares; to account strictly for all Viet workers to assure they leave the bases; and to review all procedures for final protective fire. Such measures could have—should have—been taken by every Allied unit in Vietnam.

29. *Tour 365*, 50.

30. The failure of MACV to prepare in a comprehensive fashion for the Tet offensive has recently been addressed by military historians. In *The 25-Year War*, 78, General Bruce Palmer, Jr. (commander of II Field Force and later deputy to Westmoreland), wrote: "[I]n hindsight I feel that the November 1967 agreed national estimate of enemy strength—generally lower than the CIA's estimate, which was later confirmed—probably helped reinforce the feeling in Vietnam prior to Tet 1968 that the enemy was not capable of conducting major, near-simultaneous, country-wide attacks. In turn, this may have contributed to the tactical surprise achieved by Hanoi." In *Summons of the Trumpet*, 179–180, Colonel Dave Richard Palmer asks: "Why did commanders ignore the ample evidence available to them? The answer is more psychological than military, more emotional than professional. They were victims of their own sturdy optimism and of General Giap's shrewd staging of his deception campaign. . . . [A] U.S. Army intelligence officer, who had seen and discounted all the evidence of an

offensive against the cities, was quoted as admitting, 'If we'd gotten the whole battle plan, it wouldn't have been credible to us.' . . . The Allied high command simply did not believe the evidence. The other reason, of course, . . . was General Giap's superb execution of the first phase of his plan. By fixing his enemy's attention on the border areas, the North Vietnamese leader had splendidly masked his real intentions. . . . Blinded by the ruse, officials could not see the reality. The deception plan had worked. Perfectly. Indeed, there exist in military history few examples of so effective a feint."

CHAPTER 17

1.   The Special Forces camp, as well as MACV headquarters, did receive further notice of North Vietnamese armor across the border when, on 24 January, soldiers, dependents, and elephants of the 33d Laotian Volunteer Battalion came to Lang Vei after being overrun by NVA tanks. Construction at the camp was still not complete and anti-tank mines not yet in place. Though the possibility of a tank attack was still discounted by the Americans, they did requisition a large number of LAAWs (Lightweight Anti-Armor Weapons).

2.   By June 1968, according to Dougan and Weiss, *Nineteen Sixty-Eight*, 145, MACV headquarters was estimating that about 70 percent of the VC units were composed of northern-born NVA regular soldiers. By 1970, at least in I Corps, the estimate was 75 percent (General Lewis W. Walt, *Strange War, Strange Strategy*, 172).

3.   Dougan and Weiss, *Nineteen Sixty-Eight*, 38. See also Pisor, *End of the Line*, 179.

CHAPTER 19

1.   According to Dougan and Weiss, *Nineteen Sixty-Eight*, 127, Johnson's announcement "only deepened the mood of apprehension in Saigon. . . . They believed that the United States was preparing to abandon them to the Communists. For many South Vietnamese the bombing halt and the promise of negotiations brought with them not the hope of a quick end to the bloody conflict, but an abiding fear of peace." The dangers of "peace" had long been predicted. For example, Bernard Fall described Hanoi's goals in *Street Without Joy*, 339: "As a

long-range objective, Viet-Nam must be reunified under the authority of Ho Chi Minh, although an intermediate situation of a neutral Viet-Nam may be acceptable for a period of years."

2.   The official report of American losses during the Khe Sanh siege was 205 KIA. But in *The End of the Line,* 259–60, Robert Pisor reports that a Marine chaplain kept records of the dead men for whom he offered prayers. They numbered 441. Pisor also notes that KIAs were not included from related operations or aircraft lost outside the formal map boundaries of the operation. But our headquarters did report that Khe Sanh, like Dak To, was an American victory.

3.   In MACV's Monthly OB Summary there were three levels of recognition for enemy units: confirmed, probable, and possible. However, only the confirmed units (based on two hard sources) were counted in the totals and listed with current probable location, date of contact, etc. We therefore rarely submitted write-ups for the lower two categories. But MACV J-2 would sometimes slip our submittals into the lesser categories, a more subtle form of "downward trending."

4.   Report of the Conference on DCI Assessment of Enemy Strength, 10–16 April 1968.

5.   The background of the computer episode was described in an affidavit by Colonel Russell E. Cooley, formerly of CICV OB Studies, on 7 March 1983. In it Cooley states: "Colonel Graham proposed to revise the enemy strength holding in a way that was totally unacceptable to Commander [James] Meacham [the chief of OB Studies]. . . . [I]t was Meacham's perception that he was being told to alter the historical 'data base.'" That historical data base was maintained in the CICV computer.

CHAPTER 20

1.   Rand Corporation Interview File No. AG-647, 23 October 1967.

CHAPTER 21

1.   How we "Americanized" the war, when we should have been stressing "Vietnamization," is illustrated in the Department of the Army's *Area Handbook for South Vietnam,* April 1967. It reported that the American training mission, which assisted the development of South Vietnamese military forces, numbered about 800 in 1960; 2,600 in

1961; 11,000 in 1962; 15,000 in 1963; 23,000 in 1964. The handbook reports, "The number decreased in 1965 to about 5,000 when the United States assumed a more direct combat role in aiding South Vietnam." These numbers may be the best indication of why the war went the way it did.

2.   Rand Corporation Interview File No. AG-643, 11–12 October 1967.

3.   In *Summons of the Trumpet,* 143, Colonel Dave Richard Palmer notes that by 1965 our Vietnam tactic had become one by which "maneuver elements found the foe while firepower eliminated him": the traditional tactic of "fire and maneuver" had become "maneuver and fire." In this kind of war, writes Palmer, "long-range patrols, rangers, or commando units could do the job better and more economically" than entire infantry units. (Palmer also criticizes our reliance on firepower in Vietnam [145].) Similarly, Marshall Andrews in his preface to Fall's *Street Without Joy,* 11, notes the gap between "two widely divergent military philosophies, one built on the mobility of the individual soldier, the other resting on the mobility of armies." Therein may lie the essence of the Vietnam War, or any guerrilla-based conflict.

4.   In 1986, I found Miss My. She was able to get out of Saigon in 1974, leaving her family behind (her two brothers, former naval officers, were still in Communist "re-education" camps). She is married and well.

EPILOGUE

1.   W. R. Peers, *The My Lai Inquiry,* 247.
2.   B. Palmer, *The 25-Year War,* 85.

GLOSSARY

ARVN   Army, Republic of Vietnam

Battalion, NVA/VC Infantry   Force composed of three infantry companies and often a heavy weapons company.

CDEC   Combined Documents Exploitation Center, part of MACV J-2.

CIA   Central Intelligence Agency.

CICV   Combined Intelligence Center, Vietnam; part of MACV J-2.

CINCPAC   Commander-in-Chief, Pacific Area Command. MACV (Military Assistance Command, Vietnam) reported to CINCPAC.

CMEC   Combined Material Exploitation Center, part of MACV J-2.

CMIC   Combined Military Interrogation Center, part of MACV J-2.

Combined   Conducted or operated by two or more Allied nations. In Vietnam, the term referred to U.S. and South Vietnamese cooperation.

COMINT   Communications Intelligence, intercepted radio transmissions. Also known as SI (Special Intelligence), signal, electronic, or "all source" intelligence.

COMUSMACV   Commander, U.S. Military Assistance Command, Vietnam. MACV was established on 8 February 1962, replacing MAAG-V (Military Assistance Advisory Group, Vietnam). The first COMUSMACV was General Paul D. Harkins, who served from February 1962 until June 1964, when he was replaced by General William C. Westmoreland. In July 1968, General Creighton W. Abrams, Jr., assumed the post; he was replaced in June 1972 by General Frederick C. Weyand, who presided over the American withdrawal in 1973.

Contact   According to MACV Directive 335-2, an "operation which results in an application of firepower by either VC or friendly forces. There must be reasonable evidence of VC in the vicinity of the friendly unit. Unless determined to be command detonated, mines or boobytraps are not sufficient evidence. Light resistance in the form of sniper fire while on an operation is considered a contact. Contacts are either enemy initiated, friendly initiated, or reactions to named operations."

CO   Commanding officer.

GLOSSARY

COSVN   Central Office of South Vietnam. COSVN was set up in 1951, but in 1955 it became dormant until 1958 or 1960. According to CICV study 67-037, *Strategy Since 1954,* this Communist head-quarters for the war in the South functioned as the central committee for the People's Revolutionary Party. COSVN had numerous locations in Cambodia and in III Corps, and it moved frequently to avoid detection.

CTZ   Corps Tactical Zone. One of the four sectors of South Vietnam established by MACV for command control purposes. I Corps extended from the DMZ through the provinces of Quang Tri, Thua Thien, Quang Nam, Quang Tin, and Quang Ngai; II Corps was the area of the Central Highlands; III Corps included Saigon; IV Corps, in the far South, included the Mekong Delta.

DA   Department of the Army.

Detainees   According to MACV Directive 335-2, "personnel who have been detained but whose final status has not yet been determined."

DIA   Defense Intelligence Agency, the intelligence arm of the Joint Chiefs of Staff.

District   An administrative division of South Vietnam, comparable to an American county.

Division, NVA/VC Infantry   Force generally composed of three infantry regiments, one artillery (heavy weapons) regiment, and support elements.

DMZ   Demilitarized Zone; in Vietnam, a strip five miles wide established by the Geneva Conference of 1954 generally following the 17th parallel and the Ben Hai River as a buffer between North and South Vietnam.

DoD   Department of Defense.

DRVN   Democratic Republic of Vietnam; proclaimed on 2 September 1945 in Hanoi by Ho Chi Minh. The Communist name for all of Vietnam after that date; in practice, North Vietnam only until 1 May 1975.

GVN   Government of Vietnam; South Vietnam (SVN), or the Republic of Vietnam (RVN).

Hamlet   One of several communities (usually four to six) within a village; for example, the hamlet of My Lai was part of the village of Song My in Quang Ngai province.

Incident   According to MACV Directive 335-2, an attack by assault, fire, or ambush; harassment of civilians or military; terrorism; sabotage; propaganda; antiaircraft fire.

Infrared photograph A photograph that registers heat sources. The heat from groups of bodies will print in an infrared photo.

Irregulars U.S. name for Viet Cong categories of guerrillas, self-defense forces, and secret self-defense forces.

J-2 The intelligence arm of a joint headquarters, or its chief.

JCS Joint Chiefs of Staff. The military high command and the president's primary military advisors; headed by a chairman appointed by the president.

KIA Killed in action. According to MACV Directive 335-2, the number of KIA recorded after an incident "will be based on actual body count of males of fighting age and others, male or female, known to have carried arms. . . . Personnel identified as porters, ammunition bearers, and battlefield clearance personnel may also be included when confirmed by body count."

Lao Dong Party The Communist Party of North Vietnam. Evolved from the Indochinese Communist Party formed in 1930 by Ho Chi Minh and others. Its adjunct in the South became known as the People's Revolutionary Party.

MACV Military Assistance Command, Vietnam.

NFLSVN National Front for the Liberation of South Vietnam. Organization established in 1960 as a federation of Communist and nationalist groups, but always run by Hanoi directives. Responsible for building administrative and political apparatus in units from hamlets to provinces. Usually referred to as the National Liberation Front or NLF.

OB Book· Informal name for the MACV Monthly Order of Battle Summary.

Operations According to MACV Directive 335-2, operations were categorized as search and destroy (regional, provincial, or local); combat; security; and in support of pacification.

Order of battle The disposition, strength, composition, and capabilities of units on the battlefield.

Pacification Actions and operations designed to support our Revolutionary Development (RD) program, which provided a secure environment for the local Vietnamese by destroying or neutralizing the enemy's local, district, or provincial infrastructure and/or guerrillas while also improving living conditions. President Johnson called it "the other war" and the Vietnamese version of his War on Poverty.

People's Army of Vietnam (PAVN) The Communists' name for their army, the southern component of which was the People's Liberation Army.

Phoenix program An effort initiated in 1967 to neutralize the Viet

Cong infrastructure. It evolved from a joint CIA-MACV program called ICEX (Intelligence Coordination and Exploitation).

Province   One of forty-four administrative divisions of South Vietnam, comparable to an American state. VC boundaries and names of these often differed from the ones used by the South Vietnamese.

PW   Prisoner of war. A detainee who qualifies under Article 4 of the Geneva conventions of 1949. According to MACV Directive 335-2, PW status did not extend to a terrorist, saboteur, or spy. In Vietnam the command preferred the abbreviation PW to the earlier POW. (See also Detainee.)

RD   Revolutionary Development. The GVN and U.S. program for pacification of rural population centers.

Regiment, NVA/VC Infantry   Force composed of three infantry battalions, usually with an artillery (heavy weapons) battalion.

ROTC   Reserve Officers Training Corps.

RVN   Republic of Vietnam, or South Vietnam (SVN).

Sappers   Small specialized units that engage in reconnaissance, sabotage, intelligence collection, and, especially, demolition.

SI   Special Intelligence, intercepted radio transmissions. Also known as COMINT (Communications Intelligence), signal, electronic, or "all source" intelligence.

SVN   South Vietnam, or the Republic of Vietnam (RVN).

VC   Viet Cong, from Viet Cong San, a derisive term coined by the Diem regime to mean Vietnamese Communists. The National Liberation Front rejected the name, partly because the NLF was not exclusively Communist, partly because the Chinese roots of "Cong San" did not reflect Ho's vision of the revolution (his party called itself Xa Hoi Dang).

Viet Minh   In full, Viet Nam Doc Lap Minh Hoi, or Vietnam Independence League, the front that directed the First Indochinese War, against the French, 1946–54.

WIA   Wounded in action.

BIBLIOGRAPHY

Bonds, Ray, ed. *The Vietnam War: The Illustrated History of the Conflict in Southeast Asia.* New York: Crown Publishers, 1983.

Braestrup, Peter. *Big Story: How the American Press and Television Reported and Interpreted the Crisis of Tet 1968 in Vietnam and Washington.* Abridged edition. New Haven: Yale University Press, 1977.

Caputo, Philip. *A Rumor of War.* New York: Holt, Rinehart and Winston, 1977.

Department of the Army, *Handbook for U.S. Forces in Vietnam,* 1967.

Doleman, Jr., Edgar C., and the editors of Boston Publishing Company. *Tools of War.* The Vietnam Experience. Boston: Boston Publishing Co., 1984.

Dougan, Clark, Stephen Weiss, and the editors of Boston Publishing Company. *Nineteen Sixty-Eight.* The Vietnam Experience. Boston: Boston Publishing Co., 1983.

Doyle, Edward, Samuel Lipsman, and the editors of Boston Publishing Company. *America Takes Over, 1965–67.* The Vietnam Experience. Boston: Boston Publishing Co., 1982.

Doyle, Edward; Samuel Lipsman; Terrence Maitland; and the editors of Boston Publishing Company. *The North.* The Vietnam Experience. Boston: Boston Publishing Co., 1986.

Dye, Dale A. *Run Between the Raindrops.* New York: Avon Books, 1985.

Fall, Bernard B. *Street Without Joy: Insurgency in Vietnam 1946–1963.* Harrisburg, Pa.: Stackpole Co., 1963.

———. *Hell in a Very Small Place: The Siege of Dien Bien Phu.* Philadelphia: J. B. Lippincott Co., 1966.

———. *Ho Chi Minh on Revolution: Selected Writings, 1920–66.* New York: Frederick A. Praeger, Publishers, 1967.

———. *The Two Viet-Nams: A Political and Military Analysis.* New York: Frederick A. Praeger, Publishers, 1967.

Fitzgerald, Frances. *Fire in the Lake: The Vietnamese and the Americans in Vietnam.* Boston: Atlantic–Little, Brown Books, 1972.

Gravel, Mike, ed. *The Pentagon Papers: The Defense Department History of United States Decisionmaking on Vietnam.* Boston: Beacon Press, 1971.

BIBLIOGRAPHY

Herr, Michael. *Dispatches*. New York: Alfred A. Knopf, 1978.

Hersh, Seymour M. *Cover-Up: The Army's Secret Investigation of the Massacre at My Lai 4*. New York: Random House, 1972.

Johnson, Lyndon Baines. *The Vantage Point: Perspectives of the Presidency 1963–1969*. New York: Holt, Rinehart and Winston, 1971.

Karnow, Stanley. *Vietnam: A History*. New York: Viking Press, 1983.

Krulak, Victor H. *First to Fight: An Inside View of the U.S. Marine Corps*. Annapolis, Md.: Naval Institute Press, 1984.

Maitland, Terrence, Peter McInerney, and the editors of Boston Publishing Company. *A Contagion of War*. The Vietnam Experience. Boston: Boston Publishing Co., 1983.

McChristian, Joseph. *The Role of Military Intelligence, 1965–1967*. Vietnam Studies. Washington, D.C.: U.S. Department of the Army, 1974.

Morrocco, John, and the editors of Boston Publishing Company. *Thunder from Above: Air War, 1941–1968*. The Vietnam Experience. Boston: Boston Publishing Co., 1984.

Nguyen Cao Ky. *Twenty Years and Twenty Days*. New York: Stein and Day, Publishers, 1976.

Nolan, Keith William. *Battle for Hue: Tet 1968*. Novato, Calif.: Presidio Press, 1983.

Palmer, Bruce, Jr. *The 25-Year War: America's Military Role in Vietnam*. Lexington, Ky.: University Press of Kentucky, 1984.

Palmer, Dave Richard. *Summons of the Trumpet: U.S.–Vietnam in Perspective*. San Rafael, Calif.: Presidio Press, 1978.

Peers, W. R. *The My Lai Inquiry*. New York: W. W. Norton and Co., 1979.

Pike, Douglas. *PAVN: People's Army of Vietnam*. San Rafael, Calif.: Presidio Press, 1986.

Pisor, Robert. *The End of the Line: The Siege of Khe Sanh*. New York: W. W. Norton and Co., 1982.

Porter, Gareth, ed. *Vietnam: A History in Documents*. New York: New American Library, 1979.

Pratt, John Clark, comp. *Vietnam Voices: Perspectives on the War Years 1941–1982*. New York: Penguin Books, 1984.

Rossner-Owen, David. *Vietnam Weapons Handbook*. Wellingborough, Northants., U.K.: Patrick Stephens, Publishers, 1986.

Sharp, U. S. G., and William C. Westmoreland. *Report on the War in Vietnam*. Washington, D.C.: U.S. Government Printing Office, 1969.

Stanton, Shelby L. *Green Berets at War: U.S. Army Special Forces in Southeast Asia, 1956–1975*. San Rafael, Calif.: Presidio Press, 1985.

Summers, Harry G., Jr. *On Strategy: A Critical Analysis of the Vietnam War*. Novato, Calif.: Presidio Press, 1982.

BIBLIOGRAPHY

———. *Vietnam War Almanac*. New York: Facts on File Publications, 1985.

Telfer, Gary L., Lane Rogers, and V. Keith Fleming, Jr. *Fighting the North Vietnamese, 1967*. U.S. Marines in Vietnam. Washington, D.C.: History and Museums Division, Headquarters, U.S. Marine Corps, 1984.

U.S. Army, Vietnam. *Tour 365*. 1968.

U.S. Department of the Army. *Area Handbook for South Vietnam*. 1967.

U.S. Military Assistance Command, Vietnam, Headquarters, Office of Assistant Chief of Staff, J-2. *Strategy Since 1954*. Saigon: Combined Intelligence Center, Vietnam, 1967.

Van Tien Dung. *Our Great Spring Victory: An Account of the Liberation of South Vietnam*. New York: Monthly Review Press, 1977.

Vo Nguyen Giap. *People's War, People's Army*. New York: Frederick A. Praeger, Publishers, 1962.

Walt, Lewis W. *Strange War, Strange Strategy: A General's Report on Vietnam*. New York: Funk and Wagnalls, 1970.

Westmoreland, William C. *A Soldier Reports*. Garden City, N.Y.: Doubleday and Co., 1976.

INDEX

Ablard, Charles D., 258
Abrams, Gen. Creighton, 102, 217–18, 219, 235, 254
Acheson, Dean, 14
Adams, Samuel A., ix–xii, 99, 102–5, 119, 234, 261–63, 282
administrative/service units, VC. *See* VC administrative/service units.
Aggressor Order of Battle Manual, The (Department of the Army), 211
AKA ("also known as"), 85, 224, 273
Americal Division. *See* U.S. Army Infantry.
"Americanization," 77, 93, 286
Anderson, Jack, 227
Andrews, Marshall, 287
Arc Light. *See* B-52s.
Area Handbook for Southeast Asia (Department of the Army), 75, 286
Area Order of Battle Analysis, 83. *See also* order of battle.
Armed Forces Radio, 8, 226
armor, enemy, 67, 208, 285
Army Intelligence and Security Branch (AIS), 9, 15–16, 136
ARVN (Army of the Republic of Vietnam), 17, 94
ARVN counterparts, 55, 92–94, 126, 143, 151, 155–57, 159, 200, 207, 225, 248, 253, 274
A Shau Special Forces camp, 137–38
A Shau valley, 137–38, 277, 279
Ashworth, Gen. Robert L., 41
Associated Press (AP), 191, 194, 216
attrition, 152–53
automatic data processing (ADP), 62, 86, 236, 286

B-52s, 281; and Arc Light, 45, 233, 281; in DMZ, 97; Operation Niagara, 158,

161–64, 168, 280, 282; VC reactions to, 67, 271
Bangkok, 151, 157
Baron, Robert, 261–62
Benning, Fort, 3–5, 16, 30–31, 79, 179, 180–81
body counts, 108–9, 227
border battles, 98, 278. *See also* Con Thien; Dak To; Khe Sanh; Tet offensive.
Brinks BOQ, 148
Brown, Gen. Grover Cleveland, 216
Bunker, Ambassador Ellsworth, 118

Callaway, Howard, 258
Calley, Lt. William, 258
Camp LBJ, 6, 44
Caravelle Hotel, 110
Carver, George, 102–4, 117
CBS, xi, 118, 260–62
Central Intelligence Agency (CIA), xii, xv, 99–107, 117, 119, 230, 234. *See also* Adams, Samuel A.; National Intelligence Estimates.
China, People's Republic of, 14
and First Indochina War, 13, 269
and Korea, 13, 269
and revolution of 1949, 81
and Second Indochina War, 76, 87
Cholon, 47, 193, 207, 233, 234
Christianity in Vietnam, 146
CINCPAC J-2, 99–105, 217
Citadel, The (Hue), 192
Civilian Irregular Defense Group (CIDG), 137
code of conduct (U.S. military), 20
Cole, Col. C. A., 147
Combat Intelligence in Modern Warfare (Heymont), 16